GOING TO WASHINGTON STATE

Washington State University Centennial Histories

Going to Washington State

A CENTURY OF STUDENT LIFE

WILLIAM L. STIMSON

Washington State University Press
Pullman, Washington
1989

Washington State University Press, Pullman, Washington 99164-5910
Copyright 1989 by the Board of Regents of Washington State University
All Rights Reserved
First Published 1989
Printed and bound in the United States of America

98 97 96 95 94 93 92 91 90 89   1 2 3 4 5 6 7 8 9 10

Library of Congress Cataloging in Publication Data

Stimson, William L., 1946-
Going to Washington State : a century of student life/
William L. Stimson
p. cm.
Bibliography: p.
ISBN 0-87422-056-4 : $24.95

ISBN 0-87422-056-4 (hardbound)

This book is printed on pH-neutral, acid-free paper.

Dedicated with great appreciation to

DR. WELDON B. "HOOT" GIBSON

CLASS OF 1938

As a donor to Washington State University's Centennial Publications Program, Dr. Gibson has helped to make this book possible. Over the years he has maintained strong ties with his alma mater, constantly working to improve its standing as one of America's great land-grant universities. Among his many contributions, Dr. Gibson has served as:

Founding Chairman of the WSU Foundation

an Endowed President's Associate

Co-Chair of the Glenn Terrell Presidential Scholarship Committee

a WSU Benefactor

a member of the WSU Centennial and Alumni Center committees

For his unceasing work on behalf of Washington State University Dr. Gibson has been honored as a recipient of both the Board of Regents Distinguished Alumnus Award and the Alumni Association Achievement Award.

After receiving a Bachelor of Arts degree from WSU in 1938, Dr. Gibson earned his Master of Arts and Doctor of Philosophy degrees from Stanford University. He is widely known in business and government circles around the world for his contributions to international and economic development.

Table of Contents

Foreword

A century has passed since the first Washington Legislature created what today is Washington State University. When classes began nearly one hundred years ago in a tiny building on College Hill called the *Crib*, only twenty-nine students were in attendance. Today, Washington State University has some 16,000 students enrolled and offers hundreds of classes in dozens of buildings in Pullman and throughout the state.

This book is the story of Washington State University's students. It is the culmination of two years of dedicated research, interviews, and writing by William L. Stimson, a research news coordinator for the WSU Office of News and Information Services. *Going to Washington State* is unique as a university centennial history in that it focuses exclusively on student life.

Going to Washington State: A Century of Student Life is the first of three *WSU Centennial Histories*. This will be followed, in the fall of 1989, by Richard Fry's sports epic *The Crimson and the Gray: 100 Years with the WSU Cougars* and, in the spring of 1990, by George Frykman's monumental *Creating the People's University: Washington State University, 1890-1990*. Together, these three books will present us with a definitive view of our history and will aid us in planning for the future of this outstanding University, one that we can appropriately call the "Pride of Washington"!

Samuel H. Smith, President
Washington State University
March 1989

Preface and Acknowledgments

UNIVERSITIES CUSTOMARILY USE THE OCCASION OF A CENTENNIAL TO record their histories. But few universities (I'm not sure that there are any others) feel compelled to devote a book to the history of their students. I suppose that taken collectively students seem like hurricanes, forces without discernable structure. They blow in and they blow out, and there is nothing much to be said about it afterwards except, "Whew!"

As a matter of fact, when I began contacting alums of Washington State University and asking them to tell me about their college years, I expected only some entertaining anecdotes. Then the letters—ultimately about 250 of them—began pouring in. Many of these letters were virtual memoirs, six or ten pages long and full of perceptions about youth. The writers recalled the pranks and water fights, but they also talked about a four-year period during which they chose careers and spouses, established friendships that lasted a lifetime, and learned things that helped them to form lasting attitudes about the world. Some alums were introspective about the changes they saw in themselves as they passed the critical years from age eighteen to age twenty-two on the campus at Pullman. It was WSU students themselves who showed me that a book about "student life" might go deeper than pranks and rah-rah stuff.

The pranks and rah-rah stuff, moreover, shouldn't be dismissed so quickly. Like most people with their college years well behind them, I had come to see the customs of student life as perhaps amusing, perhaps harmless, perhaps inevitable, but of course a waste of time. Now I wonder. I have spoken to and corresponded with hundreds of graduates and have noticed that there is an association between the fun they remember and their affection for the institution.

I remember one specific incident that helped crystalize this thought in my mind. One of the dozens of people I interviewed while doing research was Kenyon Bement, a 1934 graduate and now a successful business executive in Portland. When I arrived for the interview, he ordered all calls held and leaned back to regale me with memories of friends, favorite teachers, and rivalries with the University of Washington. Several months later I was sitting in an awards ceremony for the College of Pharmacy, waiting to give a slide show about the frivolities of college students, when I looked at the program and noticed that the first scholarship that would be handed out that night was the Mabel Bement Memorial Scholarship for a minority student.

It was, I learned later, a scholarship set up by Kenyon Bement, his sister, and his two brothers, all WSU graduates, to honor their mother. One reason college memories count is that they tie generations together, bringing one to the support of the other.

This book is not, however, about the consequences of student life, but about student life. I have listened to Washington State University students (including those who spoke in the *Evergreen*, the *Chinook*, and in material found in Manuscripts, Archives, and Special Collections of the WSU Libraries) and tried to put down verbal pictures of college life to go along with the photographs. The changes that have taken place at Washington State are apparent as the decades role through the ten chapters. But I think, after talking with many alums, that the thing that will surprise them most is the many aspects of college life that have not changed.

I HAD A LOT OF HELP IN WRITING THIS BOOK. TO START AT ITS INCEPTION, Vice President for University Relations Stanton E. Schmid gave me both total support and total freedom. My boss Barbara Petura, Director of News and Information, remained a source of encouragement and understanding; she was of great assistance throughout the preparation of *Going to Washington State*. I could not have asked for better support from above.

Editor-in-Chief Fred Bohm of WSU Press was a full partner in this project from the beginning. Naturally I appreciate his tireless efforts to make the manuscript one word and one comma clearer. But his biggest contribution, I believe, was that from the start he saw the possibilities of doing something other than a traditional pictorial history. Without his enthusiasm, this project inevitably would have been constricted. Editor Glen Lindeman turned an incredibly keen eye for fact on the final manuscript and captions, to the great benefit of both.

Belinda Starkie selected most of the photographs in this book from the extensive WSU Manuscripts, Archives, and Special Collections holdings. Her professional eye for revealing images will be obvious to anyone who looks through these pages. The beautiful cover design and page layout is the work of Graphic Designer Jo Savage.

Thomas H. Sanders, Director of the Office of University Publications, Printing, and WSU Press, has been a constant source of support. His encouragement and the work of his outstanding professional staff are, in large measure, responsible for turning the idea for this book into a tangible reality.

John Guido, Lawrence R. Stark, Tina Oswald, and Carol Lichtenberg of Manuscripts, Archives, and Special Collections freely offered their time and expertise, helping to locate photographs and other archival material for *Going to Washington State*.

Thanks also go to the Regional Director of Development, WSU Spokane, Dan C. Peterson, and to the Director of Campus and

Community Relations, Sonia Hussa, for their ongoing support. I gratefully acknowledge the cooperation and consideration given me by the *Evergreen* and *Chinook* staffs, personnel in the President's Office, the Graduate School, and the Registrar's Office; I thank my colleagues in News and Information Services for their comments and advice.

WASHINGTON STATE UNIVERSITY IS EXTREMELY FORTUNATE TO HAVE had a series of talented photographers record its history from the beginning. Among the earliest was William D. Barkhuff, one of the first students to enroll at WAC and an 1898 graduate. Barkhuff, as well as George Ritchey, another early photographer, took pictures under great technical constraints, but their results were excellent and sometimes dramatic. Examples of their work are included among the photographs in the first chapter (in fact, Barkhuff is visible in two of the group pictures, and George Ritchey and his wife are the newly-weds on Military Hill).

Fine photographic work also was done by Myron Samuel Huckle in the 1920s. The portraits of Orchesis dancers at Silver Lake in chapter five are his. Huckle "raised documentary photography to an art," commented Belinda Starkie, the photographic consultant who selected most of the photographs for this book.

Routine events and scenes of everyday campus life from 1910 to 1972 also were recorded by R. R. Hutchinson photographers (today, Swilly's restaurant in downtown Pullman occupies the old Hutchinson studio). Candid pictures of students in the old bookstore cafe and returning World War II veterans in temporary quarters are examples of the Hutchinsons' outstanding record of the college scene.

Upon his retirement in 1956, Paul Kies, an English professor at WSC for thirty years, became an unofficial recorder of campus life until his death in 1971. He captured images of hundreds of events on film and turned his invaluable collection over to Manuscripts, Archives, and Special Collections. Several photographs of the student demonstrations during the Vietnam era are his.

The "underground newspapers" and other printed materials from the early late 1960s and early 1970s protest period are from the private collection gathered by WSU research librarian Siegfried Vogt. These items were essential research tools for understanding that era and also served as excellent illustrative material.

Earl Otis, Virgil Barta, William Howell, Lloyd Rogers, Robert Bullis, Ed Neill, Charles Painter, Arden Literal, Catherine Bicknell Matthews, Jo Savage, and Norm Nelson all took photographs of campus life during the period from the 1940s through the early 1980s. Examples of their work are included here. Photographs of 1980s students were taken by WSU staff photographers Robert Hubner and Lisbeth Thorlacius; several are presented in the last chapters. Hubner, a photographic technician, skillfully prepared copies of original pictures for this book. Talented student photographers from the *Chinook* and *Evergreen*, almost all of whom go uncredited for their efforts, also took many fine pictures. Any who might identify their work here have my gratitude.

The balance of the photography reproduced in *Going to Washington State* was provided by individuals from their personal collections. Special thanks go to: Sandy Wilson Barrett; Henry Bassett; Thelma Mahanes Brown; Robert Bucklin; the family of Cecil Compau; Nancy Gale Compau; Bill Moos; Janet Murrow; Drex Rhoades; and Harry Weller.

There are others, too numerous to mention, who shared their memories, documents, and photographs. Without them, this book would not have been possible.

FOR THEIR CORRECTIONS AND CRITICISMS TO THE MANUSCRIPT, I WOULD like to thank my mother-in-law Marge and my mother Frances. My most trusted and diligent advisor on this project was, as always, my wife Kristine.

Since this is my second book and I have two children, it was predetermined that my work on this book be dedicated to my daughter Brie Kristine Stimson. It is a coincidence, though a happy one, that she and Washington State University were both born on March 28.

William L. Stimson
Pullman, Washington
March 1989

CHAPTER ONE

Going to State

NEW SHOES. A NEW PEN, A NEW WATCH. STACKS OF PAPER, A STUDY lamp, tennis racket, football, laundry soap, photos of girlfriends or boyfriends, a dictionary. Clothes (depending on your era and sex: long-sleeved dresses and suits with vests, white corduroy slacks, ties and flop-fronted caps, bulky knit sweaters, naval-looking "middy" blouses, cardigan sweaters, starched blouses, ankle-length skirts, sun-tans, trapeze dresses, baggy blue jeans, creased blue jeans, tight blue jeans, cashmere sweaters with matching skirts and pearls, shirts with button-down collars, bell-bottoms, mini-skirts, plain white T-shirts, tie-dyed T-shirts, message-bearing T-shirts) are folded and placed in trunks or suitcases with infinite care. During the weeks spent choosing and preparing them, these clothes have been your tangible link to college life: you have imagined yourself strolling across a campus green in them, lolling fashionably about a campus hangout in them, chatting casually with someone of the opposite sex in them. The clothes must be just right when you arrive on campus so that you'll fit in perfectly with the college crowd. "You can always tell a freshman," some snide upperclassman wrote in a September 1934 issue of the State College student newspaper. "They have a freshly cleaned and pressed look."

Then comes the day you leave for school. At the door, mom and dad say "study hard," and, God bless them, they mean it; they have a better perspective (either from having gone to college or not having gone) on the importance of what you are about to do. But they smile as they offer this advice, for they understand that you are not stumbling over luggage and burbling euphorically because you are anxious to get into chemistry class.

You hardly pause to look back as you head down the walk, but this is where you leave your parents. After four years away, you won't be a kid in this house again. Other things will intervene: jobs in other cities, military service, marriage. Going away to college is one of life's transitions, but no ceremonies mark it as a rite of passage. In fact, you are decidedly unceremonious as you dash off, looking ahead and giving no thought to what you have just left behind.

Not that parents are forgotten. Surely not! According to the 1899 *Chinook*, the premier issue of the Agricultural College's annual, the first commandment of college life should be: "Write long and loving letters to thy parents, that thou mayest receive many bank checks from home." Surviving "letters home" from all eras of Washington

OPPOSITE: *Student train, the "Seattle-Tacoma Pullman Special" bound for the State College of Washington. At center: Harold Potts, '32, in cap, leans on the shoulder of Wyman Knapp, '33.*

State's history attest that this commandment of college life was well kept. "I will need $25 by the 8th or 9th at the latest," Tom Humphrey of Kappa Sigma wrote home in 1912. "If you can spare more it will save the trouble of sending again." The request is so standard, complete with urgency, in "Dear Mom and Dad" letters of all eras, that the school might have issued forms, leaving blank only the requested amount. Parents did their best to respond to these entreaties and only occasionally asked questions. In 1921, at a time when Washington State College tuition was free and room and board were about $40 per month, one perplexed father wrote to President E. O. Holland, wondering if Sonny might be exaggerating his expenses. "He has had and spent $500 in three months and has bought no clothes."

Money was not enough. Pre-World War II students routinely sent their cheery notes enclosed in bundles of laundry for mom to wash, press, and mail back. The post office provided special, canvas-covered "laundry boxes" for this purpose. Students expected that these cartons, when returned, would contain more than just clean clothes. "We ate the cake you sent us for Sunday meal," Ralph Wood of Waller Hall wrote home in 1938. "It was certainly swell. I hope you won't think that I am hinting when I say that a similar one would taste good next Sunday." Then he added: "Stan's folks sent him three pounds of divinity today. We are working on it now."

Long after graduation, most students came to appreciate what their fathers and mothers had done for them. Only then did they come to understand that what they once took for granted—financing a college education—often required heroic effort and self-sacrifice on the part of their parents. The father of Hermine Duthie, '30, was one of many who moved an entire family to Pullman and found a job there because it was the only practical way to provide room and board for children in college. Other parents invested family savings, everything, in their children's education. Going to Washington State was cheaper, but it wasn't free, and many of those who sent kids to Pullman were the ones for whom meeting minimum expenses came the hardest. The parents of Walter Herndon, '28, a distinguished engineer who one day would help invent the automatic transmission, worked to put him through college, worked more to buy him a used car as a graduation present, then watched as the car carried their son away to a new career and a new life in the East. Parental selflessness is something people remember about their college years.

SINCE THE 1950S, COLLEGE GOOD-BYES HAVE USUALLY TAKEN PLACE AT curb sides or in driveways, beside automobiles crammed with clothes and other necessities. One 1950s student remembered, "You could tell the cars heading for Pullman by the fact that they were piled high with stuff and had a box of Kleenex in the window."

In the forties and earlier, college life began at train stations. "College Specials" leaving Seattle's King Street Station, the Union Station in Tacoma, Spokane's Great Northern Station, and others across the state, had the aura of troop trains. Crimson sweaters and

ABOVE: *"The Coast Special" arriving at the Pullman Depot, bringing students to college for the fall 1924 semester.*

LEFT: *A group of dapper fraternity men pose for a group photograph at the Pullman train station in the 1920s.*

ecstatic hellos identified veterans, while hurried trackside good-byes and uncertain strides made it easy to pick out the "freshies."

Urbane-looking fraternity men, dressed in college sweaters and rumpled cords, strode through the crowds hoping to find among the new freshmen the budding athletes, musicians, and campus politicians who would embellish their houses in coming years. The absolute minimum requirement for new recruits was that they needed a place to live, for the competition to fill proliferating fraternities was fierce.

A likely looking candidate was taken in tow by the fraternity men and earnestly told of social advantages and palatial accommodations. (Meanwhile, other fraternity brothers were working furiously in Pullman to make the house at least presentable. Bud Compau, president of Psi Nu Sigma in 1922, wrote to a sister that he had inherited a "pigsty" and was trying to get it in shape before the College Special arrived). Kenneth K. Kennedy, '31, emerged from a chauffeur-driven limousine at the Great Northern Station in Spokane and was amazed to find himself instantly surrounded by fraternity recruiters. He would be initiated into Lambda Chi Alpha for three weeks before someone asked him why a guy who rides around in a limousine owns such a modest wardrobe. He explained he was poor but, luckily, his rich uncle had put him up for a night in Spokane and then sent him to the train station in his limousine.

The College Special was a rolling party, normally to the music of what one student called "the inevitable ukelele." People made new friends, reunited with old ones, boasted about summer adventures, and anticipated the coming year as the train swayed its way over the Cascade Mountains, across the Columbia Plain, and into the Palouse. On arriving in Pullman, passengers were met by crowds of greeters. Confused freshmen had only to pay some enterprising student a quarter to get luggage delivered to campus. Then they simply followed the mob up Kamiakin to Maiden Lane and on to the Administration Building, the turreted, red brick structure that stood at the edge of campus like a gatehouse.

First impressions of Pullman weren't always exhilarating. "Westsiders" especially, accustomed to the proximity of Puget Sound, the Pacific Ocean, and perpetually green fields, were shocked to step off a train and into what looked like a desolate, whistle-stop town. Harry Weller of Tacoma, dressed in his traveling suit, vest, and felt hat, arrived already sweltering on a hot September day in 1919. With a big suitcase in one hand and a topcoat over the other arm, he started the hike up Maiden Lane, and then down the long, gravel walk to the Administration Building. The grass was brown, the trees were puny, the college appeared to consist of three or four lonely buildings with large gaps between them. "For a nickel I would have gotten back on that train and gone home. I thought this was the end of the earth."

Someone pointed the way to Ferry Hall, and there Weller was greeted by Ellen Bakke, "a motherly old soul." With smiles and patience, she told him what he needed to be doing and what was going on around campus. Then she showed him to his room and things looked more interesting still.

At home, "I was always in a room with a brother, or maybe two brothers," Weller recalled. "To have a dormitory room where I could have my own things, where nobody would bother them, I thought: *this is heaven!*"

However modest that first dorm room, there was something portentous about the empty drawers and closets, the bookshelf waiting to receive real college books, the sight of one's own study desk, and in that initial look out the window to the campus below.

ABOVE: *The campus in 1895. The buildings are, from the left: Stevens Hall, the Administration Building (now Thompson Hall), old College Hall, old Ferry Hall, and the Mechanic Arts Building.*

LEFT: *William D. Barkhuff's study desk, 1898. Barkhuff, one of the first to enroll at Washington Agricultural College, was first editor of the student newspaper and an avid photographer.*

These students were among the first to enroll in the Washington Agricultural College when it opened in January 1892.
They are, from the left, bottom row: Seaton Van Doren (son of faculty member Nancy Van Doren), "Miss Irwin," Lew Harris, Frank Booser. Second Row: Unknown, John Klemgard, Ollie Downs, Unknown, Unknown, Ernest Sharon. Top Row: W. S. Chapman, Daise Cosand, T. S. Huston, Marie Estby, William D. Barkhuff, Josie Booser, M. C. Reynolds, Unknown.

THE FIRST STUDENTS AT WASHINGTON AGRICULTURAL COLLEGE AND School of Science, as Washington State was called until 1905, arrived in Pullman in early January of 1892. Some came to town by train or on horse-drawn wagons. Others traveled to Pullman on foot, having walked the thirty, forty, or fifty miles from family farms. Their first glimpses of the new college from the bluffs surrounding Pullman were even less grand than Harry Weller's. A one-story brick building (located on a site now occupied by the parking lot between the Compton Union Building and Holland Library) perched atop the immense bulk of Campus Hill like a lonely country schoolhouse. Here, on the morning of January 13, 1892, the first student body of what would become Washington State University gathered together, twenty-five men and four women. The original five college faculty members sat at the front of the room.

President George W. Lilley, a genial Midwesterner in his late thirties, welcomed the new students and noted what a signal honor it was for them to participate in the inaugural of what was sure to become a distinguished institution. Since the president of the Board of Regents, S. B. Conover of Port Townsend, could not be present, Lilley read the president's message to the students. "The beginning is made of a glorious work. . . . I bespeak for it the love and pride of the whole state. . . ."

Everyone in the audience sat quietly as Lilley spoke. They may have even listened, since this was their first experience with chirping administrators. More than likely, they tied their eyes to the president, but turned their minds loose to gaze on a more personal vision of this momentous occasion. They were young men and women who never expected to go to college. Pick anyone from among the twenty-nine students and you could be certain (for their biographies are amazingly consistent) that he or she had grown up in the Midwest, traveled west with parents, then spent teenage years in the grueling work of establishing a new farm on the Pacific Northwest frontier. Most didn't have access to high schools, and so were academically, as well as financially, unprepared for higher education. College was for someone else, not these poor farm kids.

But then, weekly hometown newspapers throughout Washington began carrying articles about a new state college. These stories explained that the Morrill Act, passed by the U.S. government in 1862, gave each state a grant of land to support tuition-free college for "the industrial classes." Among the first actions of Washington's legislature after the territory became a state on November 11, 1889, was passage of legislation that established an agricultural school, laying claim to a grant of federal land as stipulated by the Morrill Act.

What that meant in practical terms was formulated by Edward Kimel, a member of the first graduating class in 1897: "No tuition; cost of sharing a room in the dormitory $17 a year; and board in the dining hall eight and a half or nine dollars a month. The exchequer could be helped by working [for the college] at 12 1/2 cents an hour." The way to college now seemed to be open and practicable. Those who weren't prepared for college work could begin in a "prep school," improvised by Washington Agricultural College professors, as soon as they recognized the need.

Because they appreciated what the Washington Agricultural College had done for them, these students had a fierce loyalty to it, a loyalty destined to play an important part in developing the institution that would one day become Washington State University. From the moment the college was founded it was under attack—by other towns still jealous for not having gotten the institution, by westside legislators already beginning to balk at funding a school that proposed to teach foreign languages and mathematics to farm kids, even by its own regents, who believed that President Lilley was mismanaging the building program.

In the latter of these struggles, students sided with their president. They believed that, if things had been a little disorganized that first semester, it was due to the meddling of the Board of Regents. As far as they were concerned, President Lilley was now placing the college on a solid footing *in spite of* the board.

George W. Lilley, first president of the Washington Agricultural College and School of Science. He came to establish the institution in May 1891 and was released by the Board of Regents after its first full year of operation in December 1892.

Nancy L. Van Doren, an English teacher who was one of the first five faculty members and the college's first female instructor. She was a teacher, librarian, and "preceptress" of Stevens Hall for many years. Van Doren Hall, adjacent to Holland Library, is named for her.

John W. Heston, President of Washington Agricultural College from December 1892 to August 1893. He was thirty-eight years old when he arrived in Pullman (the photograph shows him later in life). Like Lilley, he departed amidst the general turmoil that plagued the college in its opening years.

Enoch A. Bryan, President of Washington State College from 1893-1916, was the institution's true founder.

BY THE FALL OF 1892, RUMORS BEGAN TO CIRCULATE THAT THE REGENTS were planning to fire Lilley. Students dispatched a petition asking that the president be retained. The regents, on the motion of board treasurer Andrew H. Smith, voted to disregard the petition as "irrelevant" and having no bearing on their decision.

"The evident meaning was that we attend to our own business," huffed the student newspaper. Well, students had some news for the regents: "We consider that this is a business in which we ought to have some rights." In December of that first year, 1892, the board proceeded to allow Lilley's contract to lapse; then it gave the presidency to John W. Heston, the principal of Seattle High School.

Ignoring student opinion has always been easy do. In this case it was a grave mistake. Regent Smith, only a few days after he led the attack on Lilley, decided to escort the President-elect Heston to the campus and introduce him to the students.

The night before Smith and Heston ascended College Hill, students devoted a literary club meeting to discussing the situation. Someone read aloud newspaper reports of the regents' meeting at which Lilley had been fired. One can just imagine the scene, paragraphs from reports alternating with howls and counter-charges against the regents.

When Smith and Heston arrived the next morning, they were greeted by students singing, "Glory, glory hallelujah, We'll hang Regent Smith on a sour apple tree." The planned assembly began in the old College Hall with a brief talk by President Lilley, in which he answered charges made against him. According to an article written by a student for a local newspaper, Lilley "closed his remarks by wishing students happiness and success in life," leaving some of them in tears.

A professor leapt up to make some light remarks. Two other professors spoke briefly and won cheers from the students. But the mood was ominous, and at the end of the session Smith and Heston considered it wise to duck into a side room and lock the door behind them.

When they emerged, a student crowd was waiting. "Eggs!" someone shouted, and the two men made a break for the slope leading to Pullman. They were immediately showered with eggs, hastily procured from the college farm, and rotten cabbages, handy in a nearby campus garden. A few boys complained later that their aim had been ruined by the fact they only wanted to hit Smith, and that Smith ran too close to Heston. It is reported that Smith, treasurer of the college's first Board of Regents, actually cowered for a time behind a cornstalk before popping up again and scooting down the hill.

The school's first historian and third president, Enoch A. Bryan, called this a "disgraceful episode in the college's history." The students saw it a little differently. "Who that bears the name of an American," a writer in the college paper said, "would not be ashamed of living, if under like circumstances he did not experience a feeling of disgust with the [regents'] proceedings." Bryan said it took the college many years to outlive the damage of this widely reported

"The Cabbage Patch" where students obtained ammunition as they chased a new college president and a member of the Board of Regents from campus. This photograph was taken in 1892, the year of that infamous student rebellion. In the background is the original Ferry Hall, still under construction.

student uprising. Students conceded that. After reading the lurid accounts carried in newspapers around the state, the student editor concluded that citizens must suppose that when an agricultural college student knocks on a professor's door, "the professor appears with a dog and a gun, expecting to be murdered."

This "student demonstration," within a year of the college's opening, was to have important consequences. It convinced Washington legislators of what many critics had been charging before—that the Board of Regents was incompetent. The board that fired Lilley was itself soon dismissed. A new Board of Regents replaced Heston with Enoch Bryan, a powerful personality who became the true founder of the State College of Washington, as the school soon became known.

LIFE ON THAT EARLY CAMPUS WAS NOT ALWAYS SO EVENTFUL, THOUGH it was not boring either. Late in the afternoon of February 11, 1893, David Filer sat down to write a "Dear Mother and Dad" letter, the school's earliest known example of the genre. He had just returned to campus from Christmas break the previous day. In the correspondence he described his seven-mile walk from home in Asotin to Lewiston, his run up the Lewiston grade, and how he hitched a ride in a fancy sleigh to Uniontown. "While in Uniontown I blowed myself for five cents for ginger pops," he declared, "five cents for bologna and five cents for English walnuts. So you see [now don't worry mom!] I had a big dinner and got to Pullman just in time for military drill and bookkeeping."

David reported to his parents that some boys had some fun the previous night. While Professor Piper was absent from his room in the dorm, they filled his bed with snow, scattered tacks on his chair, and fixed a can of water over his door. Piper tumbled to every trap, David chortled to his parents, and wound up spending the night in

C. S. Sapp, a student in the late 1890s and one of several who dropped out of school to enlist for service during the Spanish American War.

Dr. Elton Fulmer, professor of chemistry, 1893-1916. A leader in building the college and popular with students, he was killed in a train wreck at Cheney in 1916. Fulmer Hall is named for him.

a wet bed. Curiously, David told his parents, "This morning all the students say that Piper was in a far better humor than he had been for four long months."

During these early years, most students and many faculty members lived and ate meals in Ferry Hall, a five-story dormitory completed during the summer of 1892. In the first floor dining hall, men and women sat together, eight to a table, and a contemporary report says "pleasant conversation and laughter" dominated the room at each meal. With a captive audience, the clowns were in their glory. One night, Swede Fisher held up a dripping garter snake and convinced several women that he found it in his soup. A fellow called "Knifey" earned his nickname for a sword swallowing act he performed with silverware. If the cook set hash on the table, the clowns would grip their stomachs and plead for mercy. If beef was served, men would scrape across it once with knives and call loudly for cross-cut saws.

Menus depended to a great extent on what college farms had in surplus. One season, Professor Balmer of horticulture had a large crop of beans, and these were dutifully purchased by the college. "Shortly after their introduction to the club table," a reminiscing senior said, "a vote was taken on the question of eight dollar board or nine dollar board; two ballots read for the eight dollar board, three read for the nine dollar board, and one hundred and three read for no beans."

THE OLDEST STUDENT ORGANIZATION AT WASHINGTON STATE UNIversity is the student newspaper, the *Evergreen*. Its forerunner, the *College Record*, put out its first issue within a month of the college's opening. "From that date," the 1899 *Chinook* said, "the college flourished, the paper flourished, the editors flourished, everybody flourished, excepting the printers. Vol. 1, No. 1, appeared early in February and was printed on cream satin [cloth], which has never been paid for to our personal knowledge."

At the center of organized social life on campus were numerous extra-curricular activities, including literary societies—organizations that met Friday evenings to debate questions and improve minds. The climax of the social season in 1893 was a student program jointly sponsored by the Websterian and Jeffersonian Societies. We can imagine that warm evening, June 13, 1893, 7:30 p.m. The audience, men in ties, women in their best dresses, seated in the old College Hall, a wood frame building which was close to where College Hall is now.

A brass quartet played an overture. William S. Van Doren gave an opening address. Ollie Downs sang "After the Ball," bowing to polite applause. Katie Moys then recited, with appropriate expressions and intonations, "Through Grandfather's Spectacles"; the Jones brothers followed with a mandolin and banorine duet. Daise Cosand recited her essay "Webster and Jefferson." Claude Eastman was introduced, paused to collect his mood, then launched into his song "Soloman

Students, some wearing cadet uniforms, on the steps of the Klemgard home, at the northeast corner of Reaney Park. The photograph was taken about 1895. The new Administration Building is visible in the background.

Levi." William Barkhuff read a prophecy, the quartet played, and then everyone—choir, quartette, musicians, students, and visitors—joined in singing a grand finale. Lovely evening!

Actually, when the Washington Literary Society revised its constitution in 1898, it created a position of sergeant-at-arms, someone to scour the campus and town for absent members. Their stiff collars and long dresses may have made them look like grandparents, but these young men and women were, after all, still college students. The 1905 *Chinook* described a "peanut drunk," an early form of the "kegger," that was sponsored by the Websterian Literary Society. The 1914 official college songbook included a drinking song entitled "Booze" ("I sat up the booze. . . to a party of three. . . . Then I saw things by twos, for the booze upset me. . . .") written by DeForest Cline, composer of the Washington State University alma mater, "Washington, My Washington."

THE EARLIEST STUDENTS OF THE COLLEGE WERE MORE CIRCUMSPECT about sex, as society required. Whether they were less fascinated by it is doubtful. Turn-of-the-century annuals and newspapers abound with cleverly oblique references to forbidden behavior. A photograph of a male student looking languorously into the face of a young woman in the 1899 *Chinook* is titled, "Life In Ferry Hall." One of the few students of the era to leave college papers and mementos to the university's archives was William Barkhuff, '98, first editor of the college newspaper. The collection contains a poem written by William Hull, the second editor of the college newspaper. It is called "A College Ode" and describes a Campus Hill seduction:

> The College hall a solemn stillness holds,
> While on the steps sweet Pasco and her Will,
> Hold revelry without a thought of colds.
> The whippoorwill resounds her lover's name
> The distant orchestra disturbs the calm repose,
> And Pasco feels a strange thrill through her frame,
> As Will employs his fingers neath her clothes. . . .

ABOVE: *A "shadowgraph" from the 1902* Chinook *depicting students sneaking a kiss in front of the Administration Building. This was an era when college administrators were shocked to see students holding hands.*

BELOW: *The campus as it looked from the edge of Rogers Field in the early 1920s. The buildings visible are, from the left: the original 1899 gymnasium, Bryan Hall, Van Doren Hall, and the Music Building.*

AT THE BEGINNING OF THE TWENTIETH CENTURY, WASHINGTON AGRI-
cultural College and School of Science was a handful of bright red
buildings jutting up from bare ground on an immense hill. There
were many "keep off the grass" signs, but little grass, and there were
no trees to speak of. After a rainy day, the whole area was awash in
what one student called "affectionate mud" because of its tendency
to cling to the shoes. So when it rained, wooden walkways served as
virtual bridges between main buildings.

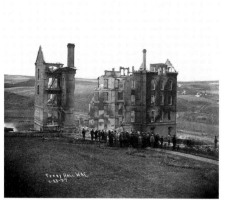

One of the reasons so little grass could be found on the campus
was the almost perpetual construction during that first decade.
Within a few years, the original "Crib" had been relegated to the
Student Cadet Corps brigade and most classes were held in the
turreted Administration Building, completed in 1894. The top (fourth)
floor of the new structure held the library; the middle three floors ac-
commodated most classrooms, administrative offices, and large
assembly hall; the physics and chemistry labs were in the basement.
Professor Fulmer's chemistry lab had workbenches for sixty students
and was often the source of acrid smells that permeated the rest of the
building.

ABOVE: *The original campus dormitory,
Ferry Hall, the day after it burned down
November 23, 1897. No one was
injured. Pullman residents housed and
re-clothed boys routed from the burning
building in the middle of the night.*

BELOW: *The annual Freshman Class
Banquet, 1898, Stevens Hall dining
room.*

In 1900, a new Ferry Hall (replacing the original, which burned down in 1897) and the four-story Science Hall were both completed. These stood opposite the Administration Building and Stevens Hall to enclose the original campus "Quad." The college's grounds began to resemble a campus.

Science Hall (now part of the Murrow Communication Center) especially bespoke serious higher education. It provided space for classes and labs in botany, zoology, bacteriology, agriculture, horticulture, and geology and sported a large natural history museum stocked with animal, vegetable, and mineral specimens donated from all over the country.* A veterinary operating room seated 150 observers. Rounded towers with windows facing three directions were specially designed so that microscopes could catch the best available natural light.

The schools of business and pharmacy were housed in the three-story frame building called old College Hall (located where Science Hall was built). Farther down the slope, Mechanic Hall, a seventy-eight by ninety-two foot brick building, held engineering laboratories. The two dormitories at opposite ends of the campus, a large power plant and various wooden buildings for hospital, greenhouse, and other purposes completed the turn-of-the-century campus. In all, there were six substantial buildings and another half-dozen lesser structures scattered across a broad, naked mound. As student Robert E. Bucklin wrote to his aunt in 1897: "The laboratories are finely fitted up, and I think a fellow couldn't very well get into a better school. I just wish there were trees and water around."

WASHINGTON AGRICULTURAL COLLEGE WAS, IN THAT FIRST DECADE, A tiny, close-knit community, more like a boarding school than a college. The entire student body gathered for "chapel" each morning, actually a secular "pep talk" (as the students called it) by President Bryan, a faculty member, or a visitor to campus. Those first students spoke of President Bryan affectionately as "Prexy," and his next senior in command was "Dad" Waller. There's an old story about Waller that has him saying to a coed, as women students were then called, "May I call you Jenny?" "Yes," she is supposed to have replied, "if I can call you Daddy." Edward Kimel, '97, recalled being on a wagon ride with a few other students and Professor Elton Fulmer. Fulmer teased a couple for "going steady" by singing "give me her promise true" in a rich baritone voice. The school was, Kimel said, "just a big student family with teachers as foster parents." This close relationship is more extraordinary than it sounds. At most colleges during that era, a strict decorum kept professors and students at arm's length.

---

* The young college had a remarkable collection of stuffed and mounted wildlife because regent Charles R. Conner had arranged for them to be donated to the school at the close of the famous Chicago Exhibition of 1893.

IN THOSE EARLY YEARS, EVERYONE PARTICIPATED IN JUST ABOUT EVERYthing. Biographical notes in the 1903 *Chinook*, for example, show that three of four class members held at least one leadership position on campus: athlete, officer in a student organization, editor, or debater. This active participation in campus life proved to be a hidden advantage for Washington Agricultural College graduates, an advantage more difficult to find at many larger schools like Harvard, where journalist-philosopher Walter Lippmann could not be part of the student elite because he was Jewish, or Princeton, where historian George F. Kennan was barred permanently from the inner circle simply because he was from the Midwest.

Of course, both universities, and hundreds of other institutions of higher learning at the time, would have been absolutely prejudicial to the third of the college's students who were female. The state college was, of course, not free of society's general presumptions about what was called "a woman's place." The *Chinook* of 1905 commented: "It has been said that a lady was not fitted for the editorship of a college paper, and not without some reason." But it went on to say: "The fact that we have had a lady editor during this entire year and a college paper that has been up to the standard of any in the Northwest in every particular, has proven conclusively that there are exceptions to the rule."

However grudgingly done, she *was* editor—an extraordinary exception to the gender rules of that era. Her entire staff was male. The editor of the first *Chinook* was Daisey T. Busby; she was also president of her class. While women tended to be the English literature majors and men the engineering majors, Mabel Taylor in the class of 1899 graduated in electrical engineering. In a sampling of activities of the class of 1903, only two students were leaders in all three branches of student activity—political, literary, and athletic. One of them was Bess Mackay, president of her class, vice-president of the Intercollegiate Oratorical Association, and captain of the women's basketball team.

A wooden bridge in "The Tanglewood," a favorite spot for students wanting to escape the attention of censorious administrators and faculty. The small woods surrounded the far side of the man-made pond that students called Silver Lake. Silver Lake covered ground that now contains Bohler Gymnasium, Hollingbery Fieldhouse, and Mooberry Track. This photograph was taken circa *1914. The lake was drained in the mid 1920s.*

WASHINGTON AGRICULTURAL COLLEGE STUDENTS STUDIED CHEMISTRY, American and European history, mathematics (trigonometry was mandatory), English literature, and two foreign languages. These basic courses were required whether they majored in agriculture or literature. Many organizers of colleges established under the Morrill Act presumed that, because land-grant colleges were mandated to do agricultural research, their general purpose was to train better farmers. This idea dictated a narrow curriculum and those institutions deserved to be called "cow colleges."

Edward D. Eddy, Jr., author of the classic study of land-grant colleges, *Colleges for Our Land and Time*, cited Washington State College as an example of a land-grant college that escaped this narrow definition. In fact, he points out, Washington State has "a long history of emphasis on English literature and languages." This was the policy from the school's earliest years. On the occasion of the Administration Building dedication in 1895, President Bryan warned the college's first students that "skill in doing things [and] mere empirical knowledge . . . are helpless to give you the power you seek." Students needed, Bryan said, a broadly based understanding of the world. That principle guided him in establishing the curriculum.

On the other hand, Bryan did not believe his young institution should adopt the classical curriculum that was widely used by American colleges at the time. Instead, he created a course of study that was given focus by specialized work in an area of emphasis during a student's senior year. This approach to learning, now almost universal, originated at Harvard, where Bryan had gone to graduate school. "The underlying idea," an early Washington Agricultural College catalog explained, " is that it is better to know one thing thoroughly than to have a smattering of a great many things." It was a very modern idea.

But that was not the most innovative part of the new college's curriculum. As late as the 1890s, only the most progressive colleges and universities saw that scientific research must have a place in academe. This was a strength of land-grant colleges, with their commission to advance agriculture through research. On this topic Eddy, the land grant historian, once again cites the example of the Washington Agricultural College, quoting from an 1898 speech delivered by President Bryan. "Truth and beauty," Bryan said, "lie no more deeply concealed in every dull clod and crawling worm of this great cosmos about us than in the mysteries of this microcosm within us." It was, Eddy points out, a radical endorsement of the value of natural science in an era when the classics were still presumed by many to contain all the knowledge an educated person needed.

As a result of the dual emphasis on a liberal arts curriculum and the natural sciences, the little school in Pullman offered an education broader than most land-grant schools and more modern than all but the most progressive established colleges. Bryan backed up his curriculum with a capable faculty. Stanford, Harvard, Cornell, and Johns Hopkins, all top-rate graduate schools of the time, were represented on the faculty at the turn of the century.

The campus at the turn of the century. Science Hall, to the right of the turreted Administration Building, was added in 1899. On the far left is Stevens Hall, on the far right, topped by the cupola still preserved on the WSU campus, is the rebuilt Ferry Hall.

How students felt about the tough requirements naturally depended on the student and the subject. "This is examination week," Buck Bucklin wrote to his sister on February 8, 1898. "I took my geometry examination today and I think I am through with geometry. I had a high class grade in modern and medieval European history, so did not have to take the examination in it. . . . French don't bother me much because I don't know anything about it."

French aside, Bucklin was one student who had a solid appreciation for quality education. In 1897, when the governor of Washington was proposing to reduce the salaries for college teachers in order to reduce taxes, Bucklin wrote to his mother:

> It may be all right to reduce expenses, but let [Governor] Rogers think twice before he reduces. . . the salary of any of the professors. We have in this institution a faculty that would be a credit to any school. If their salaries are reduced they will leave, and profs who don't begin to be as good will fill their places.

From the beginning, students at WAC took an extraordinary interest in debates over leadership, budgets, and definitions of their institution. They understood that their futures were being determined. In another college, students might depend on tradition, high tuitions, and endowments to provide the kind of education they wanted. The quality of education at Washington Agricultural College was being determined month by month.

Robert E. Bucklin, a student in 1897-1898, wrote home praising the college, but dropped out to join the army at the opening of the Spanish American War. He was wounded while fighting in the Philippines.

IN 1904, AN *EVERGREEN* EDITORIALIST WROTE, "OUR COLLEGE NAME IS a misnomer. Six of our 114 graduates from four year courses have been in agriculture. Will anyone give a sensible reason why we should continue to bear our present name?" The next year the legislature changed the name of the Washington Agricultural College and School of Science to The State College of Washington.

The fact that the college had been established under the Land Grant Acts bequeathed to it a good school of agriculture and an isolated location. President Bryan's broad outlook took "agricultural college" out of its definition and made the place a college, period. The word "State" remained in the school's name, however, and had great significance, especially for students. At the time the institution was founded, only about four percent of America's college-aged young people pursued their education beyond high school, and the main determinant of who was in that four percent was family money. The campus of the tuition-free State College of Washington had a feel different than that of the more typical, patrician and cliquish, turn-of-the-century institutions of higher learning.

All of these things helped to define the college. "Going to State" would not be synonymous with going to college. It would be a particular kind of college experience. ■

Going to State

TOP: *Silver Lake, also known as Lake de Puddle, and the first trees of "The Tanglewood." This photograph, taken from about where the Compton Union Building is now located, shows the view students had looking east from Campus Hill. The open fields were beginning to be used for college orchards and farms.*

BOTTOM: *The view from Campus Hill looking west in about 1895. Buildings of the town of Pullman can be seen between old College Hall and the Administration Building.*

TOP: *Cadet drill in front of old College Hall*, circa *1897. The original school bell, barely visible at the top of the building, was brought to the campus in its first year and is now the Victory Bell on the top of new College Hall.*

BELOW: *Students watching cadet drill* circa *1897.*

TOP: *Newlyweds pose for the camera on Military Hill* circa *1898.*

RIGHT: *The "Senior Sneak" picnic in 1898.*

First library - Administration Building

The original college library, housed in the attic of the Administration Building, "is more meagerly equipped than any other part of the institution," the Board of Regents reported to the legislature in 1900. The regents asked for money to add 5,000 volumes at once. For the first decade of the college's operation, most of the books in the library had been donated by faculty members and others.

The graduating class of 1898. They are, from the left, bottom row: Frank Booser, Will Phillips.
Second row: E. Tappin Tannet, Milton McCroskey, William D. Barkhuff, Harold J. Doolittle.
Top row: David Brodie, Cleo Busbey, Harry Thompson, Florence Snyder, Lorin Corner.

At the turn of the century, photographs were considered "portraits," and students generally followed the custom of posing with serious expressions and formal demeanor. It tends to convey the impression that this generation of students was more "serious" than others. But the impression is belied by thrusts of humor that often made their way into photographs like this one of a 1904 "athletic team."

Women's physical education class in the old Gymnasium about 1920.

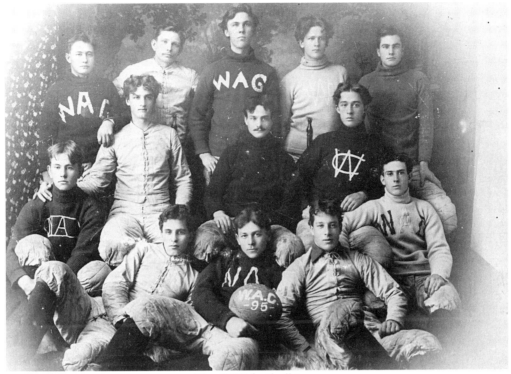

The 1895 football team.

The college orchestra in 1903, led by Professor W. B. Strong (top center).

Spirit

INSTEAD OF BEING EMBARRASSED BY ITS AGRICULTURAL CONNECTIONS, the Washington Agricultural College student body took a snob-deflating pride in it. The official yell at the turn of the century was:

Farmers! Hayseeds! Pumpkins! Squash!
W.A.C., By Gosh!

The University of Washington predated WAC by thirty years and usurped the ivy-draped, Oxbridge image. That institution was called *The University*, a phrase audibly italicized whenever they said it. That was okay with students at the new state college. Pomposity left students at *The University* vulnerable to a horse laugh at the slightest stumble. It was a game students at the Pullman college loved to play. The 1908 *Chinook* reported the results of a football game with the cross-state rival: "U of W–5. 'Palouse Cow College'–11."

The University of Washington student body president visited Pullman in 1910, five years after the name change from Washington Agricultural College to the State College of Washington. The *Evergreen* reported that he was treated with great respect and given a thorough tour of campus, "but it is to be regretted that he failed to waken in time to see the early morning brigade of Ag students with overalls, milking stools and lanterns on their way to the College barn for the practical phase of farm instruction, the 'morning chores.'"

Mind you, at this time only eighteen percent of WSC's students took any sort of agricultural class at all. The editors of the *Evergreen* were liberal arts majors and it is not likely they had been up many mornings to watch the milking. No matter. The editor was simply trying to make the point that "we're different." Students at the State College of Washington always took great pride in one particular thought; they were not students at the University of Washington.

During his visit to WSC, the UW student body president gave a speech in which he called for "a healthier and saner rivalry." Editors of the *Evergreen* suggested he preach that message on his own campus, where many people were actively plotting the demise of the state college in Pullman.

OPPOSITE: *WSC students gather for a mass "school picture" in the early 1920s. President E. O. Holland stands at front center.*

Getting ready for the dairy cattle lineup at a livestock show, 1922.

THE NEW STATE COLLEGE HAD MANY DETRACTORS, ESPECIALLY ON THE west side of the state. But they were not upset because the place was a "cow college." To the contrary, what upset most enemies of the school was precisely that the Washington State faculty was not content merely to teach agriculture. In 1909, a legislative committee visited WSC and found, among other disquieting things, a foreign language department of seven linguists, not counting the Latin and Greek teacher, an English department headed by a Harvard Ph.D., prospering schools of engineering and architecture, and a half-dozen departments with graduate students—in other words, a budding university. The legislative committee's report recommended the virtual dismantling of the state college so that it could be restarted as an "experimental agricultural school," something it contained but never was. Seattle newspapers suggested that the state college never should have been allowed to take the word "agriculture" out of its name, because that's when it started getting big ideas.

The University of Washington was an enthusiastic supporter of these attempts to cut WSC down to size. The dean of the University of Washington law school wrote a legal brief contending that there was no real reason why the state land-grant college should be the recipient of federal land-grant funds. If you really thought about it, this distinguished legal scholar suggested in a report voluntarily prepared for the state legislature that the money should go to the University of Washington.

As the conflict between the two state institutions headed toward a climax in 1916, a coincidence occurred that gave the whole affair the personal feel of a civil war. Ernest O. Holland and Henry Suzallo had been roommates and close friends at Columbia University, where Holland was a Ph.D. candidate when Suzallo was a young instructor. Then, in 1915, Holland was selected to be president of Washington State College and Suzallo was chosen to be the president of the University of Washington. As they approached their respective inaugurations, the two old friends amiably exchanged ideas about patching up differences between the two state schools. But the closer Suzallo came to taking up his new job, the more he assumed the point of view of *The University*. In one letter to Holland he had the gall to say that he was ready to help make WSC "the greatest school of agriculture in the world" if only Holland would consent to leave virtually everything else to the University of Washington.

By 1916 after both men took office, Suzallo was leading yet another attack on the state college. He wanted to take away the WSC's schools of architecture and pharmacy, end its graduate programs, including engineering, and make the place into a trade school with a feeble liberal arts college as an appendage. The two presidents, their respective boards of regents, alumni, and political supporters, prepared for war.

The showdown came in the Washington legislative session of 1917. When the struggle ended, even the University of Washington conceded that the State College of Washington's friends were too powerful; President Holland came away with the equivalent of a 49-0 victory. WSC retained complete freedom in granting graduate degrees and, once and for all, established the school's academic legitimacy. In the process, the twenty-five-year-old state college received a compliment that must have made those at the much older University of Washington wince. The legislature commissioned a panel of three educational experts of national reputation to study the situation and make recommendations on the dispute. In their final report the specialists commented: "In Washington, it might be re-marked in passing, the complete educational parity between the university and the land-grant college has long been established and is generally recognized."

THUS, THE ANCIENT RIVALRY BETWEEN WASHINGTON'S TWO MAJOR STATE institutions of higher learning was based in fundamentals: the University's distaste for competition on one hand, and the State College's interest in survival on the other.

It was different with that other traditional rival, the University of Idaho. WSC and the U of I had nothing against each other except that

A freshman rappelling down the "Stack" at the west side of campus to add his class' numerals.

they were neighbors. When University of Idaho students would come across the border for games, WSC students enthusiastically greeted them at the train station and engaged them in fist fights with practically no personal rancor at all.

For apparently, there had to be rivalries. Perhaps the young soul required a certain amount of conflict, as the body must have a certain amount of vitamin C, and there was just too little of this conflict growing naturally on a pleasant campus populated by friends. In any case, during those years when the campus was a student's whole world, rivalries proliferated almost as quickly as friendships. The creation of the Columbian Literary Society in the early 1890s postulated the founding of the Washingtonian Literary Society—someone to argue with. Because there was an agriculture college and an engineering college in the beginning, there was rivalry between the two that culminated every fall in a freewheeling, bloody combat roughly based on the game of football.

The longest running intramural rivalry was between the freshman and sophomore classes. Each fall the campus was the scene of a traditional gang war called the "frosh-sophomore supremacy fight." No one seemed to know why freshmen and sophomores didn't get along, but in the campus family they were the perpetually squabbling children. Whatever freshmen did, it seemed to irritate sophomores.

One night in the autumn of 1900, several freshmen sneaked over to the old brick smokestack that stood at the bottom of Campus Hill and painted their class number on it. When sophomores learned about it they were outraged—no doubt because they had not thought of it themselves a year earlier. The sophomores proclaimed that no freshman class should ever try such a thing again. So, every fall for the next thirty years, freshman classes designated groups of commandoes to sneak to the chimney with buckets of paint in hand. When vigilant sophomores caught them committing the forbidden act, the freshmen were roughed-up, tied-up, and forced to swear they would never again try to paint their class number on the smokestack. The culprits would swear it and then, the next week, they would sneak out and finish the paint job.

Sophomores spent a great deal of time thinking up rules to impose on freshmen, which freshmen violated any chance they got. The *Evergreen* for November 9, 1905 reported:

> The scrimmage in chapel Friday morning between
> sophs and freshies was the result of the sophomore
> proclamation. The freshmen took possession of two
> rows of sophomore seats, in this way showing their
> disregard for the rules laid down in the proclamation.
> The belligerents were quieted down by members of
> the senior class, but not before eight seats were
> broken.

Freshmen had to wear green beanies through the fall and spring, of course, and were restricted in all sorts of arbitrary ways besides.

They were not allowed to wear suits or collegiate corduroy slacks and freshman men were not allowed to escort women to major sporting events. The rules were taken seriously and sophomores enforced them with paddles. In 1911, the official sophomore "Big Stick" was initiated on the posterior of a freshman named Chester Boddy, "who felt greatly honored," according to the *Evergreen*.

By then an effort was made to control the freshmen-sophomore rivalry by formalizing a day-long competition between the two classes. The juniors and seniors designed a list of brutal contests to pit the freshmen and sophomores against each other. Then they sat by, Roman-like, and watched the excitement.

A typical contest placed several woolen sacks stuffed with straw, weighing 125 pounds each, in the middle of a field. Forty freshmen and forty sophomores then fought to see who could drag the most bags back to their respective goal lines. Though slugging had to be outlawed after the first competition, tying up opponents with ropes remained legal. These all-day competitions ended with tugs-of-war

"Crosley gets his for not having a 'fez,'" circa *1936. The fez was a crimson and grey cap shaped like a "Shriners" hat. All males were required to wear it the day before and the day of football games.*

Freshmen and sophomores competing in the annual supremacy bout, 1912.

across Silver Lake, the man-made pond that once occupied the area where Mooberry Track is now.

In the 1911 contest, neither side could muster the energy, after a full day of battle, to pull the other into the lake. The *Evergreen* reported:

> The contest was called a tie when darkness inter-vened and many were the protests from both camps, the froshes claiming that the sophs were "crooked" in digging holes with shovels for braces, and in having twenty-six men on the rope. The sophs came right back and claimed that their opponents substituted new men for tired ones, and so it goes.

THE INTRODUCTION OF FRATERNITIES TO CAMPUS IN THE DECADE following the turn of the century brought yet another source of rivalry, one with a more troublesome aspect. Competition among fraternities for status reached a point where a varsity football quarter-back might look around for a fraternity brother before he lateraled the ball. That led to the formation, in 1913, of Crimson Circle, an honorary that invited membership from all men's living groups to join together in supporting the school as a whole. Among the Crimson Circle's early successes was the inauguration of an annual song, yell, and skit competition, first held in 1914. It was for the 1914 contest that J. DeForest Cline wrote "Washington, My Washington," the song cho-sen as the WSC Alma Mater in 1919.

In 1913, Crimson Circle organized the first of twenty annual "Campus Days." On this day each spring, classes were cancelled and the entire student body organized into work parties to make im-provements to the campus. Engineering students supervised the building of sidewalk forms and poured concrete. Horticulture stu-

ABOVE: *"Late nighters."*

OPPOSITE, TOP: *"Come on in, the water is fine." Tug-of-war across Silver Lake in the freshman-sophomore supremacy bout, October 7, 1910.*

OPPOSITE, BOTTOM: *"Push Ball" game in the freshman-sophomore competition, October 6, 1911.*

dents supervised the planting of trees and bushes. Pullman citizens loaned the hundreds of hand tools that were used. That first year alone, 750 feet of sidewalk was poured and thirty wagon loads of sod laid. At noon, the laborers ate a lunch prepared by a group of women students. Brush and debris cleared from the campus produced a house-high bonfire for everyone to gather around that night. As much as the campus could use improvement, the real purpose of Campus Day was the creation of "school spirit."

For students of the era before World War II, college was more than a center for academic training; it was an exercise in society building. Student leaders worked to create an almost utopian community where everyone participated, everyone had fun, and everyone gained so much from the experience that they would treasure the memories for the remainder of their lives.

That goal could not be reached if students just sat in their rooms and prepared for classes. Student leaders, editors, and those who wrote letters to the *Evergreen* constantly warned their peers of the dangers of "apathy," a subversive force which, if left unchecked, threatened every accepted campus value—action, fun, athletic victory, and togetherness.

An article in the 1904 Christmas issue of the *Evergreen* titled "The Ideal College Man" explained:

> A student may master his studies, but if he does nothing more, he. . . loses the most valuable part of his college education. Perhaps the greatest gain of a college career comes from association with fellow students and from active participation in the many forms of college undertakings.

Above all, the article said, "the ideal college man is a man capable of genuine enthusiasm for his alma mater."

"Noise Merchants" Lusker McCroskey, Harold Holt, and George Gannon, ready for the 1914 football game with Oregon Agricultural College.

THE ULTIMATE MEASURE OF STUDENT BODY FORTITUDE WAS THE
Saturday athletic contest. For another school to schedule a football or
basketball game against WSC was considered a deliberate insult, and
the entire student body was called upon to respond. Getting a solid
turn-out for rallies and games was the most important test of student
leadership.

The seriousness with which the students took on these responsibilities is clear from the way they spoke of them. Most topics
discussed in the student newspaper—administration pronouncia-
mentos, academics, broken hearts, etc.—were treated with a standard drollery. The proper collegiate attitude toward life was amusement. When President Holland and the dean of women announced
new social rules, the *Evergreen* headline was: "Prexy Holland and
Dean Annie to Stop Necking on Campus."

But when the topic was a weekend football game, the tone turned
deadly serious. "Idaho has an admittedly strong team backed up by
an intensely loyal and enthusiastic student body," the *Evergreen*
intoned gravely in 1905. "It is up to us to send the biggest and most
patriotic band of rooters ever sent over the line." "The championship
of the West is at stake," a 1916 *Evergreen* editorial warned its readers.
In these circumstances, it asked, "Does one with true school loyalty
slight services or evade responsibilities to his college?" Adults seemed
to think that all that rah-rah stuff just happened spontaneously, which
showed how much they knew. "Annually we are confronted by the
necessity of rejuvenating what seems to be a declining college spirit,"
an editorial writer scolded in 1923. But doing so was a sacred
obligation. "Students think they won't be missed if they don't attend
the rallies," the *Evergreen* said in 1935. "We would certainly be in a
fine mess if everyone felt this way about our rallies." Fusty professors,
shut up in their campus offices with windows tightly closed against
the excitement outside, were likely to think all the hoopla over sports
was proof students were not serious. On the contrary! True irrespon-
sibility, any student leader of this era would have said, was to skip a
rally or a game, particularly if it was for the selfish purpose of
furthering one's career by studying. If you accept that student leaders
saw "spirit" as campus patriotism, an obligation to both past and
future, then you understand that their dedication, energy, and ingenuity was something to be admired, not lamented.

THIS "SPIRIT" WAS CONVERTIBLE TO OTHER CAUSES, WHEN THE CAUSES
seemed worthy. At the outbreak of the Spanish American War in
1898, the Washington Agricultural College Student Cadet Corps
petitioned the governor of the state to send them into federal service
immediately. When Governor John R. Rogers refused, football players Robert E. Bucklin and C. S. Sapp and a half dozen other students
went immediately to Uniontown and enlisted. A Navy recruiter
appeared before the WSC basketball team in 1918 to argue that they

shouldn't be playing games while their country was at war. Even the recruiter was surprised when the entire team enlisted on the spot.

Nor would it be fair to write off such enthusiasm as just another manifestation of "college kid" frivolity. Lee C. Lewis was a fraternity man and one of those who wrote sardonic commentary for the *Evergreen* and *Chinook* between 1914 and 1916. Two years later he was in France with the American Expeditionary Force. In a letter to his mother he described having seen a homeless woman and her daughter picking through the rubble of their bombed-out house. If he was doing anything to stop such tragedies, he wrote, he was glad he was a part of it. "Perhaps I should not have written this way, for I don't fear anything, but something might happen and I'd like you to know how I felt about it all." He was killed at Château-Thierry a month later. However much the nation fretted about its frivolous college students, there were no complaints about them when the chips were down.

ABOVE: *Typical "Joe College" in the 1910s and 1920s.*

RIGHT: *Student quartet, 1920s.*

IN PEACETIME, HOWEVER, THE ENEMY WAS THE UNIVERSITY OF WASH-
ington, or whoever happened to be the invading team of the week.
Who could count the late Monday nights, the long Tuesday afternoons, the laborious Wednesday evenings spent inventing and
painting spirit-generating jewels like "Mush the Huskies" and "Milk
Ma's-Cow."

If the team was leaving on a train for an away game, a thousand or
more students would form a serpentine and snake their way through
campus and to the train station for a noisy rally at trackside.*

Rallies for home games were held in the large, vacant field where
Holland Library now stands, or in the "Old Quad" on the downhill
side of Bryan Hall. A Friday night in football season: thousands of
students and townspeople bump shoulders in the crisp, October air
and cheer themselves into a boisterous mood. Spotlights slash
dramatically through the dark. A trumpet rips the night air and the
crowd responds with a roar. The president of the college mounts the
stand and wishes the team good luck with as much emotion as the
dignity of his position allows. The student body president and other
"big men on campus" ascend the platform to pronounce their faith in
destiny. The yell king and his two dukes (there were no female
cheerleaders until 1940) raise their megaphones and hoarsely flog
the crowd into a happy mob.

Here is how a participant would experience it: there is no need to
request silence when Coach "Babe" Hollingbery gets on the platform;
the mere sight of him brings a hush to the crowd. He speaks in what
one student described as "his halting way," his tongue catching on
every other word as he consciously controlled his stuttering. The
speech impediment has an ennobling effect, suggesting a show of
humility by one for whom it was manifestly unnecessary. It also gives
the sentences a dramatic punch. "Well," Babe might have said to the
hushed crowd, "we're not fooling ourselves about our opponent. But
the boys worked hard, . . . and, . . . well, . . . just maybe we've got some
surprises in store for them!"

When the eighty-five-piece band bursts forth to the pounding
rhythm of

> Fight, fight, fight
> for Washington State. . . .**

participants don't so much hear as they feel it in some repository of
thrills buried deep in the chest.

For homecoming games, these rallies were held around a bonfire
that began as an architectural masterpiece of boxes, doors, tree limbs,
cardboard boxes, outhouses, fence posts, road signs, and whatnot.

---

*In the twenties, students often gathered in Bryan Hall Auditorium to listen to the
away games over a radio rigged to a giant speaker. The lights were dimmed so
that a flashlight could follow, on a screen prepared to resemble a football field,
the movement of the ball as each play was described.

**Words by Zella Melcher, '19; music by Phyllis Sayles, '19.

As a matter of courtesy to local residents, WSC students tried to steal as much of this material as possible from across the state line in Moscow. This was no doubt appreciated by local residents, but was of limited help, since University of Idaho students simply came to Pullman to steal the materials for their own bonfire.

It was customary, in the twenties, for students at WSC and U of I to try to ignite each others' homecoming fires prematurely. In 1924, Washington State outdid itself by equipping a student with incendiaries and an airplane to bomb the University of Idaho pyre. Unfortunately, in buzzing back and forth looking for his target, the first and only Cougar air force pilot irritated a farmer, who shot at him with a duck gun and forced an emergency landing.

When games were over, and victories won, the Intercollegiate Knights announced the results by ringing the Victory Bell.* The length of time they rang it, working in shifts, depended on the immensity of the victory, and sometimes, when the Huskies were thoroughly drubbed, the clanging would go on and on, late into the night, echoing through the campus, penetrating dorm walls, the library, the Cougar Cottage, insinuating itself into every conversation and every thought.

THE SUPREME CAMPUS VALUES OF "PARTICIPATION" AND "SUPPORT" applied to dances, drama, and debate as well as sports. Campus citizenship meant serving with enthusiasm on the dance decorating committee just as surely as it meant trying out for the basketball team. But sports appealed most directly to the core of college values: action, comradery, conformity, risk, rivalry, mischief, and sincerity. Football was the major sport from the beginning because it epitomized what students thought life ought to be—and that was not fun and diversion but danger and dedication. Sports were supposed to be heroic, not entertaining. Post-game descriptions of games in the *Evergreen* took on an almost Homeric diction:

> On the roll of honor, at the top of the list, stands
> the name of Heintzelman, who, but his second
> chance this season, played a marvelous game, espe-
> cially in the defense. Battered and torn by the ma-
> chine-like interference that came around his end time
> and time again, he gave no thought of numbers and
> invariably stayed with the rushing mass of opposing
> brawn and speed until he had captured his man. The
> awful strain told on him physically, but his 140
> pounds of pure nerve and fight brought him up on
> his feet again, ready for another onslaughter [*sic*].
>
> *Evergreen*, November 15, 1910

*The same bell that called the first students to class in 1892. It still rings after football victories.

OPPOSITE, TOP: *Mud-caked glory. WSC beats Idaho 18-0, November 4, 1909.*

OPPOSITE, BOTTOM: *Rogers Field fans.*

That was part of a story describing a losing effort. Imagine student body awe when suddenly in 1915 the team defeated Oregon 28-3; Oregon State 29-0; Idaho 41-0; Montana 27-7; Whitman 17-0; and Gonzaga 48-0.

Students were in a tizzy, fans ecstatic. Sports editors all over the West ransacked their vocabularies for verbs powerful enough to put behind the name Washington State. The creator of this marvel of a team, William "Lonestar" Dietz, part Sioux Indian and a dandy who sometimes posed in full Indian regalia, received a telegram late in the fall of 1915: would Washington State College be willing to face Brown University, champions of the Ivy League, on New Year's Day in Pasadena, California? This proposed "Rose Bowl" (the first of the modern series, preceded only by a false start held in 1902) would match a Western college against Ivy Leaguers to see if football out West was to be taken seriously. Before the eyes of the nation,

1916 Rose Bowl team. Coach "Lone Star" Dietz (with cane) next to actress Hazel Daley.
The squad "co-starred" in Brown of Harvard, *a 1917 film.*

Washington State College would defend the West against the long-standing Eastern dominance of college football.

Students and townsfolk thronged the Pullman railroad station. Coach Dietz gave a modest speech declaring that the Eastern team did not know the trouble it was in. A blast of steam, a whistle, and the train pulled away.

It was prearranged; since there was no radio, the campus power plant whistle would signal the score that New Year's Day in 1916, counting out first WSC's score and then Brown's. By late afternoon, those on campus waited nervously. The air was suddenly filled with blasts from the deep-throated whistle—16 of them. Then the pause for Brown's score and—nothing! When the team pulled into the Pullman station a few days later, a "wild, howling, cheering" crowd greeted them. Fans jammed Grand Avenue for blocks. Pullman Mayor Harley Jackson was on horseback dressed up like a Sioux Indian.

THE ONE THING THAT HAD MARRED THAT FAMOUS SEASON WAS—YOU might have guessed—the University of Washington. WSC had played the cross-state rival in Seattle in 1912, 1913, and 1914. It asked that in 1915 the UW come to Pullman, but the University "refused to come out of its backyard," as the *Evergreen* put it. It thus avoided meeting the most devastating WSC football team in history. The cross-state series was resumed again in 1917 (WSC 14-UW 0) but ceased again in 1920; this time the University didn't want to split gate receipts fifty-fifty. That spring "Doc" Bohler, athletic director and track coach, had to threaten to cancel a track meet because the University's coach wanted to pit the standard twelve-man WSC traveling team against a fifteen-man UW team. Somehow, whenever Washington State had problems, it was with the University.

The worst of all came on the night of November 16, 1919. Three weeks earlier the WSC football team had pursued California so relentlessly, in beating it 14-0, that a San Francisco cartoonist drew a beleaguered California Bear trying to free itself from a Northwest cougar.

Cougar! Independent, indigenous, powerful, beautiful. Students realized instantly that this feline perfectly captured what it meant to attend WSC. Within a week the Cougar was adopted as the official mascot and student leaders managed to round up a stuffed specimen to show at the next game.* It was stored on the porch of Bryan Hall in the meantime, and before WSC even got a chance to display it at

*For a detailed account of how the Cougar came to be the school's mascot, see the companion volume to this book: Richard B. Fry's *The Crimson and the Gray: 100 Years with the WSU Cougars* (Pullman: Washington State University Press, 1989). Washington State College acquired its first live mascot in 1927, a gift of Governor Roland Hartley. The Cougar was soon nicknamed Butch after Herbert "Butch" Meeker, the ferocious 140-pound quarterback who led the team through the successful 1928 season. It was perhaps coincidental, but Hartley was a political enemy of University of Washington President Suzzalo.

a game, the mascot was stolen by a marauding band of University of Washington students.

Thereafter, the only problem with the missing, stuffed Cougar was that it was in the hands of the Huskies. It was an insult Cougars could never forget—were not allowed to. As a matter of fact, every time the schools' football teams met, the trophy was paraded around the football field by UW lettermen. It was a galling sight to every Cougar, but most of all to Frank Douglass, WSC "Rooter King" that fatal year of 1919, and later a Seattle pediatrician who never missed a WSC-UW match, and who always flinched when the UW brought out the captive cat.

The situation came to a head in 1932. The night before the annual game, WSC students descended upon a downtown Seattle store where the Cougar was on display (along with a Golden Bear from the University of California at Berkeley). The Washington State students were unable to retrieve the Cougar, but managed to block the store's doors so Husky lettermen couldn't take their prize to a pre-game rally. The episode was reported in the Seattle *Post-Intelligencer* under the headline "Co-Ed Keeps Husky Men Under Lock and Key."

> Blonde and beautiful Jeanette Olsen of Washington State College last night prevented 10 University of Washington athletes from taking Husky campus trophies from Littler's haberdashery store, where they have been exhibited for the past week. Directing a siege upon all doorways from six to seven-thirty in the evening by WSC football players and students, Miss Olsen made it impossible for Washington to display the Stick, Cougar, siren and other trophies at the school's pre-game parade.

That night WSC students stole a stuffed Husky mascot and the UW "Big Stick."

At the game the next day, the Huskies were naturally expecting an attempt by WSC to retrieve the stuffed Cougar. At halftime when the stolen trophy appeared, it was borne on the shoulders of four fleet-footed Husky lettermen, who would break for their side of the field at the first sign of trouble. Other UW lettermen armed with clubs surrounded the Cougar to delay any attackers. The Huskies paraded the Cougar before their own rooting section, then looped around and moved toward the Cougar bleachers, hooting and grinning.

Cougar Yell King Walley Halsey and his dukes, Milt Wyatt and Ken Bement, watched the show with arms folded. When the Huskies came abreast, Halsey and Wyatt suddenly knelt down as Bement placed his foot in their cupped hands. They lifted up with all their strength and Bement went sailing through the air over the heads of the Husky guards. He came down on the Cougar, toppling the platform and its bearers.

This was the prearranged signal, and every male WSC rooter ran out of the stands and overwhelmed the Husky guards. Husky rooters responded by streaming out of their own stands. The brawl that followed delayed the second half of the game a half hour and made national newsreels. In the melee the Cougar was ripped to shreds, never to be paraded again. The game ended in a 0-0 tie.

At the bottom of the pile, Bement found himself pinned to the ground next to an older man who had been one of the first out of the stands. While they waited for the pileup to thin so they could move, Frank Douglass, former rooter king, smiled and shouted to Bement that he had waited a long time for this moment.

Many things have changed about campus life. The famous rivalries between freshmen and sophomores, aggies and engineers, fraternities and independents, have all cooled. The oldest rivalry of all, with the University of Idaho Vandals, is all but forgotten. If a WSU student goes "over the line" now it is more likely to take a class under joint instructional agreements than for a raid.

So it is possible for rivalries to cool and to be transformed into mutual respect and cooperation.

With anyone but the Huskies. ■

Spirit

"Serpentine" on Rogers Field before the WSC-Oregon Agricultural College contest, October 14, 1910.

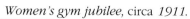

Women's gym jubilee, circa *1911.*

RIGHT: *President Bryan and an associate eating lunch at one of the early "Campus Days."*

BELOW: *Students building a sidewalk in front of Ferry Hall on "Campus Day,"* circa *1914*

LEFT: *Two of the five male "Bosses" overseeing work on "Campus Day," circa 1914. Five women "Bosses" organized the noon meal.*

BELOW: *Students constructing a sidewalk to Van Doren Hall, May 2, 1913.*

WAC campus, circa *1904. Foreground buildings include, from the left: Science Hall (now part of Murrow Hall), the Administration Building (today's Thompson Hall), the original College Hall (a wooden structure; moved a couple of times), and the Gymnasium, which partially obscures a view of Stevens Hall. Football team practices in front of the gym.*

May Day, 1912. Presiding, from the left: Harry Chambers, Anna Taylor, and Isabelle McRae.

Students form a "W" on Rogers Field at halftime of the WSC-Idaho game, October 21, 1910. Note Silver Lake in the background.

Sigma Nu brothers "Got," "Alonzo," and "Breadth," circa 1910. "Breadth" was a football player.

A student football team representing the class of 1912.

Sleeping Porch Politics

BEFORE WORLD WAR II STUDENT GOVERNMENT WAS NOT THE UTILITAR-ian thing it would become later, an agency through which students could negotiate with the administration. It was occupied instead with tasks like planning pep rallies and homecomings, raising money to hire bands for major dances, and for choosing school newspaper and yearbook editors.

These were important assignments, but not tasks that raised major issues or divided student opinion. Nevertheless, campus politics claimed large amounts of time and energy from many of the best students, including, for example, Edward R. Murrow. The game itself was the attraction. Students played politics as if it were an intramural sport, allowing would-be leaders to test their abilities in competitions given zest by traditional campus rivalries.

Like these rivalries, campus loyalties were defined in terms of living groups. Where you stood on issues depended on where you bedded down. If you slept in the rambling houses along fraternity row on the north side of campus, you probably considered yourself a member of the social aristocracy that ruled campus affairs as a natural right.

If you slept on the other side of Campus Hill, in Ferry, Stimson, Waller, Pine Manor, or another of the men's residences, you cynically conceded to the fraternities their power, and perhaps helped to plot one of the rebellions against it that erupted every few years. In the inter-war era women did not occupy leadership roles in campus political life. Sororities generally supported fraternity candidates, while leaders of the men's dormitories made their appeals to the class loyalties of those who lived in women's dorms.

THE EARLIEST STUDENT ELECTIONS AT WSC WERE ESSENTIALLY PERSON-ality contests. To understand how this situation changed over time and how campus politics became more complex and more interest-ing, a tour of student housing before World War II is useful.

Ferry Hall, the four-story brick edifice that once stood where the Eastlick Biological Science Building is now located, was the only men's dorm for the first thirty years of the campus's existence. Since men were the undisputed rulers of campus politics in this era, Ferry wore its cupola (now preserved just uphill from where the building

OPPOSITE: *Ferry Hall dormitory room at the turn of the century.*

Four friends in 1923 (top) and 1973 (bottom). From the left: Jack Dodd, Harry Weller, Glenn Maughmer, and Harold Eddy, all class of 1923. Though hardly keeping in contact for a half century, they kept tabs on each other in the alumni newspaper. They met again at the 1973 golden reunion.

once stood) like a crown. Countless ad hoc "fraternities" were formed in Ferry Hall based on interests in sports, academics, hunting, politics, or simply that nebulous affinity called friendship. Harry Weller, the forlorn Tacoma boy described in chapter one checking into Ferry Hall, quickly formed friendships with Glenn Maughmer and Harold Eddy. Maughmer was a brilliant, mischievous engineering student; Eddy a somber, World War I combat veteran, a head waiter, and a role model for men living in Ferry. This friendship lasted a lifetime.

What initially brought Weller, Maughmer, and Eddy together was an interest in amateur crooning. In the early 1920s commercial radio had not yet reached Pullman. Except for an occasional band brought in for a dance, what music students had was necessarily home made. Weller and his friends would practice the latest songs around the Ferry Hall piano and then, on certain pleasant evenings, assemble in front of a women's dormitory and hold forth. The titles of songs they sang, "I'll Tell You My Dreams If You Tell Me Yours," or "Let Me Call You Sweetheart," sound as if they were written to be sung in the dark of mild spring evenings, baritone and tenor voices rising up to smiling faces gathered at open windows.

Those women's dorms, Community and McCroskey, were built in 1921 with money raised from community bond sales after the

Vera Kidwell, Ann Matsen, and Eunice Thrift, circa 1913.

Washington Legislature refused to allocate the funds (thus Community's name). Like Stevens Hall, these dorms and Duncan Dunn (completed in 1926) accumulated traditions and alumni until they became de facto sororities; a woman did not just live in McCroskey Hall, she was a "McCroskey girl."

The main advantage of dormitory life was the opposite of the main advantage of fraternity or sorority life. In dormitories, people had not been pre-sorted and they learned to live with all types. Dorothy Jeanette Carroll, '38, remembered all the types. First, there was the roommate who borrowed clothes without asking. Next came the intellectual, "aloof, serious, well-organized." That roommate had a vast vocabulary; while sharing a room with her, Carroll said , "my own increased at least two-fold." Her third roommate was Mary Huggins, who would attend her in her wedding after college and become a life-long friend.

Dorothy liked McCroskey Hall better than Duncan Dunn for a special reason. Duncan Dunn was directly across the street from Lambda Chi fraternity. And one warm day while she lounged about her room casually dressed, she heard a husky, male voice through the open window shout, "Hey, Dorothy!" She nearly fainted before she realized that the voice had called "Hey, Doherty!" for Roger Doherty of Lambda Chi. "Roger was evidently much in demand," Dorothy said, for she suffered near heart failure dozens of times before she changed dorms.

Stevens Hall residents in 1922. Kneeling in front is an impromptu band with comb and wax paper "kazoos" and the ubiquitous ukelele.

AFTER WORLD WAR I, WSC'S ENROLLMENT GREW AT THE RATE OF ABOUT 100 students per year.* Construction of Community, McCroskey, and Stimson halls with public subscriptions was one answer to the expanded need for housing. The same emergency spawned "co-ops," like Pine Manor for men and Linden Cottage for women. Those who lived in them did their own cooking (or chipped in to hire a cook), took turns waiting tables and doing the dishes, did all the repairing and painting that was required, and were generally autonomous of the college administration. "Strangely enough," Ralph Wood wrote to his parents shortly after moving into Pine Manor in 1942, "almost no formal pressure is necessary in order to make the fellows come through with the work. Group pressure can be very strong when one slacker means that his companions will have to work that much harder." Doing for themselves extended to nearly every detail of daily life; when the Pine Manor barber was about to graduate in 1940, he trained Robert DeVlemming to give the house haircut.

The most common form of off-campus living in the twenties and thirties was the boarding house. Mom Thornton's, across A Street from Delta Delta Delta sorority, was typical of the dozens of boarding

ABOVE: *"Mom" Thornton sitting on the porch of her "A" Street boarding house, 1938.*

BELOW: *"Mom" Thornton's boarders.*

* To estimate the college's regular enrollment for any given year up to World War II, roughly figure 100 students for each year of the century—thus, in 1910 the school had about 1,000 students, in 1920 it was about 2,000, and so on. More exact figures are: 2,045 students in 1922-23; 3,033 students in 1929-30; 4,155 students in 1937-38.

houses that surrounded the campus. Mrs. Thornton, "a kindly and jolly lady with a ready smile," took in students, ranging from freshman football player and future student body president Chris Rumburg, to pharmacy graduate student Junichi Tomita of Hawaii, and the tall gray-haired lady from New York who loved to share gossip around the dining table.

A calm not typical in other student housing prevailed in boarding houses. Occasionally there was a ruckus, like the time an engineering student at Mom Thornton's wired another boarder's bed to an electrical outlet. But for the most part boarding houses operated and were treated as home. Mrs. Thornton, called "Major" or "The Maj" by boarders, liked to discuss the prospects of the college's athletic teams at the dinner table. Most boarders were men, and they spent a lot of time kidding the Thornton's two pretty college-aged daughters, Genevive and Geraldine. The "painfully shy" houseboy Glen Davidson, an industrial arts major, was often the butt of little jokes— like the time everyone around the table took turns salting his dish of ice cream as he went back and forth to the kitchen. When he finally looked up from dessert and asked, "Does yours taste a little salty?" the burst of laughter was that of a family at one of its own.

The only cheaper way to live than the attic room of a boarding house was that amorphous category called "batching it." This could, of course, mean a nicely appointed apartment on Maiden Lane, where some football players with proud fathers lived fabled lives that included beer in the icebox and unchaperoned female visitors. More typically "batching it" meant you were scraping and scavenging to survive as best you could while trying to get an education. This was nobody's choice of living accommodations, but it provided some famous stories. In 1932, for example, physics major Peter E. Kragt arrived in Pullman three days before fall semester started. He next purchased a thousand board feet of lumber and proceeded to build a tiny cabin on a borrowed piece of land. It was finished the day school opened. By boiling potatoes on a small stove and by joining no groups that charged dues, he figured he lived on $140 for the entire school year. That story of survival won an essay contest on the subject "How I Economized Last Semester" sponsored by President Holland. But it wasn't as unusual as it may sound. In 1932 Bob Sandberg and Bob Cheatham, two Spokane friends, built an eight-foot by sixteen-foot shack in Spokane. Then they had it towed to Pullman, where journalism professor Joe Ashlock allowed them to put it in his backyard. They hooked up to Ashlock's water, sewer, and electricity for a dollar a month.

Most "batchers" rented tiny basements, attics, or garage rooms. Wilber B. Gilbert, '37, shared a basement with five other guys. "We ate lots of oatmeal, chili, and cheap cuts of meat," he recalled. "When one of us got cookies from home, we'd draw straws to see who had to go and 'liberate' a quart of milk [from the doorstep] at one of the apartment houses."

Scavenging was an unrecognized WSC tradition. Sororities that left windows open to cool the kitchen were legendary for involuntarily

generosity with their cakes and pies. Farmers went into their vegetable gardens in the morning to find them neatly harvested overnight.
The college's apple orchard was considered a sort of natural student-
assistance program. In the 1930s the college chicken farm had to be
guarded by watchdogs and floodlights.

Between the two world wars, the Washington State College
student body was largely made up of kids who didn't have enough
money to go to school. The agricultural depression that followed
World War I kept their parents poor until the Great Depression made
things even worse after 1929. In 1921, the school administration
estimated that eighty-three percent of the students were earning at
least a quarter of their expenses. Vet student Vernon Cline, '23, was
typical of many students who considered study the fun part of
college. He got up at 3:30 a.m., worked in the dairy barn until 8 a.m.,
drank a glass of cream for breakfast, then started classes. Times were
even tougher in the next decade with the onset of the Great Depression.

Dropping out for a semester or a year to earn money was a
common practice throughout the thirties. By dropping out, and then
back in again when he could afford it, Rolf Jorgensen, '36, earned
every penny of the $1,555 depression dollars it cost him to go through
college, and he finished in seven semesters by taking correspondence courses during the periods he was working full time.

Dan Eagle, '39, opened his own art shop in desperation. He was
soon making such good money, hand decorating dance programs
and doing other design work, that he couldn't afford to take another
job after graduation. Shirley Stewart, '37, earned college expense
money by canning and selling her own brand of jam. Typical part-
time jobs for women involved cleaning and babysitting in private
homes in return for room and board. Many male students worked on
farms surrounding college. Robert Holz, '37, got up early on Saturday
mornings to walk three miles to a dairy farm owned by two bachelor
brothers. There he spent the day washing dishes, scrubbing floors,
cleaning animal stalls, pitching hay, and removing boulders from
fields. Then he walked back to Sigma Chi for dinner. All this for $2.50
a day.

Perhaps the most common job of all, for both men and women,
was working in a kitchen. If an honorary called the Order of the
Soggy Apron had existed, it would have been the largest one on
campus, and perhaps one of the proudest. Edward R. Murrow made
it through his freshman year washing dishes in a sorority. William
Bugge, '23, a future director of the Washington State Department of
Highways, gained early experience organizing massive tasks when
he worked as a scullery boy for the Robinson Restaurant and Bakery.
Left alone at 11 p.m. with the dirty dishes of 150 banqueters in the
gym, he carried the glasses, plates, cups, and silverware into the
shower room, arranged them in the shower stalls, and turned on the
hot water. Ten minutes later he turned off the water, stacked the
dishes, and went home.

"Around campus," 1926.

BECAUSE HE WORKED EVERY NIGHT AND ALL DAY SATURDAY, "I COULD not enjoy many privileges of college life," Bugge would say much later. "I fully realized the loss I was experiencing, but in the final analysis it was the situation I had to live with."

In the scheme of campus politics, people like Bugge were important. They didn't have the time to get involved in student government, but they still voted. In fact, their votes represented the margin of victory for dormitories over Greek Row anytime the dorms could arouse sufficient excitement among the "independents."

This hardly seemed right to fraternities. They, after all, were by constitution and inclination dedicated to campus leadership. It was no voting day issue with them, but one of the main reasons for their existence. Fraternities and sororities considered themselves to be the campus's natural aristocracy.

The first local fraternity was formed in 1905 when an informal club at Ferry Hall moved out and rented an old house on the other side of campus. Several other "locals" organized soon thereafter. Kappa Sigma became the first living group to get a national charter on campus in 1909, followed a year later by Sigma Nu, then Alpha Tau Omega in 1911, Sigma Phi Epsilon in 1912, Lamba Chi Alpha in 1914,

Sigma Alpha Epsilon in 1915, and Phi Delta Theta in 1918. The first nationally chartered sororities were Phi Beta Phi and Alpha Delta Pi, both installed in 1912. Alpha Chi Omega followed in 1915, and Delta Delta Delta in 1918.

Fraternity and sorority members gave up dorm rooms and moved into old family houses along residential streets, especially Linden and Colorado, and Greek Row was established. These were anything but posh addresses. In the mid '20s the most inviting room in the original Alpha Gamma Delta sorority house on the southeast corner of Colorado and Thatuna had a plain parlor with an old upright piano, rocking chair, davenport, fringed rug, and a single Maxfield Parrish print on the wall. The kitchen was so bad that three different cooks quit in disgust. In the basement, black-eyed rats scurried around the laundry tubs.

It was no simple matter to explain to entering freshmen why they should pay higher fees to live in such places, not to mention enduring the truly rigorous hazing that, in those days, included sleepless nights and bruising hacks for fraternity pledges. Yet students joined in droves. Whereas fraternities and sororities housed only a small portion of the student body at the end of World War I, five years later, in 1922, about one in three students lived in a Greek house; by 1930, over half the students on campus were members of a fraternity or sorority.

One reason for this growth was the constant and persuasive recruiting. When a fraternity or sorority decided you should join, it was hard to say no. If you told Greek recruiters their monthly bill was too high, they would respond with a convoluted explanation showing that though the bill was higher, the expense was less, because house dues included many social events one would surely pay for separately otherwise. If you said you just didn't have the money, they

"Local fraternity" Psi Nu Sigma,
circa *1923.*

At home in Sigma Nu, circa 1923.

would offer to get you a job (which they could do, through ex-Greeks who had businesses downtown). If you said all you came to college for was to study mathematics and play in the band, they would call up *their* math whiz and member of the band and have them come over to meet you.

The most impressive thing was that they went to such lengths to recruit you at all. Somebody (and big shots, at that) really wanted you in their organization. The appeal of fraternities and sororities wasn't so much that they were exclusive as that they were *inclusive*. No matter how many great people you might meet in a dorm, there was always something of the hotel about it: waxed hallways, numbers on the doors, people moving in and out all the time. The fraternity or sorority house, on the other hand, had the asymmetry of a real home. You got familiar with the feel of the banister on the stairway, the worn spot in the couch, the view of the trees through the front window in fall, winter, and spring. In a smaller group and a much smaller structure, relationships had the cumulative, implosive nature of family. The guy who hacked you with the most relish during initiation might turn out to be the one who, two years later, got you through statistics class.

WSU's oldest living fraternity man, Floyd Smith of Yakima, remembered, three-quarters of a century later, the evening gatherings in 1912 and 1913 at Alpha Zeta. The other guys—Harry Chambers, the debate champion, Hackenschmidt "Hack" Applequist, the muscle-bound but cheerful football star, and all the others—would lounge about the chapter room in the evening swapping stories. Sooner or later Jock Whitesall, a tall skinny kid, folded his long legs under the piano bench and began pounding away at the keys, while the whole group harmonized the latest songs. It was, the ninety-six-year-old fraternity man said, "a wonderful bunch of fellows."

ALONG WITH THE MISTY FEELINGS THERE WAS THE SOCIAL OIL THAT, LIKE the community hair oil in Theta Chi, came with fraternity membership. Everyone knew, even those who had to admit it grudgingly, that if you were looking for social life, Greek Row was where the action was.

There was a sense among Greeks that if you weren't in a fraternity or sorority it must mean that (as one thirties era fraternity man put it) "you had less personality, less on the ball." Actually, the thing most non-Greeks had less of was money. Not that Greeks were rich kids; there weren't many of those at WSC. But students who lived in the dorms were often so poor that even the few dollars extra a month it might cost to live on Greek Row was impossible, not to mention the wardrobe and other trappings of formal social life of the era. "I think many of us envied the frat men, and if we could have afforded it, would have pledged fraternities," said Matt Strauss, president of Ferry Hall in 1925 and later a school superintendent. He turned down invitations to join fraternities because he barely met the costs of college as it was. Though he had many friends in fraternities, "I was made to feel by some [Greeks] that I was one of the 'unwashed,'" he said.

Independents reciprocated by typifying fraternity men as (as a 1918 *Evergreen* article said) "lounge lizards and fireside artists" whose pretensions to superiority were ridiculous. Everyone on campus came from "the same common stock," the *Evergreen* article noted. It was curious how "plebeian ancestry does not follow one into his fraternity."

These social fissures were not serious; they were simply another manifestation of spontaneous rivalries that were always bubbling up on campus. The gap between fraternity members and non-fraternity members meant less at WSC than at most other colleges in the country. On a small campus populated almost exclusively by the children of working and middle class parents, everyone associated with everyone.

But small social distinctions provided the basis for campus political division. Members of fraternities and sororities got to know each other well because of an almost constant round of dances, "firesides," and impromptu social gatherings. In contrast, as one fraternity man put it, "independents were more difficult to get acquainted with." This difference became the mainspring of student politics from 1920 to 1940.

From their first appearance in the 1910s, fraternities dominated leadership in campus politics by vigorously recruiting those considered "big men on campus." There seemed to be no issues in student politics; a candidate's main argument for himself was a list of sports honors, debate competitions, editorial offices, and other services to the campus. Such types were just the ones heavily recruited by fraternities. It wasn't hard to lure them away from homely old Ferry Hall, which, with its mere 100 tenants, was not even much of a political base.

But things changed in 1922. That year Stimson Hall was completed and opened to 200 male students. Located on the other side of   *Stimson Hall in 1923.*

Campus Hill, Stimson had attractions to rival those of the social fraternities. With its august colonial façade, leather furniture, and courtyard fountain, it was the most luxurious student residence in Pullman. Its long, hardwood lobby was indisputably the best dance floor on campus—and of such advantages were campus political empires made. A lot of engineering majors chose Stimson, and engineering carried great prestige. Many ROTC leaders also chose Stimson, and in those days ROTC was an a major organization and an important part of campus life. Stimson developed an elite image that it retained long after other men's dorms were constructed.

Stimson housed mostly freshmen. They were guided through their first year in college by a cadre of upperclassmen, who served as floor monitors and waiters in the Commons, a community dining hall built in 1924. When these waiters gathered around a table for their own meal before they began serving the others, they discussed campus affairs and became a de facto party caucus. They organized the Stimson Senate in 1922 "to promote better unity, definite action and group spirit." This senate became the official center of "Independent" (non-fraternity) politics. Ferry Hall waiters (serving upstairs in the Commons) were natural allies, and of course these waiter-leaders had the ears of the dorm dwellers for a political message three times each day.

Stimson Hall became the political base of such renowned student leaders as Frank Cleary, Hugh Tinling, Felix McLarney, Frank Misner, and Fred Weller—all names that turned heads on campus. Stimson had not even been officially named in 1923 when Frank Misner of "New Dorm" was elected student body president—the first non-fraternity man to hold the position in eight years. The following year another Stimson Hall man, Fred Weller, the likeable and loquacious debate champion (and brother of Harry Weller, recently of Ferry

Leaders of the newly organized "Stimson Senate," which guided the new dormitory in campus politics.

Hall), defeated two fraternity men who had divided the Greek vote between them.

It became obvious to fraternities that they had better cooperate with one another. The Commons conspiracy would defeat them every time if they continued to divide Greek Row votes. Cooperation was not a new idea and, in fact, a mechanism for bringing it into being already existed in the form of a "secret" intrafraternity organization called Theta Nu Epsilon, TNE for short. TNE existed as an unofficial organization at many colleges and universities across the country, though there was little, if any, cooperation between campuses.

Theta Nu Epsilon had been at WSC since about 1912 or 1913, but hadn't prospered. It was first mentioned in print in the 1920 *Yellow Jacket*, a broadside issued every year on Campus Day to shake up administrators and others. The article said:

TNE pin, 1920s.

> Theta Nu Epsilon has been a sinister factor in State College politics for many years, but at no time has it been more evident than it is today. There is but one acknowledged member on the campus and he is unwilling to show his pin. But not long ago, he came out with more than intended when, under the spell of demon rum, he announced that initiations had been held this spring.

Because it insisted on acting in secrecy, most fraternities initially opposed TNE. The secrecy, however, besides being fun, was also based on one practical consideration. If it were generally known that fraternities and sororities were coordinating their voting, non-Greeks would do the same, and, being more numerous, could win any election.

After the back-to-back wins by Stimson Hall candidates in 1923 and 1924, the major fraternities set aside their quibbles and began to cooperate under the auspices of TNE. Winning campus elections was a matter of getting organized and of getting enough cooperation to deliver a block of votes. Organization and cooperation were what fraternities did best. Once fraternity leaders put their minds to the problem, the independents were practically swept from the field. A fraternity candidate won the next election, and for the next ten years TNE ran the campus.

Most students did not even know there was an organization called Theta Nu Epsilon. It existed without written rules, formal meetings, or elections. Each major fraternity had two members. They were not elected, but were handpicked by other TNEs based on leadership potential. Robert E. Bucklin,* '25, recalled how flattered he was to be approached by two of the biggest of big men on campus and told, more or less, "You've been singled out as a campus leader by us insiders." He had some vague notion of a secret organization, but until that moment, no idea of who belonged to it.

---

* Son of Robert Eben Bucklin, the loyal student quoted in chapter one.

Bucklin was chosen for TNE membership because he was *Evergreen* editor and active in student government. TNE members had to command respect in their own fraternities so that they could "deliver the vote" to anointed candidates. Some TNE members ran for student offices, while others worked behind the scenes.

Even fraternity members might not know for sure who their TNE representatives were. This lent an air of mystery to the whole thing that college men loved. People "in the know" might whisper: "Smith is TNE." If no one whispered it, Smith might have to whisper it himself, since it was, after all, one of the most prestigious affiliations on campus.

The initiation of new TNE members usually took place each fall at a drinking party around a bonfire in some remote field. Business meetings were held in carefully guarded basements or chapter rooms in one or another of the fraternities. The most important TNE gathering was the one held to broker campus offices and other prizes for the year. The student body presidency and editorship of the *Evergreen* were supposed to rotate among participating fraternities. But this depended somewhat on the candidates available, so that a fraternity due the presidency might agree to barter the position away for some other consideration—perhaps the sports editorship for one of the guys, or a list of campus committee assignments. There were also two yell king and dukes, seven members of the board of control (as the student council was called at the time), class officers, and various other positions to be discussed. Many a Homecoming and Harvest Ball queen was chosen at TNE meetings.

TNE was wise enough to give something to everyone, including "the dormies" and off-campus students. If a worthy dorm candidate planned to run for a lesser campus office, TNE might agree to support him, especially if his popularity was such that he might win anyway. But leaders from the top six or seven fraternities effectively controlled student activities, from pep rallies to dealings with the administration. "Unless you were a member of one of these," said TNE member Kenneth Kennedy, "your chance of getting one of the campus plums was pretty remote."

TNE connections went beyond campus politics. Someone might announce at a meeting that he or one of his fellow fraternity men was now in the business of contracting to decorate for major campus dances, and so would appreciate support from the campus social chairmen. Such useful business connections put some of WSU's best known graduates through college.

The college administration was tapped into TNE via Earl Foster, the college's "graduate manager," a sort of supervisor of student activities. Foster worked with TNE members as the student leaders they were.

The combination of the traditionally high Greek Row voter turnout and sheer growth (19 fraternities and sororities formed between 1916 and 1929) would have made united fraternities and sororities difficult to beat in any case. TNE husbanded this power expertly. Candidates were usually well-chosen and needed little help in winning. The odds could be improved further during the nomination process by a suggestion that "everybody knows he's the logical guy." Everyone had to be impressed, for example, when a football star stood up during nominations and gave a heart-felt speech on behalf of the candidacy of a campus debate champion, or when the present student body president impressively took notice of a lowly sophomore by nominating him to the board of control. These seemingly spontaneous nominations were carefully planned. Sometimes it was not planned carefully enough. Students remember with amusement the time TNE member Randall Henry (student body president in 1930-31 and later a prominent Spokane physician) leapt up and with great conviction said, "I nominate. . . ," then stood blank for a moment and finally leaned over to ask his associate who the agreed-on candidate was to be for that position.

TNE power in this era is illustrated by an incident that involved two of the most famous names in WSU student history. For some trans-

Kappa Sigma fraternity brothers; Edward R. Murrow sitting front center. Note the stylish, unwashed, corduroy pants. The influential fraternity played a key role in Murrow's election as student body president.

gression against TNE, the Sigma Nu fraternity had been frozen out of student politics during the late twenties. Mel Hein,* a Sigma Nu and football star, became acquainted with Edward R. Murrow. One day Hein asked him over to Sigma Nu for lunch. Murrow, a TNE member and student body president, decided that the Sigma Nu fellows were okay. He gave the nod and, just like that, Sigma Nu was getting campus positions again; Hein found himself on the student board of control.

When there were differences of opinion among the fraternities, TNE handled them as a national political party does. The 1931 election provides an excellent example. Art McLarney, baseball and basketball star (and younger brother of Stimson Hall's Felix McLarney) declared to the TNE that he wanted to run for student body president. The problem was that he was in Lamba Chi, a fraternity that had student body presidents in 1927 (Ruben Youngquist) and 1928 (Erwin McDowell). TNE had already agreed that 1931 was to be Psi Nu Sigma's turn. But McLarney was adamant.

Lamba Chi members were ready to forsake TNE to support McLarney if it came to that, and he was certain to attract other Greek votes on the basis of personal popularity. The worst threat was that McLarney would align with Stimson Hall, where his brother, Felix, was still fondly remembered.

TNE members who had graduated, but still kept a paternal eye on campus affairs, tried to mediate. They invited McLarney to meet in a Spokane hotel room and there reminded him that benefits of TNE membership did not end with graduation. There were continuing contacts, perhaps even jobs. Wouldn't he step aside and avoid upsetting the whole system? McLarney said no deal, whereupon TNE did the wise thing and made him its official candidate.

The rotation among fraternities got back on schedule in 1932 and 1933. Then a long-simmering rebellion finally erupted. Carl Brewster, a speech major (who three decades later would be the voice heard narrating National Aeronautics and Space Administration documentaries) led a coalition that made TNE an issue for the first time since 1920. Brewster ran on a ticket with vice presidential candidate Carl Uppman, president of Phi Delta Theta, Mel Hackedorn, son of a popular veterinary medicine professor, and Larry Giles, a Phi Delta Theta and candidate for editor of the *Evergreen*. Brewster, Hackedorn, and Giles were all "town boys" who had attended Pullman High School and so drew considerable support from students who lived with their families off campus.

These challengers published a flyer called *The Campus Politician* that said their purpose was "to be no permanent political faction but to serve only in a time of need as a uniter of the majority of the students until the undesirable organization labelled 'T.N.E.' is ousted from the campus."

---

*A member of the 1931 Rose Bowl team and an All American, Mel Hein later played football for the New York Giants and was elected a charter member of the Professional Football Hall of Fame.

THE CAMPUS POLITICIAN

PULLMAN, WASHINGTON, MAY 14, 1934

OFFICIAL PUBLICATION OF THE ALL-CAMPUS PARTY

Vote a New Deal at W. S. C.

Organization Lists Capable Candidates

With the All-Campus party pre-
complete ticket, th:
tomorrow
vears

EDITORIAL

THE TRUTH ABOUT T. N. E.

(A front page editorial in the Friday, April 20, 1934 issue of the Oregon State Barometer, official publication of the Associated Students of
Oregon State college.)

about 1916 or 1917 an Oregon State fraternity received a small
folder from Chicago in which appeared "The Truth About
"—two blurby paragraphs which boiled down the informa-
organization appearing in that old standby Bairds
at once that the paragraphs were smoothly hypocrit-
the true nature of the order except that a clue
—a stein.
State were inter

All-Campus Party Purpose Explained

The purpose of the All-Campus
party is to obtain equal representation for every student on this campus
in the student government and extra-
curricula activity of the A. S. S. C. W.
The party was organized to be
permanent political faction
serve only in a time of
uniter of the majori'
until the

their student body
present a certified
from the registrar's
effect that they are
tudents.

of all candidates has
including scholar-
t hours. With Hal
hn Bley formally de-
tion for the athletic
iginal field of seven
r that body has been
e. No further declina-
en received from can-
ugh the possibility of
ker candidates looms
voting time approach-

the circulation of
ature on the
nd tomorrow,
publishing a
raph about
presidential
tall any pos-
allenging the
eligibility of
ates. Eligibil-
ion has been
for all, and

"All-Campus" Publishes Communistic Newspaper

Circulation This Afternoon Marks First Appearance of Radicalism in Present Elections; Disturbers Corrected on Stand of Managing Editorship of Evergreen

Confident that all parties concerned would enter the election race tomorrow on the basis of equality and fairness the Evergreen went to
press this morning with no more comment on the election than the
above non-partisan discussion of the three presidential candidates, and
the banner story on election rules. Following the appearance of the
All-Campus party "Campus Politician" this noon, the presses were
stopped, and space made for a brief
comment.

The "Campus Politician" marks
the first apearance of socialism
radicalism in politics on this
us, and was printed in the
the Palouse Republic w'
printers refused to be con
such a venture, althou
tions this afternoon
all were offer
the publi

Ad Club Winner Will Be Named

announce

Smith, p
slowly tl
ous cro
sentative
work of
honorary

The
Marjor
Kappa
Clarkst
Omega
Griffith
Calgar
Brooks
Clarkst
Beta P
zer, K
welah;
Dormi
Baker,
burn; I
Phi, P
selhorn
Pullma

Dorotl
introd
st

In 1934 when independents published the
Campus Politician *challenging TNE control of*
campus politics, the fraternity-controlled
Evergreen *treated it as a revolt of the masses.*

That struck TNE as extremism. The TNE-controlled *Evergreen*, under the headline, "'All-Campus' Publishes Communistic Newspaper," gravely reported: "The 'Campus Politician' marks the first appearance of socialism and radicalism in politics on this campus." Of course, no ideologies were involved; "communistic" and "socialism" were merely the choice epithets of the day.

Students outside the Greek system had long assumed that one of the things TNE could control was the vote counting. At the urging of these independents, President Holland appointed a committee to oversee balloting, which that year was run under rules more strict even than national elections.

On election night Brewster beat football star Phil Sarboe* by about a hundred votes out of the over 1,700 cast. The turnout was three times as high as that in the previous year, when TNE had a firm grip on things. The Independents also won the key positions of yell king and editor of the *Evergreen*.

The next year, challengers ran a full slate once again, this one headed by John Evans of Stimson Hall, colonel of the ROTC cadet corps. The first plank in his platform was "To remove TNE and its principles" from campus. But TNE had regrouped. It set aside thoughts of rotating privileges and went straight for a candidate thought to be unbeatable, Ed Goldsworthy, *Chinook* editor, letterman on a championship track team, poised, popular. Goldsworthy won handily.

Neither Goldsworthy nor his successor, the affable baseball player Marion "Tex" Brotherton, winner of the 1936 election, were campus politicians. They were drafted to the cause in an emergency by TNE. The essence of TNE's strength was its ability to select, groom, and put forward solid fraternity candidates, whether they were TNE members or not. To TNE, the vital thing was that, when such a leader emerged, he be carefully brought into the fold, so that he would be a supporter, not a challenger.

They overlooked Chris Rumburg and failing to spot and recruit this big man on campus turned out to be a mistake. The problem was that Rumburg had been a late bloomer. He didn't live in a fraternity during his freshman year, or even a dorm, but in a boarding house. When Rumburg turned out for the freshman football team he spent most of his time sitting on the bench.

Al Olsen, '36, roomed with Rumburg in Mom Thornton's rooming house that first semester and recalled that Chris was so discouraged about not catching the coach's eye that he contemplated quitting the team. Olsen then left school for a semester to earn money. When he returned to school the following year, he visited a girl friend in an apartment on Maiden Lane. Her roommate, a pretty blonde popular on campus, was dressed in an evening gown and ready to go out. "The doorbell rang and who should appear but tall, blonde, and handsome Chris. He was resplendent in a tuxedo, white shawl, and a topcoat. I remember thinking, 'You've come a long way, buster.'"

Nancy Sampson, student body secretary walks with Chris Rumburg, the student body presidential candidate who successfully ran against TNE control of campus politics.

---

* And head football coach at Washington State 1945-49.

Fellow football players thought the same thing each year as the bench-sitter worked his way up to starter and then to captain of the team. He did it by being an outstanding leader rather than through native athletic ability. In the meantime, he was also rising to a top position in ROTC and had joined the Alpha Tau Omega fraternity. But no one had invited him into TNE.

When Rumburg announced he would lead the Independent ticket in the 1937 election, TNE knew it had problems. It was the first time in fifteen years that two Greek candidates had opposed one another. Rumburg did what McLarney had threatened to do six years earlier: use his personal popularity to divide the fraternities and, at the same time, form a coalition with the dorms. Even then, he won the election by only fifty-eight votes out of 1,910 votes cast. But he won. "I have always felt," reflected one TNE member, "that this marked the beginning of a rather slow decline in TNE's influence."

The following year, 1938, TNE member Don Whalen was elected without opposition, but that was a last hurrah. While TNE did not disappear, it was henceforth merely another party offering a slate of candidates for office. The long era of secret brotherhoods, of bonfire beer busts where all the anointed hoisted their steins with the left hand, of Murrows who put friends on boards of control with nods of the head, of smoke-filled rooms where student presidents and Harvest Queens were chosen—that era was over. The worst that can be said of TNE is that it was undemocratic and that it deprived some non-members of their chance at holding a student office. The best that can be said is that it's leadership choices bore the test of time, as many of its members and candidates are included among the luminaries of Washington State's alumni.

IN THE SPRING OF 1939, "POLITICS POPPED LIKE FIRECRACKERS ON A Chinese New Year," the *Evergreen* reported. A fraternity man, Bob Littlejohn of Beta Theta Pi, represented the Independent Party, fragmenting the fraternity vote again. The fraternity party chose the popular football star Ken Devine of Sigma Nu. Campus buses carried Devine's name plastered across their sides, while Littlejohn's name was emblazoned across Bryan Tower. Devine won, but by only sixty-seven votes out of 2,130 cast.

The 1940 campaign was "the wackiest political drive on the Washington State campus since the Rumburg-Arthur rumpus of four years ago," declared the *Evergreen*. It featured "a street dance, a fire hose that backfired, hundreds of sign-smeared jalopies, perhaps a dozen rotten eggs and two simultaneous political rallies only 50 yards apart." Don Greeley, president of Tau Kappa Epsilon and fraternity candidate, won the presidency by a small margin. The Independents won vice president and nine of thirteen other positions.

Each year's breathtaking finish spurred rival factions to bigger efforts in the next election. In the spring of 1941 Kirk Gebert, Phi Delta Theta and captain of the basketball team, and Jim Zimmerman, basketball player and incoming president of Kappa Sigma, ran as a president/vice-president ticket for the fraternities. Carl Ronning, boxer and president of Pine Manor men's co-op, and Richard Gay, Stimson Hall Senate member and managing editor of the *Evergreen*, represented the Independents. The *Evergreen* estimated that one rally brought out 1,300 students. The campus was awash in signs and pamphlets. Cars mounted with loudspeakers patrolled campus streets while candidates feverishly canvased living halls.

On election night students crowded into the Women's Gymnasium and the roars went up with each posting of a new count. At 8:30 p.m., with over 1,700 votes posted, Gebert, the fraternity candidate, led Ronning by five votes. That increased to eighty-three votes, then dwindled to a seven-vote lead at 11 p.m. At 10 p.m., Richard Gay, the Independent candidate for vice president, led his opponent Jim Zimmerman by one vote. Just before midnight the final votes were posted. Gebert, the fraternity presidential candidate, won by six votes out of 2,818 cast. Gay of Stimson Hall beat Zimmerman by twenty-three votes. Eighty-two percent of the student body had voted, a record that still stands. It was perhaps the most feverish campaign and election night in the history of WSC student politics, a fitting climax to two decades of competition between fraternities and independents.

Two years later, the Independent Party finally overtook the fraternities and began its own long era of dominance. But that was 1943, and students were too preoccupied with World War II and events beyond the campus to be much concerned about student politics. When the war ended, it turned out that some portion of student attention had been permanently diverted to affairs in the outside world. Campus politics would never again command as much interest, energy, or ingenuity from so large a portion of the student body as it had when the campus was a world unto itself. ∎

$\mathcal{S}$leeping Porch Politics

Areal view of WSC, 1923. Note the cut-stone arch at the west (lower) entrance to campus.

"Student life" in Ferry Hall, circa *1910.*

"Ann," circa *1920.*

Front steps of Community Hall, 1926.

ABOVE: *Going home on vacation, 1926.*   BELOW: *Students at the Pullman train station.*

Campus campaigning.

A women's literary society meeting, circa *1909.*

Stevens Hall dormitory room, circa *1915.*

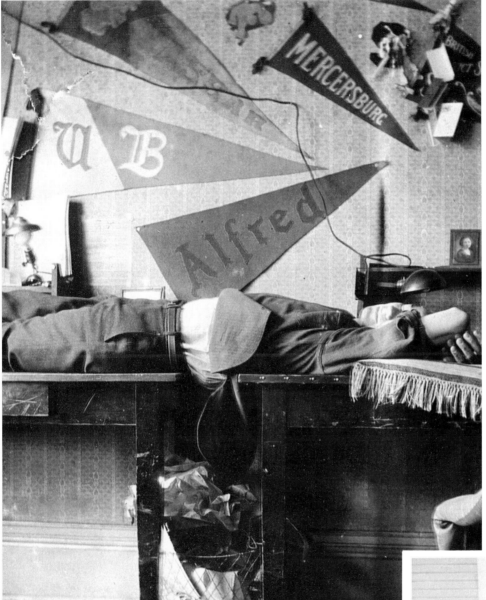

Overworked; student of the 1920s takes a break.

Frat brothers, circa 1922.

Social Life in the Shadow of Dean Annie

ONE OF THE THINGS THAT DEFINED LIFE AT WASHINGTON STATE COLLEGE
was its isolation from the rest of the world. Those trains that arrived
in Pullman at the beginning of each semester docked like ships from
distant ports; once you disembarked you were pretty much there for
the season. Few students had cars to take them to Lewiston or
Spokane for a weekend. The campus had a radio station, but since
radios were not allowed in dorm rooms, electronic media intruded
very little on student life through the 1930s. Visiting speakers came
to campus once or twice a month. Some students subscribed to
national magazines and passed them along. Most walked downtown
to take in a movie once or twice a week. The Green Lantern (later the
White Owl) on Maiden Lane had a dance floor and sold hamburgers.
Otherwise there was little entertainment except that which students
made for themselves.

It sounds like a prescription for boredom, but the actual effect was
just the opposite. Because students had to create their own entertainment, social interaction was intense; the campus was a hive of
activity. A couple weeks after arriving at WSC in the fall of 1920,
freshman Gladys Chellis wrote to her sister:

> Went to Moscow Friday to see the football game
> between WSC and University of Idaho. . . . Thursday
> night they had the big rally and night shirt parade
> then a big bonfire. . . . Friday night I went to the Stray
> Antler's dance with Mr. McNeil and Sat. night to the
> Dairy Club Dance with Mr. Lowry and yesterday to
> the show with Mr. Boyd. . . . Am dated up for next
> weekend too.

Activity was doubled or tripled by the fact that all of it had to be put
together by the students themselves. A dance usually meant a band—
which translated into many afternoon practice sessions for one group
of students. Since there was no ballroom on campus, the gym had to
be disguised; that meant evening planning meetings for the dance
committee and two days of hard work. In one way or another,
students were constantly thrown into group activity. The absence of
television meant every dorm had its skits and talent shows. The
unavailability of canned music spawned choruses and barbershop
quartets by the dozens.

OPPOSITE: *Budd Bankson, of Theta Chi,
with Publications Ball Queen candidates, 1939.*

The *Evergreen* covered campus life with the detail of a small-town paper and had a constantly entertaining stable of budding crusaders, satirists, and cartoonists. Literary magazines were always being born and every spring the whole campus waited—some nervously—for the unsigned lampoon (with changing names, including *Yellow Jacket* and *Claw*) that had as its express purpose the embarrassment of everyone it mentioned.

The center of that pre-World War II campus was the "Old Quad." The Administration Building, with its quaint turrets, stood at the lower end, on the Pullman side of Campus Hill. At the North end stood Stevens Hall and the other women's dorms, and opposite them was Science Hall (now part of Murrow Communication Center) and, just beyond, Ferry Hall. The grassy expanse in between was a busy town square. When the sun was out, it was a place to throw down the books and sit for a little socializing.

At the top of the Old Quad was Bryan Hall, with its big clock tower looming overhead. This was the busiest building on campus. The

"Old Quad" below Bryan Hall after "chapel hour," circa 1914.

Library reading room, north wing of Bryan Hall.

twice-a-week, all-campus convocations were held in its auditorium and its hallway was a common meeting place. The library, used for social gatherings as well as study, was small but impressive. The main reading room had a scholarly appearance of depth and order with its row upon row of heavy oak tables, each with a line of lamps down the center. The book stacks were overhead in a circular mezzanine that hovered above the reading room like a halo.

"Hello Walk" was the sidewalk that linked the entrances of Bryan, Science, and Ferry halls. It was the axis of campus life, and the tradition was that when you were on it you should smile and greet everyone you passed. This was to show what a friendly place WSC was, and many a freshman male got his rear hacked for forgetting it. It was no great problem, however, since the college was small enough in the 1930s that most people recognized practically everyone on campus. "If you didn't know the name, at least you could say 'she's in Alpha Chi,' or whatever," recalled Nadine Fisher Klock, '37.

At the northern terminus of Hello Walk, across the street, was the bookstore, a wood-frame building located on the site of the current Students Book Corporation. The campus coffee shop in this building consisted of a long fountain with Coca-Cola levers, ice cream scoops, and, across a narrow isle, a dozen high-backed booths. The dark wood of the booths and dim lighting gave the room a sombre cast. But throughout the day and late into the night the cozy room resounded with greetings, laughter, and "a constant din of chatter," as one student put it. In January 1936, the *Evergreen* reported that the coffee

ABOVE: *Bookstore fountain, 1927.*

BELOW: *"Chatter" in the bookstore coffee shop.*

shop sold 600 cups of coffee on an average day. And many students drank Coca-Cola. This small snack bar and the Cougar Cottage, another Coke-and-hamburger dispensary near the fraternities on Colorado Street, were the only "student unions" on campus until after World War II.

Winters during the twenties and thirties were cold and long. Cross-country skiing was popular and there was even a ski jump off the ledge now occupied by the Compton Union Building. Many fraternities owned toboggans and these could be seen careening down Campus Avenue any time the snow was right. The skating pond at the edge of the football field was one of the most popular ways to spend a bluish winter afternoon. Bonfires usually crackled nearby for warming.

In warm weather, one of the most common dates was a walk of several miles along one of the roads or railroad tracks that stretched out from Pullman. The men might take along a small-calibre rifle to shoot at gophers; they might also bring a blanket to spread out on a grassy hill or under a shade tree. This was called a "fussing blanket," whether or not it was actually used for fussing. The term means kissing, and it was so pervasive in its time that it is no wonder that deans of women were suspicious. The campus telephone book, primarily a listing of student numbers, was called "The Fusser's Guide."

The main romantic retreat, until it was removed in the mid-twenties to make room for Bohler Gymnasium and Mooberry Track, was The Tanglewood, a little thicket at the edge of Silver Lake that hid a few paths where couples could be alone.

The other romantic spot on campus was Roundtop, the steep rise north of Campus Hill. It offered an oasis of grass and trees at the top and, looking back at the lights of campus at dusk, a sense of remoteness. In 1922, Don Stewart, '22, led Betty Redington, '22, to this enchanted spot and, overcome by the moonlight and the smell of her hair, heard himself asking her to marry him. He remembers Betty smiled up at him and said yes. Sixty-five years later Betty remembered it differently; she recalled that she smiled up at him and said she would have to think about it. But the both remembered, a lifetime later, how this unspectacular hill seemed so remote and romantic to a couple of young lovers.

Skaters on Silver Lake; Rogers Field in the distance, 1924.

The plot of a book about college life is boy-meets-girl. Arthur Bonn, '31, first laid eyes on Marjorie Faulkner, '24, the future Mrs. Bonn, at the Methodist church, where he had gone for the free food. Carl "Tuffy" Ellingsen, '31, the football star, was paired up with Virginia Kuhn, the future Mrs. Ellingsen, by a friend organizing a swimming party on the Snake River. That was perhaps the single most exciting thing about college; you never knew but that this might be the day your life changed. It leant a certain electricity to daily life. In this atmosphere (and here one must invoke personal memories), hearing him call your name from across the street, or seeing her push a lock of hair behind an ear and steal a glance your way, could be the highlight of a college career, and nobody else even noticed.

But the broken heart was also a campus commonplace. In this era when everybody knew everybody and social life was conducted quite publicly, one could not even suffer quietly. The 1922 *Chinook* carried a page of photographs of couples which had split up during the academic year. Just about everyone in school in the mid-twenties knew the story of handsome and popular Eric and his girl friend Sally, a blonde many thought to be the prettiest woman on campus. He returned from a winter tour with the glee club to find that Sally was now seeing another guy. Eric's fellow glee club members decided to make one last appeal for their disconsolate partner, and so one night

Sunday outing, 1922.

assembled outside Sally's sorority and sang a popular song of the time, "Whatever Came Over Sally," in a pleading way that brought tears to the eyes of the residents of three adjacent sororities. To no avail. Sally married the other guy.

A 1937 graduate remembers that when men's groups came to her dorm for social get-togethers called firesides, "men invariably chose all the pretty, vivacious girls and left me shrinking on the furniture. Then the next day the phone rang and rang for all the others, but never for me!" A half century later she could credit the experience with making her more sensitive to the feelings of others, but that was no consolation to the college girl.

Even when things went right, sometimes they went too right. Archie Buckley, '30, a football, basketball, and baseball star, asked Mary Maude Hungate, '29, for a date. But she already had a date—with a guy who had asked her out two weeks before at the end of a class, and then rather oddly never said another word to her. Handsome Archie Buckley could date every woman in school before he ever got back to asking Mary Maude a second time. She decided in her own mind that if the other boy didn't mention their date again before Friday, he must have forgotten, and she would then be free to say yes to Archie. Which she did.

On the Saturday in question, Archie was walking to the Pi Beta Phi sorority to pick up Mary Maude when he ran into an old friend going in the same direction. They did not discover until they got to the front door that they were calling for the same girl. Mary Maude, hearing her sorority sisters gasping and laughing, gathered what had happened and refused to come down from her room. Confusion reigned. Finally a sorority sister rescued the situation by offering to go out with either of Mary Maude's dates. The other guy volunteered to drop his claim and left with the sorority sister. Mary Maude came down to face Archie, to whom she profusely apologized and eventually married.

In dealing with the riptides of romance, students felt pretty much on their own. Adults must have gone through the same things when they were young, but somehow they seemed to have forgotten. To them, a kiss had become a terrible thing and a party something to be scrutinized and patrolled. These were attitudes that college students would never understand.

If any group of people on campus exercised positive and lasting influences on student social and moral development, it was the lowliest of adult "guides," the housemothers. Many genteel and understanding ladies, like Mrs. Seymour of the Pi Phi house, Anne Sims of McCroskey Hall, and Rose Weatherford of Duncan Dunn, are fondly remembered as sincere advisors in matters of morality and etiquette, which they treated with equal gravity. They didn't snoop, but they expected women to be good and were themselves living advertisements for what they considered ladylike behavior.

Mrs. Baake of Ferry and Stimson halls was so respected by male students that anyone using improper language within her hearing would incur the wrath of the whole house. She earned this loyalty by tempering rule making with genuine affection. She loved her boys, and her motherly ways have became a part of the college legend. Students at WSC in the early 1920s recall that one of her residents in Ferry Hall was a married student whose wife taught school in a distant town. Whenever the wife was able to visit on a weekend, Mrs. Baake packed her bag and went to visit a friend so the young couple could stay in her apartment.

Housemothers were also teachers of practical skills. Dorms, fraternities, and sororities had weekly "formal nights," when everyone appeared for dinner attired in suits or dresses and groomed for a social event. The housemother would pace the group through the social niceties—punctuality, before-dinner chit-chat, choosing the right fork, and carving the meat. Whether or not they appreciated these lessons at the time, many students subsequently blessed housemothers for their efforts.

By his own admission, Weldon B. "Hoot" Gibson was probably as untutored socially as any student at Washington State College. His uncle, the renowned Cougar coach, Buck Bailey, brought him from the parched landscape of a Texas farm to play center on the football team. Hoot joined Beta Theta Pi and, without a clue as how to act, was plunged into what seemed a sophisticated social life. His salvation was the housemother of the Beta House, Hulda Bergquist, who took him under her wing and offered guidance and instruction.

Hoot borrowed clothes and depended on his fraternity brothers to show him how his wardrobe should be arranged. One evening, as he was standing in the house doorway preparing to leave for a formal event, one of the brothers said, "Hey! Where's your sash?" This fraternity brother proceeded to explain, with a side glance at the others, that since Hoot was the only one going to the dance from Beta House, he was the fraternity's ambassador, and custom required that he wear a big red ambassadorial sash across his chest. Hoot had never heard of this before, but ever-helpful brothers quickly found a scrap of red cloth and made a sash. Hoot, the garish red cloth hung across his torso, was about to step out the door on the way to his first date with a sorority woman, when Mrs. Bergquist called him over to explain that the sash was a joke. Brothers will see you embarrassed for a laugh; mothers won't.

At the center of campus social life was The Big Dance. It was, like The Big Game, a universal campus experience, a cynosure by which lives were navigated for weeks beforehand. Fraternities, sororities, and dorms placed their reputations on the line when they put on their big dance. Individual social reputations were made through an invitation to the right dance—say the Pi Phi formal or the annual Crimson Circle formal.

There was, of course, more than one Big Dance. There were dozens, each with its own audience and social rating. On one typical Saturday night in January 1936 there were no less than eight semiformal (suits and party dresses) dances on campus. Theta Chi filled the

Harvest Ball, 1932.

*Leona Saunders,
1933 May Queen.*

chapter house with flags, Lambda Chi danced in a graveyard motif, and Duncan Dunn held a "moon dance." At Chi Omega "a myriad of billowing balloons" bobbed from the ceiling, the *Evergreen* reported, while "colored spotlights glowed softly from the corners and revolved from the ceiling."

The big, all-campus dances included the Varsity Ball, Military Ball, Crimson Circle Honorary Ball, Publications Ball, Harvest Ball, Junior Prom, Homecoming, and Campus Day. They were formal, with invitations mailed and requests for *RSVPs*. Women attending these affairs received corsages from their dates, and usually gifts of compacts or other mementos. Upon arrival, the couples (young men in tuxedos and young women in formal gowns) were obliged to shake hands with the older patron and patroness of the event and engage them in a brief conversation. "Quite a chore," remarked Lylia Appel Miller, '29. Partners for each dance were predetermined by a dance card contained in the tasseled invitation. This listed each dance of the evening, and each listing was followed by a blank line. During the week before the big event, the man (or the woman when the affair was sponsored by a dorm or sorority) went to friends and scheduled dances for the evening, filling the empty spaces on the card.

Occasionally an organization would thrill the campus by bringing in a big-name band. But in those days, when so many young people studied music, there was no shortage of good local bands and orchestras. Bing Crosby's first band came down from Spokane and played for WSC functions in the early 1920s. In the mid-1930s, Fran Pearson's student orchestra was a drawing card for any event.

In more recent decades, a college dance became just something to do on a weekend. It is one of the more striking changes in college life. In the decades before World War II, "The Big Dance" had an antebellum glamour about it. It was a truly memorable occasion. This might be a little school amidst the wheat fields all week, but on Saturday night men wore tuxedos and women wore elaborate gowns and Wilson Road became Park Avenue. The gymnasium, which the day before echoed with bouncing basketballs, was now festooned with soft crepe arcs and disguised by cleverly placed lights. The hardwood floor was hidden under cloth-covered tables arranged nightclub fashion around the dance floor. At nine o'clock, college boys, hair painstakingly combed and cheeks double shaved to a ruddy glow, smiled at college girls, radiant and fragrant after four hours of primping; together they swayed across the floor to the warm liquid music of trombones and saxophones. It was intoxicating.

Dance booklet.

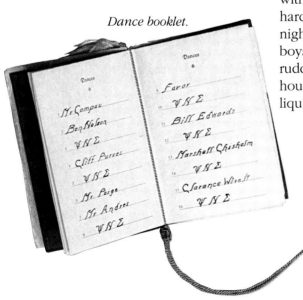

AND IF IT WASN'T, THE PUNCH MIGHT HAVE BEEN. EVEN DURING PRO-hibition, liquor was fairly easy to obtain and a part of many important college functions. At the 1929 ROTC encampment, a member of the military band managed to sneak back to his fraternity for a few drinks before the big parade. "As we watched the band pass in review," recalled C.R. "Mac" McCabe, '32, "Scott was having difficulty in keeping in line and getting his clarinet in his mouth. The companies watched and wondered what the reaction of the review officers must have been." That same year President Holland abolished Crimson Circle, the major men's honorary, because of drinking at initiations, dances, and even the annual Campus Day. Two years later the president allowed the organization to be reestablished. He didn't know that one of the charter members of the reconstituted honorary was WSC's main bootlegger.

Holland was a teetotaler who considered drinking a moral, not a practical, issue. Even after the Twenty-First Amendment repealed national prohibition in 1933, WSC administrators continued to en-force their own alcoholic ban on campus, though with no great success. Fraternity men could have whiskey delivered by a local milk man by telling him to bring a bottle of "heavy cream." A top science student in Stimson Hall kept a large supply in his room and sold it to friends at a modest markup.

Student attitudes toward this particular mind-altering drug were ambivalent. It was a part of college lore, of course, that where the rest of society saw hazards and taboos, a student might crash ahead, for

"Burning the midnight oil [Stimson Hall]"—used in a recruitment brochure, circa 1935. On the back of the original picture, an administrator instructed the printer: "Be Sure *and paint out the tobacco can before photographing this, also blot out bottle on right shelf or trim it out of picture."*

he (less often she) was somehow exempted from consequences. Recalling the outright dangerous homemade alcoholic concoctions he and his friends drank during prohibition, a 1931 graduate said, "We were no more careful about what we ingested than students are today." Another strain of opinion on campus held booze to be a source of weakness. In at least one major fraternity, coming in drunk was an offense that brought even upperclassmen humiliating hacks. Drinking was still enough of a social taboo in the 1930s that some women became livid at a date who returned from the men's room smelling of alcohol.

STUDENTS WERE ALSO SEXUALLY PROMISCUOUS, IN THE VIEW OF ADMIN-istrators. In fact, what was "sexually promiscuous" usually depended on whether it was done in view of administrators. In 1920, even students agreed that serious and repeated kissing, or "fussing," as students called it, was improper. "If you were a nice, decent girl, it simply wasn't done," said Helen Schwartze Landerholm, '22. But there was nothing wrong with holding hands or slipping an arm around a waist. Or was there? Once on an outing, Helen Lander-holm's fiancé casually put his arm across her shoulder. "Helen!" a male professor said in horror, then looked away. The arm was quickly retracted. Students were often surprised at what elders considered wicked. When, in the early twenties, women started "bobbing" their hair, cropping it off at the neck, college administra-tors put in calls to sorority leaders to urge them to put a stop to the radical fad.

This cultural gap between the generations could only grow during the 1920s, a time of rapid change in social behavior. Young people in general were the quickest to take up new ideas and fashions, while college administrators and professors of the early twentieth century lived lives exceptionally sheltered from currents of change. Next only to ministers, society expected college officials to be models of propriety. Many of them remained unmarried, a state of life recom-mended both by low pay and the old British professorial tradition. Professionally, of course, most scholars were trained to revere the past. No wonder that, as they watched each new generation bend society's rules a little further, they were genuinely perplexed.

Students were no less puzzled by college authorities. The typical college student was unmarried but of marriageable age, and there-fore had no more serious business than searching for a lifemate and for happiness itself. And here came administrators with all their silly rules of comportment! Student disdain for administrators was the disdain of infantrymen for military theorists. What did "they" know about the real world? Ellen Baake, the beloved housemother of Stimson Hall and Ferry Hall, was an advisor to the Alpha Gamma Delta sorority. She regularly gathered the women and gave lectures on how to deal with "gentlemen." "When she got to the place where she warned that holding hands would only lead to trouble, it was hard to keep a straight face," recalled Dorothy Siebenbaum McLarney, '29. "By then we knew that holding hands was safer than letting them roam."

By the thirties, the big question about necking—as fussing came to be called—was not if, but where. With "Lover's Lane," the little tree-lined path that cut through the hillside around the football fields, and many other dark spots on campus, this was no problem in warm weather. But most of the college year was cold, and in an era when few students owned cars and almost no one had a private apartment, finding a place to say goodnight was a considerable dilemma. After a dance or party, couples would have to go around campus rattling doors in college buildings to see if one had been left ajar. The fieldhouse was a good prospect. Richard Gay, '42, said the ROTC trucks in the fieldhouse were nice places for smooching. "It was dark in there, so one would have to tap on the truck first to see if it was occupied," he said; sometimes all of them were. If the fieldhouse was locked up, you might try the stadium ticket booths. If that failed, you took her back to her dorm.

STUDENT MORALITY WAS THE RESPONSIBILITY OF THE DEAN OF WOMEN, a position established in 1912 by President Bryan. The job was upgraded from that of "Preceptress of Stevens Hall" and given authority over women living off campus as well as on. When he put this reform into effect, Bryan was amazed to discover (he said in his history of the college's early years) that "women living in private homes had hardly realized that it was anybody's business to interfere with their private affairs."

Of course it was the college's business to interfere with their private affairs! No dean of women ever doubted that. She worked on the domino theory of human emotions, assuming that anytime young men and women were in sight of each other, a scandal was brewing. To do her job, a dean of women needed to know what students were wearing, when they were coming in at night, who they were with, whether they had ridden in a car—in short, every detail. She trusted the morals and good judgment of college students not one whit.

The opinions of a dean of women were of no particular interest to students, for, ironically, no counsel was valued less than that of the very person who theoretically served as their moral guide. The dean's view of life was so outlandish that students simply could not have taken her advice seriously.

Her rules, however, were a nuisance. Women had to be in at ten in the evening on weeknights and midnight on Saturday. There was nothing wrong with those hours, if you preferred to be in at that time anyway. As a matter of fact, many women depended on curfews to send ardent beaus home at a reasonable hour. But there was no flexibility, no faith that a reasonable excuse would be accepted. A young woman of twenty or twenty-one years might be attending a sanctioned event—say the annual counting of votes for a student election—and yet have to wait nervously to hear whether the dean of women had given a dispensation, or whether all the women had to scurry back to the dorm to get in under the clock. Young women actually had to bow out of Professor Potter's famous evening philosophical gatherings so they could get back to their dormitory at the arbitrary hour of ten o'clock. Somehow deans of women seemed to confuse their curfews with morality itself. The earliest account of student life at WSC left by a female is that of a woman who lived in Stevens Hall in 1902. She recalled that one of the big social events was for students to go, closely chaperoned of course, by sleigh or wagon to a nearby farm, to be entertained by a farmer and his wife. But the evening was always cut short because Mrs. Van Doren, the Preceptress of Stevens Hall, insisted that the women be back by ten in the evening. "As they were all in their late teens or early twenties," she asked sixty-five years later, "was that necessary?" It was a question that stood at the center of conflict between students and administrators for decades.

THE FIRST WASHINGTON STATE COLLEGE DEAN OF WOMEN WAS Rhoda White, a truly fierce character in campus mythology. During her 1912 to 1920 reign, she decreed, among other things, that male and female students could not walk together after seven in the evening and that chaperones must accompany even the most casual Sunday afternoon outings. Students called her "Dean Rhoda White Horse To Death" because she was said to have once driven a horse until it fell over dead. You can bet this was just the kind of cruel story

9 p. m.

Stevens Hall "preceptress," from the 1904 Chinook.

Dean of Women, Annie M. Fertig, in 1926.

students would make up to capitalize on a name like "Rhoda," except in this case it was true. After a much publicized 1913 Pullman trial, Rhoda White was fined for driving a horse until it collapsed. Earl Wegner, for whom the veterinary building is named, gave expert testimony against her. President Holland fired her in 1920 for, among other things, riding students too hard. She was replaced by Miriam Gerlach, who enforced the same rules with a bit more subtlety. She quarrelled with President Holland over other matters and was replaced by Dean Annie Fertig in 1924.

"Dean Annie," as she was known to students, was a squat little woman with a bun on the top of her head and a slashing gaze. She was brisk, definite in all of her statements, and seldom smiled. She was good at her job, in so far as her job was to catch wrongdoers. The Monday after a dance, several women who had attended might receive messages that Dean Annie wanted to see them. Immediately.

Did they see anything *unusual* going on in the kitchen during the dance? Ronald Jones was at the dance, wasn't he? Did you talk to him? Sitting coolly behind her desk in the Administration Building she was a clever interrogator. She asked questions to which she knew the answers, and a young woman who did not cooperate would be excoriated on the spot. Women were put in the position of having to prove their own innocence by implicating others. This applied as much, if not more, to "good girls," for Dean Annie made it clear that you could either be with *them* or with her. Some were with her; Dean Annie had her partisans among women students.

But most students, even the well-behaved, considered her a tyrant. Isobel Keeney Leber, '28, who as a student assisted former president Enoch Bryan in writing his history of the college's first years, found Fertig to be a "stern, uncompromising woman" who chose to be "more of a dictator than a counselor or friend." Dorothy E. Brown, '28, a member of the student-faculty committee on social rules, remembered that Dean Annie promulgated all sorts of strange regulations, such as a requirement that there be an average of seven square feet for each person at a party. Dealing with Dean Fertig was different than dealing with President Holland. "She tended to dictate policy," said Dorothy Brown. "He always delved into all aspects of a question before making a decision." Many students found that if you got through to President Holland, you were likely to get a fairer hearing.

Dean Annie tended to be arbitrary in her dictates. In 1934, for example, Joe Caraher of Lambda Chi went to get what he thought would be a routine approval for a dance that would feature decorations and costumes of the Bowery, a raffish neighborhood of New York City in the 1920s. Without giving a reason, Dean Annie said no to the plan. She suggested instead that the fraternity decorate with balloons or something. Caraher argued that much of the work had already been done and the guys were planning on this. Dean Annie said no.

Of course, Lambda Chi went ahead with the dance, and of course Dean Annie put the house under social restriction for the remainder of the year. The case is typical of the run-ins students had with Dean Annie almost constantly. She censored the *Chinook, Evergreen*, and programming on the campus radio station at will. When Rhoda LeCocq, '37, wrote a play about a woman who won a lottery and traveled to Europe, Dean Annie tried to stop production on the grounds that any woman traveling so far alone could be assumed to be heading for immoral adventures.

Dean Annie's tendency to issue spot decrees was probably the source of the many "phantom rules" such as: women should not wear red dresses because the color inflamed male emotions; if a woman sat on a man's lap in an automobile, a pillow must separate them; if two women are sunbathing, at least one of them must be sitting upright at all times. There is no evidence that these rules were ever enforced or even existed. But nearly all students believed they did.

No one knew exactly what the rules were because they were not written down. This was a long-standing complaint of students. In 1934, student body president Carl Brewster managed to get a student-faculty committee appointed to publish the rules. Dean Annie took the position that it was impossible to formulate rules that would cover every contingency. In other words, she did not want to be hemmed in. Whether it was due to Dean Annie's opposition or not, Brewster's committee came to naught. The rules remained pretty much whatever Dean Annie decided they were.

But ultimately it was not her rules that made Dean Annie so unpopular with so many students. It was her manner. In theory, she was supposed to be a guide for students; in reality "we were scared to death of her," said Geraldine Thornton Kruiswyk, a student in the mid-thirties. Kruiswyk told a story that sums up hundreds or thousands of students' views of Dean Annie. A train was about to leave Pullman and Kruiswyk was sitting on it talking with her boyfriend before he left. Suddenly Dean Annie appeared at the railroad car entrance. "Are you leaving on this train?" she demanded of Kruiswyk. The young woman answered no; Dean Annie said, "Then get out!" Mrs. Kruiswyk was still amazed, fifty years later, when she recalled the event: "Just like that, *'Then get out!'*" President Holland and many a housemother managed to enforce rules while transmitting a sense of affection for young people. Dean Annie never did.

THE FIRST OVERT ACT OF REBELLION CAME IN DECEMBER 1934. TWO popular students, Jerry Camp and Georgia Hendron, had secretly gotten married, but word got out when a local newspaper published the license. At that point the two decided to have a reception on campus. When Georgia went to Fertig's office to get routine approval, Dean Annie icily forbade any party and instead made it clear that she felt that rather than be proud, the two students should be ashamed. Georgia left the dean's office in tears; soon thereafter the campus was in an uproar. On December 15, a Friday night, 300 fraternity men serenaded Georgia's sorority, pointedly without the dean's permission. "This was the first mass demonstration of any kind on this campus in recent years," the *Evergreen* reported, "and it was felt that it expressed general student sympathy." An accompanying editorial said this "decent demonstration" would help atone for "the wrong that had been done to them—that of being subjected to derogatory remarks and accusations of disgraceful behavior."

President Holland at his desk.

Sixteen months later, in April 1936, a guest speaker addressed the students in one of the regular campus convocations. In summary remarks after the speaker's presentation, Dr. Holland gave students a typical little administrator's homily about how students must always be prepared to take control of their own lives. Afterwards, a group of sophomore men were walking from the convocation to their fraternities for lunch when one remarked that maybe students *should* take control of their lives. Maybe they should do something about Dean Annie and her rules.

Communication was easy along fraternity row on a sunny spring day, and that very afternoon fifteen or twenty fraternity men gathered at one of the houses to discuss the possibility of some sort of protest. The big strike of '36 was planned in a series of quickly arranged gatherings that proceeded something like this. Someone would say, "We need a statement of demands," or "Who can line up Stimson Hall support?" One of a couple of dozen students draped across the furniture or seated on the floor would call out, "I'll do that." An amazing thing about the 1936 student strike—something students never were given credit for—was that it could be so well organized in four days. The key was a long tradition of strong student leadership, honed by years of experience preparing student political campaigns and sports rallies.

All of this activity took place on a Thursday and Friday. By the weekend all leaders in dormitories, sororities, and fraternities were brought into the plan; they called numerous meetings to explain to their groups what was going on. Campus artists set to painting picket signs. Football player Chris Rumburg was sent to Spokane, where he was known from his high school football years, to visit and win over newspapers and radio stations. Mimi Frank went to Seattle to talk to the media, and her pretty, downcast face appeared in the Seattle *Post-Intelligencer* under the headline "They Treat Us Like Children."

Through the weekend there was no other topic of conversation on campus. That Saturday in the Cougar Cottage, the little snack bar on fraternity row, Weldon B. "Hoot" Gibson of Beta Theta Pi held up a hand folded into the "okay" sign and said "Viva la revolucion!" It became the rallying call of the strike and was duly illustrated and explained on the front page of the Seattle *Post-Intelligencer.*

When the students decided they needed a chief spokesman they faced a problem. The feeling was that a spokesman had to be an upperclassman with perfect credentials, a real heavyweight. On the other hand, seniors who had this kind of status were only a month away from graduation, and so were especially vulnerable.

The problem was solved when Robert Yothers, a pre-law student who, marveled one student, "sounded like an adult when he spoke,"

Protest march in front of College Hall, May 5, 1936.

volunteered to run the risks. Some guys in other fraternities were disappointed the spokesman was not one of theirs, but they consoled themselves with the thought, as one put it, "if somebody was going to get kicked out of school it might as well be a Phi Delt."

The most remarkable thing about the strike was the unanimity among students. Lettermen, top students, student government, even the ROTC band, joined under the umbrella of the "The Student Liberty Association." This was one issue in which fraternities and men's dorms were as one.

There were, however, two important exceptions to this solid front. Student body president Ed Goldsworthy and *Evergreen* editor Larry Giles hung back. Both were personal friends of Dr. Holland and believed a strike would hurt him more than it would help students. Nevertheless, neither disagreed with the basic claims of the strikers. Goldsworthy was on the track team and he said it was pretty obvious to WSC athletes visiting other campuses that other students did not have to put up with Dean Annie-type rules.

On Monday, May 4, a copy of a flier bearing one inch letters saying "We Demand" and an announcement of a protest parade the next day were delivered to Dr. Holland. The president's response was in the

Demonstrators wait across from the Administration Building (now Thompson Hall), while student leaders meet inside with President Holland.

best tradition of college administrators:

> No one can object to this parade if it is handled in an
> orderly manner, since the fourth hour is a free period.
> . . .(A)ny attempt at a strike affecting college hours
> and college work will accomplish nothing. In the
> end, any changes must be the result of a friendly,
> frank discussion between college authorities and the
> students themselves.
>
> Before any student joins a strike involving absence
> from his classes he is urged to communicate by letter
> or telephone with his parents and learn definitely if
> the father and mother will approve the action.

The next day, when students gathered in a cold drizzle for the parade, some of the signs read: "Pop Says It's Okay" and "Momma Says Yes."

It was not the signs but the sheer numbers of students gathered on the downhill side of Bryan Hall that got the administration's attention. The student newspaper estimated 3,000 students showed up; Associated Press estimated 3,500. This would comprise nearly the whole student body.

At 11:15 that morning, the ROTC band (out of uniform), supplemented by members of various dance bands, struck up a ragged Sousa March and the mob began to move. The mood was lighthearted as the students paraded in a big loop past the bookstore, along Campus Avenue, past McCroskey Hall and Stevens Hall, and finally to the Administration Building. Faculty members and townspeople lined the streets as the students passed. Some applauded, some glowered.

Students went to great lengths to prove that they were not "radical." One large sign declared "We're Not Reds." At the Administration Building the entire group stood at attention while the band played the Star Spangled Banner. Then a yell leader led a cheer for the faculty.

Yothers, accompanied by an early instigator of the protest by the name of Jerry Sage and a half-dozen other students representing various living groups, strode in to meet with Holland. One of the members of this negotiating group, off-campus resident John Hafenbrack, recalled that Holland's attitude was imperious, that of a king receiving complaining subjects. Leonard Zagelow of Stimson Hall thought Holland's attitude remarkably self-composed "under the circumstances."

The student negotiating team made its complaints as Holland listened. Lunch was brought in and the meeting went on for almost three hours. In letters written later explaining the situation to outsiders, President Holland said it was the work of "poorer students." He probably had wished it were so. Yothers was Phi Beta Kappa and Sage soon would be. One person who knew both said the difference between them was that Yothers was "brilliant and sober" while Sage was "brilliant and brash." The previous fall Yothers had been chosen as one of two students to represent WSC in competition for a Rhodes

Scholarship. He would go on to be an attorney, a legislator, and an official of the Republican Party. Sage, a big blond football player, was known to some as "the wild man" because he would try anything that looked interesting. His general unruliness was directed toward a more formidable authority a few years later, when he made a series of daring escapes from German prisoner of war camps, adventures that made him the subject of a motion picture and a number of books after the war.

The combination of the two personalities must have taken its toll on poor President Holland. Yothers, the articulate political science student, would logically and methodically argue Holland toward concessions, to which Holland would concede, but then seek a counter concession. Yothers would put the question to the other representatives, and Sage would say no. Once Holland pointed a stern finger and said, "You pain me, Sage!"

At three in the afternoon the campus steam plant's whistle sounded, announcing that the meeting with the president was over. The entire student body packed into Bohler gym, covering one side of bleachers and much of the floor, to hear the results. The discussion at this mass meeting was reported by a secretary, sent to the meeting by the college's librarian. The secretary recorded that, "Although there was

WSC students in Bohler Gymnasium listening to the protest leaders' report on President Holland's response to their demands. They voted to postpone a strike at the first meeting, but the next day reversed their decision.

much show of feeling and considerable spirit was demonstrated, the meeting was very orderly."

Sage rose to describe the confrontation in the Administration Building. "The president was very courteous and only a few times fired up," he reported. "He tried to soft-soap us, as we expected." Holland had not resisted the demands but had insisted that only the faculty senate could approve some of them.

"It sounds like the old Holland stall!" shouted Brent Schumacher from the audience. "We have the faculty on the run and the press behind us. Why not strike now and bring the thing to a head!"

Others stood to endorse that sentiment, but Yothers argued for patience. He thought striking without clear cause would lose support of the faculty.

Sage concurred. "Thursday we will really blow the lid off if things don't go the way we want them to go."

By a voice vote students agreed to postpone the strike from the following day, Wednesday, to Thursday, to see what the faculty would do.

The next day students met with a faculty committee. Afterward, Sage and Yothers had to report, once again, that nothing had been resolved. They gave this report at an impromptu gathering of a few hundred students on Rogers Field. At this meeting Sage read a telegram from C. W. Orton, president of the Board of Regents, who students had invited to campus to act as mediator: "I suggest you keep your shirts on," the regent said in his telegram. "Remember that while the college is being operated for the benefit of the students, it belongs to the citizens of the state and if the students don't like the way it is run, it is their privilege to leave."

That evening students once again packed into Bohler Gym. Yothers recommended that the strike be put off for another day, to give the faculty a chance to meet again. The response from the packed bleachers to this recommendation was instantaneous and emotional: *No!*

Sage was now all for going ahead with the strike, as were others who stood to speak. The studious Herman "Dutch" Hayner (who thirty years later would himself be a WSU regent in an era of student unrest) warned his fellow students that Holland was simply trying to hold them at bay. When the question was called, not half a dozen voices voted in favor of delaying the strike again.

The newspapers made much of the fact that students were going ahead with the strike though they had gotten virtual guarantees from the president that their demands would be met. One observer suggested that perhaps "they were just having too much fun to stop." There may have been some of that. But other students recall being suspicious. It just didn't seem likely they could have won that easily. President Holland was respected as an administrator but was not famous for his flexibility. Dean Annie did not listen to rebuttals, much less give way to them. To many students it seemed likely that they were being maneuvered toward the end of the semester, when they would be disbursed and defeated automatically.

Late that night President Holland telephoned Yothers and asked him to come to the president's mansion. When Yothers arrived, he was surprised to see the president looking haggard and distressed; Yothers had no idea Holland was taking the matter so hard. The president asked what it would take to stop the strike. Yothers responded that students wouldn't accept a promise; the demands had to be signed. Holland seemed to find this humiliating, but sat down at the desk in his den to sign the demands. For the first time Yothers realized that the president considered the strike a personal defeat; he felt sorry for Holland.

There was no way of calling another meeting, however, and at seven the following morning pickets went up around all classroom buildings. The whole thing was meticulously organized. Committees of influential students were assigned to monitor access to buildings. Lettermen cruised the taverns in Pullman to make sure no one was brewing up mischief. Above all, strike leaders wanted no untoward incidents that would divert attention from the issues they were raising.

Except for a few foreign and graduate students who were given special exemptions, no one tried to cross picket lines. Wayne Miller, '37, was on picket duty with Frank Stojack, a football and wrestling star. "I will have to admit," Miller said later, "I was somewhat

"Strike Day," May 7, 1936. Protestors block entry to the Mechanic Arts Building. Note the "rooter caps" worn by male students—a symbol of campus loyalty.

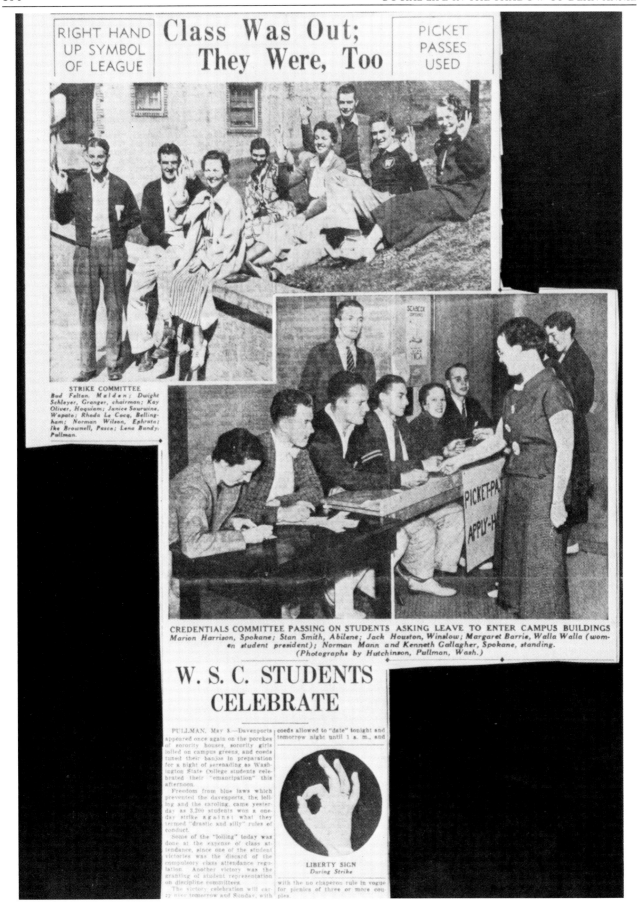

RIGHT HAND UP SYMBOL OF LEAGUE

Class Was Out; They Were, Too

PICKET PASSES USED

STRIKE COMMITTEE
Bud Felton, Malden; Dwight Schleyer, Granger, chairman; Kay Oliver, Hoquiam; Janice Sauvaine, Wapato; Rhoda Le Cocq, Bellingham; Norman Wilson, Ephrata; Ike Brownell, Pasco; Lena Bundy, Pullman.

CREDENTIALS COMMITTEE PASSING ON STUDENTS ASKING LEAVE TO ENTER CAMPUS BUILDINGS
Marion Harrison, Spokane; Stan Smith, Abilene; Jack Houston, Winslow; Margaret Barrie, Walla Walla (women student president); Norman Mann and Kenneth Gallagher, Spokane, standing.
(Photographs by Hutchinson, Pullman, Wash.)

W. S. C. STUDENTS CELEBRATE

PULLMAN, May 5.—Davenports appeared once again on the porches of sorority houses, sorority girls lolled on campus greens, and coeds tuned their banjos in preparation for a night of serenading as Washington State College students celebrated their "emancipation" this afternoon.

Freedom from blue laws which prevented the davenports, the lolling and the caroling, came yesterday as 3,200 students won a one-day strike against what they termed "drastic and silly" rules of conduct.

Some of the "lolling" today was done at the expense of class attendance, since one of the student victories was the discard of the compulsory class attendance regulation. Another victory was the granting of student representation on discipline committees.

The victory celebration will carry over tomorrow and Sunday, with coeds allowed to "date" tonight and tomorrow night until 1 a. m., and

LIBERTY SIGN
During Strike

with the no chaperon rule in vogue for picnics of three or more couples.

disappointed that no effort was made to cross the line, as I am sure the picketing would have been more than informational."

Lettermen of the Gray W Club were assigned responsibility for policing the strike. Dwight Scheyer, Northwest discus champion and president of the Grey W Letterman's Club, said only one incident was reported. One of the lettermen apparently mistook a young professor for a student and gave him a hack for trying to cross over the picket line.

Later that morning a student saw President Holland emerge from the east entrance of the Administration Building, where two chairs, used by strike monitors earlier, now stood empty. When Holland saw the chairs, he stepped back and kicked one as hard as he could, sending it rolling across the grass.

Holland visited several classroom buildings and found them virtually empty. He told two women students who were picketing that if he found them there in an hour he would expel them. They related the threat to a reporter and the story was sent to newspapers by Associated Press.

Holland lost the battle, not because students were undisciplined, but because they were too disciplined. "Other than efforts of a few to 'stir things up,'" reported the *Spokane Chronicle*, a paper which took a dim view of the whole thing, "the strike has been without customary disorder." This left the media with nothing to talk about except the student gripes. It was front-page news all over the Northwest and radio reporters were broadcasting from campus.

President Holland also knew he did not have the solid backing of his faculty, many of whom agreed with student complaints about Dean Annie and chaffed under a similar set of authoritarian rules issued by the president himself. Yothers and a few other student leaders considered the strike as much a protest against Holland's treatment of faculty as it was against Dean Fertig's treatment of students. One thing that made the strike so unanimous among students was that they had been getting clear signals from their teachers that they did not have to worry about recriminations.

Soon after Holland returned from his morning tour of the campus, he sent for student body president Ed Goldsworthy. When Goldsworthy arrived at Holland's office, he was shocked by the president's appearance. "His color was bad. He was obviously highly agitated about the whole thing," Goldsworthy later recalled.

President Holland told Goldsworthy that he had agreed to all the student demands and he couldn't understand why they persisted in the strike. He asked Goldsworthy to see if something could be done to bring the thing to a close.

Goldsworthy went to strike leaders and had little trouble persuading them to call a "truce" so that another vote could be taken. Hundreds of students squeezed into Bryan Auditorium to hear Goldsworthy and Joseph Knott, a well-liked agriculture professor, call for an end to the strike. Yothers joined them on the stage to add a passionate argument that the students had won the battle, and that the wise thing to do was to stop and collect their winnings.

OPPOSITE: *The Seattle* Post-Intelligencer *provided extensive coverage of the WSC strike.*

Sage and others rose to dissent. The auditorium resounded with impassioned declamations for both sides, equal cheers following each so that individuals in the audience could not guess which way the ultimate vote would go. Finally a motion was offered to suspend the strike until the faculty could act, and the yeas prevailed. At 4:30 that afternoon the faculty committee endorsed President Holland's concessions to the students. The strike was officially over.

That night the strikers gathered in Bohler and watched as President Holland, Professor Knott, and Bob Yothers entered the gym together. The students jumped to their feet and roared their approval. Holland assured them that they had been heard and that the episode would not be held against them.

The next day students read Dean Annie's response in the *Evergreen*. She said there never had been rules against wearing emotionally inflammatory red dresses or taking blankets on picnics. She said she had not bothered to comment on such things before because they "were so absurd that it seemed that no member of our college group could possibly give them credence."

The statement was terse and officious. It conceded nothing, not even that she might have communicated better. "The whole thing sounded like Dean Annie," one striker remembered thinking after reading it.

Though the students had never suggested it, Dean Annie Fertig and Dean of Men Carl Morrow* both resigned immediately after the strike. Whether it was their decision or Holland's remains unclear.

True to his promise, President Holland set up a student-faculty committee which adjusted curfew hours, provided for fairer hearings for accused students, and, for the first time, published the rules governing student social life. The committee also eliminated one of the more long-lived WSC student gripes: a draconian rule that took a full semester credit away from any student who missed even one class on the first day of school after a vacation.

Holland reneged in only one detail, and it probably revealed better than anything his feeling about the whole affair. The day before graduation, the president telephoned Bob Yothers and told him not to bother showing up for the ceremony. Yothers would not be getting a diploma.**

In this Holland was, judging from letters received from the public during the strike, pretty much in agreement with the larger community. Typical of the advice given to the president during the strike was a letter from a father who recommended that Holland, "appeal to the high honor and self-respect" of the young people. "Failure to re-

---

*Carl Morrow was a huge, quiet man who, at most, complied too readily with rules of conduct that students resented. He had, however, gone out of his way to help young men with personal problems and had assisted others in finding employment. Many students believed he received a "bum rap," being forced to depart at the same time as Dean Fertig.

** He was already admitted to law school, however, so it made little practical difference. Yothers got his bachelors degree from WSC in 1956, after he had become a prominent attorney and active in Washington politics.

spond to this fine appeal," said this father, "should be followed by immediate expulsion." A Spokane accountant had voluntarily polled other businessmen in that city. "The sentiment seems to be," he wrote to Holland, "that recognition should be given to meritorious complaint, if such there be, but only after the student body has been purged of contaminating loafers. Approval was also expressed of the application of the severest discipline to leaders of insubordination."

Who was going to feel sorry for college students? By any estimate they comprised one of the most privileged sectors of American society. In truth, students didn't feel sorry for themselves. Dean Annie's rules may have been irritating and condescending, but even students did not contend they were a threat to life, liberty, or even the pursuit of happiness.

On the other hand, students were not inclined to feel apologetic for defying these rules. While the public assumed campus restrictions were for the students' own good, students themselves could see from the bureaucratic way they were applied that these rules were more administrative convenience than moral guidance. College administrators, charged with controlling the behavior of thousands of exuberant students, yet ill-equipped for the task and disinclined to devote much time to it, piled on restrictions and hoped that would accomplish the task. Administrators could afford to be quite sloppy about this rule making, for what could students do about it?

That is why every generation of students at Washington State College rebelled against *in loco parentis*. Most did so quietly. Long before there was a strike against curfews, the issue had been noiselessly protested on innumerable dark nights via the first-floor windows of women's dorms. The oldest contributor to this history of student life, Floyd Smith, '13, gave the earliest of a long line of accounts of boosting girls through Stevens Hall windows after hours.

The students of 1936 were different only in that they rebelled openly. Why were they the ones to do so? Because somebody happened to have the idea, because Dean Annie had by this time offended so many that it only required the merest suggestion, and because, as Jerry Sage said, "it was a nice spring day." ■

Social Life in the Shadow of Dean Annie

WSC campus, 1937.

Pullman, circa *1940*.

Busiest spot on campus, 1920s-1930s; the post office (right) and the old bookstore/coffee shop (left) on Thatuna.

Equestrians uphill from Science and Bryan halls (now the Holland Library lawn), circa *1925*.

*Weekend date walking along one of several
railroad tracks leading out of town.*

*Jitney bus in front of the old bookstore, 1926. WSC Vice President O. L. Waller walking by at far left;
student Bruce Curtis, Pullman, at center facing camera .*

Student Bookstore, 1927.

Women's quartet, 1925-1926. From the left: Vay Kerns, Kathleen Pugh, Agnes Dilts, and Vera Bohlke.

ABOVE: *Stevens Hall parlor, 1918.
Placard at left reads: "Have nothing
in your home that you do not know
to be useful or believe to be beautiful."*

LEFT: *Cora Griffen, 1935.
College coeds led the way in the
emergence of "The New Woman"
in this era.*

Class

PRESIDENT HOLLAND ALWAYS BELIEVED THAT THE STUDENTS WHO WENT on strike in 1936 had been influenced by faculty members. He was right. Claudius O. Johnson, for instance, the acerbic young political science professor, was considered a special mentor by the two main leaders of the strike, Bob Yothers and Jerry Sage. Like other students, Yothers and Sage admired Johnson's irreverent wit, his bold assessments, his casual demeanor. He was clearly an influence on the strikers.

Not that "Claudius O." (as students called him out of earshot) ever approved of strikes. In fact, when leaders told him of their plans he warned that they probably would get into trouble and accomplish nothing. But the warning was ignored. They had been in his American government classes; they had read his book, *Government in the United States,* which took as its theme the idea that in America there is no such thing as authority without limits. In the first chapter they had read Johnson's scoffing refutation of those who considered Thomas Jefferson an extremist. Jefferson's claim for the right of revolution "because of the arbitrary acts of the King," Claudius O. had written, was "perfectly good English political theory . . . by which Englishmen had overthrown two kings." As far as students were concerned, overthrowing a dean because of arbitrary acts was perfectly good American political theory.

One of the things that happened to students in college was education. Between the big games, before band and play practice, interspersed with the more urgent calls of school politics and romance, were all those mornings spent in those big boxes of light called classrooms. No scene of campus life is more familiar to every college student: the tiny desks, the wall of windows, the indistinct smell of floor wax, the scratching and tapping of chalk on the blackboard, the clock pushing its way through the rhythm of a fifty-minute class, the reedy voice of a teacher trying to elucidate some portion of the universe—the molecule, the Roman Empire, the parabola, Milton's theology.

Lucille Olive Davis, '16, who happened to be the only student to leave the WSU archives a full set of class notes, accumulated a stack of blue-lined loose-leaf sheets several inches tall. Though containing only the faintest outline of discussions that went on in the classroom, and only a hint at the ideas that entered Lucille's mind, they are, nonetheless, an impressive compilation of knowledge. They show

OPPOSITE: *Science lab, March 11, 1930.*

ABOVE: *Drafting room.* BELOW: *Classroom, 1920.*

Lucille following a history teacher through the Renaissance and French Revolution, recording a psychology teacher's characterization of crowds as "sedulous, irrational and simple-minded," and taking a math teacher's word for it that $2x^2+3y^2=10$. In various places in the notes she defines "syllogism," "ethical dualism," and "education." In a sociology class she wrote down: "There is no great elemental difference between races." Another place she quoted George Bernard Shaw: "Britain is an island which regards its customs as the laws of humanity." She wrote a paper on unemployment and answered the test question: "Show the relationship between the economic environment and the family as an institution."

Students might, on occasion, doubt that anything so pretentious as an "education" happened during those endless fifty-minute sessions. But there is no denying that something about their thinking changed along the way. Certitudes loosened to make room for new possibilities. Little by little, more things were added to make the world more complicated, and occasionally an idea registered that suddenly made it more simple. Learning is almost a subversive thing—undermining ignorance even while a student may not be paying attention. After dutifully taking a series of poetry classes, Lylia Appel Miller, '29, idly picked up a book and "to my astonishment," she declared, "I discovered I liked poetry."

When ideas are stamped upon a student's mind, their clarity and durability bears a direct relation to the weight of the personality of the one who did the stamping. Claudius O. Johnson and his ideas were an influence on many of his students for the rest of their lives. At an age when young people were looking for role models, examples of what they ought to be, Johnson was somebody they could admire. He literally "wrote the book" on his subject. *Government in the United States* was used at colleges and universities all over the country, including some Ivy League schools. It was, like Johnson himself, blunt and irreverent. A half century before "value-free learning" became a concern in education, Johnson wrote in the preface: "I dare believe that 'on the one hand . . . on the other' represents less than a complete discharge of our responsibilities." The best students felt his good opinion was worth having. Indifferent students were impressed by him too. Showing up for class with a partially completed assignment was to be avoided at all costs. Claudius O. was likely to fix a stare on the unprepared student through those thick glasses, as if he were marking this moment when he had finally met a person who truly doesn't mind wallowing in ignorance. It was withering. Few chose it over the alternative of preparing for class.

Entomology fieldwork.

---

* Later, she became the wife of Professor Homer Dana, for whom Dana Hall is named.

JOHNSON WAS A REMARKABLE TEACHER. YET, JUDGING FROM STUDENT tributes to other professors of the era, he was hardly an exception in his own department. Others remember historian Herman Deutsch. "His lectures made you feel as if he had lived it all," recalled Wilbur B. Gilbert, '37. "You didn't want to miss a word." Kenneth Kennedy, '31, nominated William Bossenbrook as the star of the department. "He was one of the best teachers in history that Washington State ever had. He could make it come alive." A student who contemplated history under the likes of Johnson, Deutsch, and Bossenbrook might also attend the course on Northwest history taught by Enoch Bryan, founding president of the college. Howard R. Bowen, '29, who would himself go on to a distinguished career in education as president of three universities and author of ten books, remembered Bryan as one of the educators who influenced his life.

That was just one department. In his autobiography, Bowen also remembered Fay Clower in economics as a "marvelous lecturer" who was responsible for opening his mind to social issues. But the best remembered teacher in that tiny department was Richard Heflebower, a precise, well-organized lecturer—and good friend—remembered by business executives all over the Pacific Northwest.

It's remarkable how often students who went to Washington State College because financially they had no options, later count themselves lucky for ending up there. The reason is that, no matter how

Instruction in tractor mechanics.

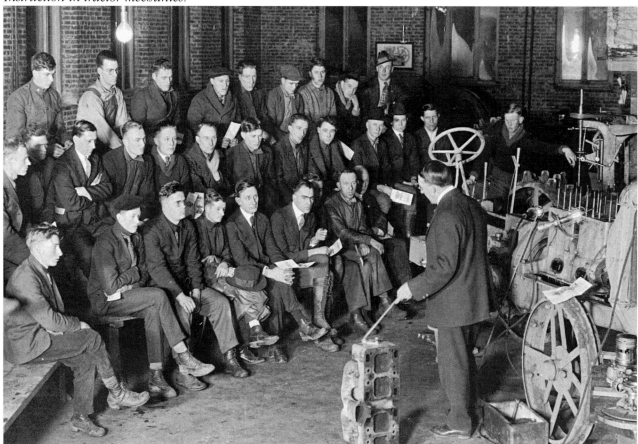

big or rich an institution, the basic thing it can offer an undergraduate student is a handful of first-rate teachers, and the State College had those. Walter Herndon, '28, went to work for the Cadillac Company in Detroit. A few years later he was on a team of three engineers that invented the automatic transmission. Later in his career, Herndon was head of a division of General Motors, hiring and supervising the work of hundreds of engineers representing every engineering school in the country. He never felt, he said, that any of them had a better education than he got at the State College of Washington.

Perhaps that is not so surprising for a college that was established to emphasize agriculture and engineering. But art? An art student at WSC in the 1930s could study with the well-known portraiturist Worth Griffin or the frenetic experimentalist George Lasner, who, according to Randall Johnson, '37, "was miles above the setting he was in." An art student between 1935 and 1941 might also have taken classes from a tall, gaunt teacher by the name of Clyfford Still. Still, who earned his masters at WSC and then stayed on to teach, painted immense canvases, oddly shaped figures, and brilliant yellow wheat fields, and hung them in the art gallery in Science Hall. Some people on campus thought he was a little crazy and the rest thought he was a genius. He never lectured about art. But the intense teacher also was capable of leaning over a student's painting and making a comment that struck like lightening in a black night, showing everything at

Home economics, bread making.

Art students, 1938.

once. Students were in awe of him. "If he even stopped to look at your painting, you knew you had something," said art major Alice Burke Schuchman, '39.

In 1941, Still went to San Francisco, where he became one of the founders of American Abstract Expressionism. He was to become one of the century's most important artists, "a mythic figure in American painting" (according to *Time* magazine) who "created a highly original and compelling artistic statement" (according to the New York Metropolitan Museum of Art *Bulletin*).

Not every teacher was distinguished, of course. Students also remember, with chagrin, the old professor who came unprepared every day and rambled through the hour, or the education course that was not *about* third graders but *for* third graders. Others are remembered as characters rather than as teachers. Professor N. G. Covington, teacher of a standard biology class, had emigrated from Eastern Europe and spoke with a barely intelligible accent. He teased women and insulted men so perpetually that it was said that the four-foot-long walking stick he carried around campus was for protection. He was famous for his standard threat to an erring student: "I geeve you *flonk!*" If really upset, and he often was, he would shout: "I geeve you *dawble* flonk!"

Good teachers could have many different styles. The manifest friendliness and warmth of engineering and mathematics professor Royal D. Sloan was part of his charm. "Some teachers you like to work for, and he was one of them," said Florence Johnson Chisholm, '27. His colleague, mathematics teacher Morris Knebelman, could be sarcastic, cool, or could shout, "That's childish!" at a disappointing student—yet was also cited as an excellent teacher. His patience in answering after-class questions "saved my life when I entered Harvard graduate school," said Ralph V. Wood, Jr., '43.

Whatever the style, however, former students generally mentioned two qualities found in good teachers. The first was competence. Students listened when they sensed that a teacher knew what he or she was talking about. The second was caring—about students, or at least about education. For all his odd ways, students sensed that Clyfford Still wanted them to be the best artists they could be. Walter Herndon, the General Motors inventor, attributed his satisfaction with his WSC education to Professor Eri Parker. "I always thought that he gave me very special attention," said Herndon. Joe H. Irwin, '36, could never forget that Professor Heflebower in the business department cosigned, without being asked, a bank loan for him so that he could continue in college. Norm Thue, '30, for decades a well-known Spokane musician and music teacher, said you worked harder than you sometimes wanted for Herbert Kimbrough simply because he seemed to care a lot about your progress and you couldn't stand to disappoint him. Ken Bement, '34, recalled that boxing coach Ike Deeter always asked about his studies, his job, and other things. In a way, that "made you know he was interested in *you*." The feeling was reciprocated, Bement said. "We loved the guy." Long after the training and the field strategies of coaches like Deeter, baseball coach

OPPOSITE: *C. Ross Greening's cartoon appeared in the 1936* Chinook *at a time when the art department was coming under the influence of Abstract Expressionism. Greening, '36, an athlete and student leader as well as an outstanding artist, took up flying while in college. Early in World War II, he flew a B-25 on the famous Doolittle bombing raid over Tokyo. Later, while flying missions over Italy, Greening was shot down and captured. He died in 1957 of a disease contracted while a prisoner of war.*

Irene and Frank Potter in the garden of their B Street house.

"Buck" Bailey, and football coach "Babe" Hollingbery ceased to have any significance, their players remembered them as teachers of important human qualities. A typical remark was that of football player Joe B. Hill, '37, who said of Hollingbery, "Any young man who came under his influence was better because of it."

THESE TWO QUALITIES, COMPETENCE AND CARING, WERE POSSESSED IN abundance by the college's most famous teacher, Frank F. Potter. During Potter's association with WSC, from 1912 to his death in 1959, WSC had ten students selected as Rhodes Scholars, more than any other separate land-grant college except the Massachusetts Institute of Technology. Nine of them considered Potter, a classics scholar and philosopher, their special mentor. The number of students who went from a tiny college to study at Oxford University in England is directly attributable to efforts by Potter and his wife, Irene, to help groom young men to compete.

Clarence M. Schuchman, '38, remembered noticing him on campus: "a very preoccupied elderly man who seemed not to notice the world. He walked along leaning slightly forward in an almost pre-hippy shuffle, wearing his inevitable brown suit and tie, carrying his inevitable brown leather briefcase." He displayed the absentmindedness that seems to accompany powerful concentration. Potter's wife told of the time he stopped for a moment to watch some construction on campus and became so engrossed he forgot to go on to class.

This famous teacher had no flamboyant teaching style—he was not a Murray Bundy, the English department chair who became a Shakespearean actor to teach Shakespeare. Potter spoke softly when he lectured; not even his mouth seemed to move very much. Dorris West Goodrich, '42, remembered his expression as placid, "but with an air that suggested that he expected something interesting about to happen."

Potter's special method of getting through to students was to pay attention to them. When Clarence Schuchman got into one of Potter's classes he found the impression was different than the "very preoccupied elderly man" he had seen on campus. "Now *you* became the focus of that intense preoccupation," Schuchman said. Because "He clearly considered everything we had to say to be worth listening to and thinking about." said Frances Handy Maurier, '42, "We all, without realizing perhaps why we were doing it, tried much harder to think clearly and logically before putting forth an idea." Jane Cauvel, '51, who became a professor of philosophy herself, said Potter simply assumed an interest and sincerity on the part of his students and "we tried our best to live up to his expectations." Because he genuinely seemed interested in her efforts, said Mildred Sherrod Bissinger, '33, "I always felt exhilarated on leaving the classroom, and happy to write a paper for him." His students always tied their motivation to an affection he seemed to instill. "It was not so much what he said or did," said Grace Gockley Click, '33, "but the warmth of his personality which I didn't forget."

Potter believed in the Socratic method, the back-and-forth of question, response, counter-question. "The joy he took in clear thinking was evident," said Russell McCormmach, '55, one of the Rhodes Scholars. Somehow—perhaps it was because he was utterly devoid of personal ego (he didn't care at all if he won a chess game, just so they were good games)—Potter could turn ten thousand volts of intellect on a person's idea without the slightest injury to the person. Toward others he always displayed what Donald Bushaw, '49, described as a kind of "meticulous decency" that assured anyone that he would never give injury. Potter didn't so much propound The Great Ideas as embody them.

In 1929, at the age of forty-nine, Potter married Irene Michet, a forty-year-old assistant professor of English. Almost immediately their house at 815 B Street, the second house down from Colorado, became an unofficial extension of the college. Monday evenings the music-listening group gathered. Wednesday afternoon the doors were thrown open to anyone interested in a "general discussion group." Friday afternoons the "Rhodes group" gathered. Friday night was chess night (Irene once described the conversation on a chess night as: "Good evening. Check. Goodnight.").

The Rhodes group was slightly more structured than the others, since its purpose was to prepare a group of twelve or fifteen promising young men for the Rhodes interview by acquainting them with as wide a variety of learning as possible. Faculty members of every discipline were invited to lead discussions. One recalled that presenting a paper before this group was "as demanding as preparing and presenting a paper to a professional society."

An invitation to any of the afternoon or evening gatherings at the Potter house was to the more brainy student what a position on the football team was to the more brawny; it was both recognition and a

Experiment in a science lab.

Tinting lantern slides for botany instruction, circa *1910.*

Vet medicine, 1925.

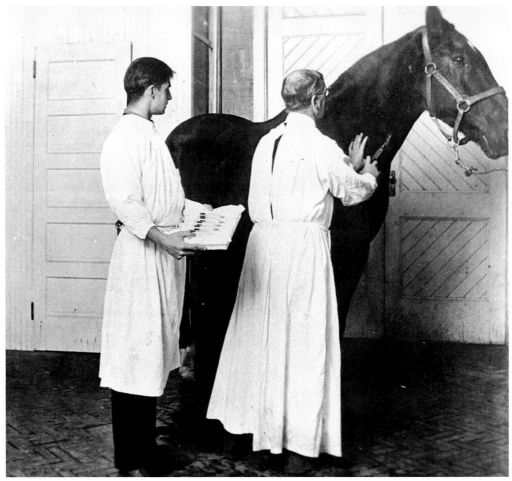

chance to exercise one's abilities. It was also a prized social event. "You rang the bell," recalled Mildred Bissinger, "and Doctor Potter came to welcome you and you were ushered into the charming living room, which was always spotless and fresh. In front of the fireplace two easy chairs faced each other. *Their* chairs." "I was aware," said Ellen Franzen Dissanayake, '57, "of all the books, the fabric wallpaper in the living room (not the flowers or prints that were on the houses of people I knew), the set of Proust, the restrained lighting, the atmosphere of refinement and simplicity."

Potter sat by the fireplace, slightly hunched in his chair, one leg crossed over the other and kicking rhythmically. He tended to let the conversation have its head, only occasionally stepping in, in his Socratic way, skillfully to place a question or a fact. If he was going to speak, he began with a little throat-clearing growl. Frances Handy Maurier, '42, remembered: "When it was a no-holds-barred affair and a whole roomful of highly opinionated young people was almost in an uproar as we tried to out-talk each other, that 'hrumph-hrumph' from Doctor Potter sitting in the corner would quiet us all in a flash. We all knew something worth listening to was going to follow." Irene Potter, vivacious and witty, alternately filled the cookie dish and plunged into the conversation. "When she did," recalls Maurier, "she was as well worth listening to as he was, and that's saying a lot."

Discussions were never chitchat, but not seminars, either. If the prearranged topic led into another subject that promised rich ore, there were no objections to following it. People remember topics of discussion ranging from the causes of revolutions to Ernest Hemingway's place in literature and whether you might fairly describe the way ballet dancers walk as "waddling."

By the time a student stepped back out into the cool air of B Street, he or she had had a genuine taste of the life of the mind. It was somehow bound up with the taste of Mrs. Potter's cookies, with the warmth of the fire, with Doctor Potter's gentle personality, and it was fun.

WHAT MAKES THE CASE OF THIS ONE WSC TEACHER STAND OUT IS THE accident of there being a Rhodes Scholarship. This provided some sort of measure of what is notoriously unquantifiable: the success of education. The tiny college was competing with every college and university in the United States for the prestigious scholarship for study at England's Oxford University, and doing very well.

But the Rhodes Scholars represented only a side project, a fraction of what Potter did for students. And Potter represented only a fraction of what was going on at the college. Potter was tutoring his first Rhodes Scholar, Earl Pritchard, in 1930. That same spring, 425 seniors across the country took a chemist's civil service examination. In this nationwide competition, the two top scorers in analytical chemistry were George Ward and David Reid, both of Washington State College. Ward and Reid were classmates of another WSC success: Edward R. Murrow.

Unidentified experimenter at work in a wheat lab as it appeared when Charles Glen King, '18, studied chemistry at WSC. King, later a professor at the University of Pittsburgh, discovered vitamin C in 1932.

One of Homer Veatch's famous debate teams, circa *1938. From the left: Jim Davis, Ed Lockhart, James Duree, and Remo Fausti.*

Murrow was one of those students who always counted himself lucky that economic necessity had delivered him to WSC. He had arrived on a campus that had an operating radio station (kept running by the personal ingenuity of engineer-inventor Homer Dana), which many colleges did not. WSC offered what may have been the only— was certainly one of the few—radio-broadcasting courses in the nation, the personal inspiration of Maynard Daggy. Murrow was coached in debate by an enthusiastic young teacher by the name of William Homer Veatch, who was destined to post one of the winningest records in intercollegiate debate and become a charter member of the Pi Kappa Delta national forensics honorary. Murrow, a budding genius, found the tiny, underfunded college fully prepared to educate him. How this could be so offers an interesting case study in higher education.

Fate did not ordain that WSC should have a great speech department. The early drama department had about it unmistakable signs of high school thespianism. In 1911, an *Evergreen* reviewer, straining to be kind, was forced to report that scene changes in the school play lasted a half hour or more, "during which the audience became weary and fretful, which was so pronounced at the time of the closing scene of the play that the principles were unable to say their lines." (The reviewer was less than convincing when he added: "Outside this defect the play was a decided success.")

In 1920, President Holland hired Nathanial E. Reeid to head the department. Reeid, tall, well-dressed, urbane, saw drama and speech as vehicles to polish the college student. "He put great emphasis on those little things we don't think much about," recalled one of his students, Glenn Maughmer, '23. "If you were going to shake hands with someone or make a gesture with your right hand, you would make sure your right foot was out so that you would have a balanced feeling. Those elementary things that he drilled into people became so basic and so clean that you never forgot them. After taking that course I don't think anybody would ever feel ill at ease anywhere."

Reeid coached students in speaking from the diaphragm, not the upper chest. He explained the importance of cadence, pitch, and stress. He had them repeat a sentence like, "And in the morning he was dead," each time stressing a different word, to see how meaning changes depending upon which word is emphasized. Students were required to memorize long passages and deliver them interpretively.

Under Reeid's direction, the amateur WSC theater suddenly was full of life. In the spring of 1921 alone it produced seven different plays. Reeid chose two casts for each play, both of which performed for students, but only the best of which would travel off campus.

In the summer of 1922, Reeid rented a theater in Spokane and staged twelve plays developed over the previous years. Two-hundred students were involved. With the profits from admissions, he purchased $5,000 worth of theatrical equipment for the Bryan Hall stage.

By the time Reeid announced in the spring of 1924 that he was leaving to take a position with a New York City play publisher, he turned over to successor Maynard Lee Daggy what was almost certainly the best drama and speech department in the Northwest. Just a few years later, one of Reeid's students, Addison "Tad" Richards became one of the last stars of the silent movie era. But, as in the case of Potter's Rhodes Scholars, such successes are only hints of the real impact. Glenn Maughmer went on to a successful career, not in theater or speech, but in engineering. "I am convinced," he would say sixty-five years later, "that a substantial percentage of what success I've had in business was due to the fact that I had training from Professor Reeid."

Another of Reeid's devoted students was Ida Lou Anderson. She was an intelligent young woman of twenty when she entered his class. But it seemed she was destined to excel at almost anything other than speech and drama. A childhood case of infantile paralysis left her tiny, frail, and with a hump on her back. She felt so ostracized because of her appearance when she first arrived at college that she almost dropped out of school.

Her college years exactly overlapped Reeid's tenure. A teacher like this was a godsend to a young woman with exceptional oratorical talents and a love of poetry. Her school notebooks, now in the WSU archives, show her assiduously recording his lessons, from the anatomical explanation of voice to the interpretation of poetry. Reeid recognized her talent and deliberately selected plays for production which would provide parts in which her physical disabilities would not be an obstacle.

By the time she graduated in 1924, Ida Lou Anderson knew she had a vocation. She went to the University of Chicago to earn a masters degree in speech and then returned to the State College as an instructor. Miss Anderson, the young woman who felt like an outcast when she entered college, quickly became one of the best-liked teachers on campus.

She was a strange sight when you first saw her walking across campus, moving the spindly legs forward with a twisting motion at the hips. She was so small that she had to look straight up to talk even

Ida Lou Anderson, '24, (holding the plate and wearing glasses) as a WSC student.

to other women. She wore wire rims with darkened glass because light hurt her eyes. The face was not pretty but very pleasant, even wise. The voice, surprisingly deep, though still feminine, was wonderful to listen to. She was immensely well-read (in one fifteen-month period she read, according to a list in her personal papers, seventy-one books) and could discuss world politics or baseball. Typically, she would enter a room full of people and within five minutes everyone would be gathered around her.

The remark Leonard A. Mitchell, '30, that he took but one class from her, and, "It was without a doubt a highlight of my college experience," was a common feeling among students. She seemed to want to take personal responsibility for the future of each of her students, and she thought everyone ought to be in her classes. It was common for her to approach a student who had just given a speech or talk and say: "You have ability! You should be in my class." Or, to a yell leader: "You are ruining your voice! You should be in my class."

The curious thing is that she showered the same attention on the hopeless cases as she did the young stars. Football players who signed up for "Interpretation" because it sounded easy found themselves, after losing a clash or two with Miss Anderson, drilling until they could give a reasonable interpretation of "Ode to a Daffodil" or Marc Antony's funeral oration.

Norm Thue, '30, remembers his excruciating efforts to give the simplest speech in her class. It seems when he spoke his head moved in and out, and some claimed his ears moved. The result was that three sentences into a speech the whole class was howling with laughter. After a few aborted speeches, Ida Lou shuffled to the front of the room and fixed a stern look through the wire rim glasses. "Norman is a wonderful musician and he needs to develop a stage presence. By laughing at him, we are hurting his future career." One of Professor Reeid's tenets had been that voice alone, if properly used, can control any situation, and his student Ida Lou was the embodiment of the truth of it. When Thue started to speak again the class was absolutely quiet. But finally, Thue recalls, he heard someone lose control and burst out laughing. "I looked over—and it was Ida Lou!"

In Ida Lou's first year of teaching, 1926, a young man by the name of Egbert (later changed to Edward) Murrow signed up for her class. He was a business administration major but soon switched to speech.

Ed Murrow was not one of those successes about whom people later say, "who would ever have thought!" Fellow students remember him as a little different than other college boys when he arrived, and

Commencement, 1922.

a lot different by the time he graduated in 1930. He was six-feet-two, handsome, smart, and had an unusual maturity about him. Close friend Paul Coie, '30, described him as "calm, almost aloof" in manner. Though he gave school politics a high priority, he was not much interested in other standard college diversions, pranks and the like.

His brother Lacey was a member of Kappa Sigma when Ed arrived, so Ed joined one of the powerful fraternities on campus. This and his natural abilities led to his being elected student body president as the candidate of the fraternity organization (see chapter three). The same seriousness and mastery of organizational work brought him promotion to commander of the ROTC brigade. He acted in several plays and some students thought, with his looks and all, he might head for Hollywood.

He received A's in speech and B's and C's in other courses, which was presentable considering the fact that he spent great amounts of time on extracurricular activities. He had the reputation of being able to breeze through classes without studying. Fraternity brother Donald E. Stover, '30, was supposed to share a study room with Murrow one year, "but I do not recall that I ever saw him study there." He apparently did have something like a photographic memory. Hermine Duthie Decker, '30, who appeared with him in many school plays, had dinner with Murrow in 1961, thirty years after they

Edward R. Murrow and friends, 1927. From the left: Esther Stilson, George Stapleton, Betty Ramsbeck, and Murrow.

graduated. She recited one of her lines from a play they had both acted in. Murrow said, "No, that's wrong," and gave her another version. When she got home and looked it up, he was right.

He could stand up at any occasion and deliver five or ten minutes of off-the-cuff remarks which sounded as if they had been practiced for a month. But there was something behind the glibness. Lylia Appel Miller, '29, a champion debater, remembers Murrow in a debate class laying down an impressive argument. Then, "a worried frown crossed his brow," she recalled, and Murrow said, "Now I wonder—is that right?"—much to the consternation of debate coach William Homer Veatch, who pointed out that the rightness of the matter was not the point of the debate.* Veatch himself recalled a similar instance. Murrow was not on the debate team, but Veatch talked him into entering the Pacific Coast Forensics League debate tournament in the extemporaneous category. When Murrow's turn came, he launched "one of the most beautiful talks I have ever heard from a student." But four minutes into the talk, "the ideas broke down," Veatch recalled, "and he limped through the rest of the speech." When scores came out Murrow placed fifth out of nine contenders. Veatch asked Murrow what happened, and Murrow's response, as Veatch recalled it, was: "Prof, I got halfway through and discovered I didn't believe a damn word I was saying. I tried to straighten it up in the last three minutes of the speech, and I'm awfully sorry, but I just couldn't straighten it up."

MURROW TOOK NINETEEN SPEECH COURSES IN EIGHT SEMESTERS, NEARLY all of them from Ida Lou Anderson. Beyond that, the two spent untold hours together talking about literature, politics, the nature of man, the nature of people they knew. The six-foot-two Murrow and the four-foot Miss Anderson were a familiar sight walking across campus together, "he carrying her books," recalled Dorothy Darby Smith, '31, "she looking up at him, both of them so engrossed in their conversation."

Ida Lou, who admired intelligence, integrity, and talent, found in Murrow her perfect student. In return, she could supply what Murrow's restless mind and ambition craved. She knew how to adjust and tune an already accomplished speaking ability. (To simulate the conditions of radio broadcasting, where the speaker has no one to look at, and the listener has no visual cues to aid the meaning, she would have him sit behind a screen to read aloud). She led Murrow to books, ideas, and preached to him the stoic philosophy of Marcus Aurelius, that of "expecting nothing, fearing nothing," but trusting that doing one's duty will provide happiness.

During his senior year, Murrow attended the National Student Federation of America at Stanford University, an association of student governments that tried to exert some influence on national

Ida Lou Anderson, speech instructor at WSC.

---

* This incident took place, appropriately, in Science Hall, which is now part of the Edward R. Murrow Communication Center.

Edward R. Murrow returns to WSC, 1942. He was on a brief visit to America after the famous "This. . .is London" broadcasts.

and international affairs. During one of the debates, Murrow rose to decry the lack of seriousness on the part of college students. The speech so impressed a group of influential delegates that they persuaded him to run for the presidency of the organization. He won and the job took him to New York after graduation. When his tenure in that position ran out he was hired as an assistant to the director of the Emergency Committee for the Aid of Displaced German Scholars, an organization formed to rescue intellectuals being persecuted in Hitler's Germany. Shortly after he completed that assignment he went to work for the CBS Radio Network as a low-level organizer of radio shows. In a few years he would be responsible for all CBS news from Europe as the continent was enveloped by war.

All this time he corresponded with Ida Lou Anderson. When he had finished the work on the rescue of German scholars, Murrow had sent a copy of the final report to Ida Lou, writing on the cover: "The credit goes to my partner, who gave me the power to do it." This was no idle flattery from an appreciative ex-student. About the same time, Murrow wrote to his fiancée, Janet Brewster, to explain that another person, Ida Lou Anderson, "is very much a part of my life and always will be."

> She taught me to love good books, good music, gave me the only sense of values I have . . . I've talked over in letters every decision. She knows me better than any person in the world. The part of me that is decent, wants to do something, be something, is the part she created. She taught me to speak. She taught me one must have more than a good bluff to really live.

Meanwhile, Ida Lou was charming new generations of students. Her classes were so popular, Dean Kimbrough said, that students had to be turned away. And she was always there to reassure former students as they went through the travails of launching careers. Bob Sandberg, '36, wrote to her that he felt he should reverse a decision he had made, except he was embarrassed to have others see him do so. She wrote him: "I would not be much concerned. Anyone who does very much over a period of years grows accustomed to occasional times 'when his face is red.'"

But she was not there just to reassure; when the situation called for it she could be about as gentle as a football coach. She visited Victoria, B.C. in the summer of 1936 and stayed up late one night to hear the radio program of one of her best students, Art Gilmore. What she heard didn't please her. Before going to bed she wrote him an eight-page letter that began, "I am not going to quibble, so get ready to take it straight." She told him he had adopted the "foam and fluff" of a false radio-voice gaiety. "Where on earth is that full rich tone of yours? ... You're giving it very little exercise, and let me tell you, Art, when you lose that, through neglect, you'll never even come within shouting distance of anything big in radio."

"Apparently," she continued, "no one else is saying anything to you except complimentary things. . . . I love you and can't stand such carelessness." She told him he had a naturally great voice that only needed to be used correctly to be great. He had to work on the technical points they had discussed in school—use of the tongue to enunciate and the mouth as a resonator. Beyond that the key was sincerity. "Most of the time, I don't feel your mind is on what you are saying or reading. . . . You pause and phrase. But *you* just aren't behind what you are saying."

She summarized that there were no tricks to being convincing on the radio. If he worked at his profession, his voice would show his sincerity and an understanding of what he was about. "A voice, in short, is only the fine instrument of something far greater than itself, which is the whole man."

Two nights later she could hear a difference in Gilmore's announcing. Then she received a letter from him profusely thanking her for the scolding. She replied, "You certainly proved you could take it on the chin with a swift and intelligent comeback. That pleased me more than anything."

Gilmore, who went on to become a nationally famous announcer for, among others, Red Skelton, one of the top comedians of the forties and fifties, kept the letters from Ida Lou for the rest of his life, proof of a teacher who had really cared about him.

Ida Lou was such a stoic that no one knew the pain she felt or how weak she was becoming. In the late thirties, she spent much time between one day's class and the next lying in a darkened room, listening to a series of college women read to her. Finally, in 1939, she was forced to give up teaching and move to Corvallis, Oregon, where a sister could help her mother take care of her. With this clear sign of serious health problems, letters of concern poured in. Murrow, now reporting from London, had shipped to her the most powerful radio on the market, with instructions that she listen to him and tell him how he was doing. She answered with a telegram suggesting the pause in his sign on "This . . . is London," a signature that is now famous.

People on campus figured she had collapsed from overwork, what with teaching several classes, advising endlessly, then writing those long letters to former students. When she responded to President Holland's letter of condolences, Ida Lou said: "None of you must feel that I was the least bit overworked. . . . I loved every minute of it, from the day I first walked into a classroom."

In that letter to Holland she added: "The air lanes are so full of voices I know. Those boys have been a comfort during this long, lonely, difficult winter." By this time her students were working all over the Pacific Northwest, including major stations in Spokane, Tacoma, and Portland. Art Gilmore had become an announcer for Warner Brothers in Los Angeles, James Campbell was broadcasting in Chicago, and, of course, Murrow was just becoming one of the most famous voices in radio as the Battle of Britain began.

Ida Lou's health steadily declined until she couldn't eat and slept only fitfully. She was taken to a hospital to be fed intravenously. One afternoon she had a conversation with a nurse about her fourteen-year-old nephew Bill and what fascinating creatures adolescents are. The next morning, September 16, 1941, a nurse turned around to fetch something and Ida Lou closed her eyes and died. She was forty-one years old.

Murrow sent $350 to President Holland to pay for the publication of a book of memorials to her. In his contribution to the book, Murrow wrote that Ida Lou's students knew "we had been in the presence of one who was, in the true sense of the word, greater than anyone we had met or were ever likely to meet." At the time he wrote this, Murrow was in daily contact with people of the stature of Winston Churchill and Dwight Eisenhower.

Before Ida Lou died, she could already see that her "masterpiece," as she called Murrow, was headed for greatness. Through his war reporting, his innovative social reporting, his stand against the demagogue Senator Joseph R. McCarthy, and his work to make broadcast news responsible, Murrow became the most revered reporter in American journalism history. His biographers, wondering what produced this giant, inevitably came across the story of a teacher at the State College of Washington by the name of Ida Lou Anderson. ∎

Class

WSC students pass in front of Bryan Hall on their way to class one morning in 1939.

ABOVE: *Early
twentieth-century
agricultural
equipment.*

RIGHT: *Hand sewing
in Van Doren Hall.*

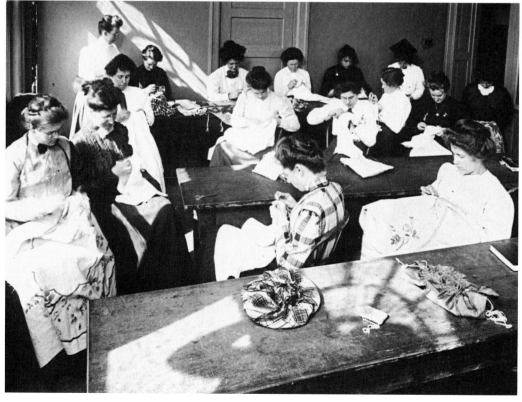

ABOVE: *Foreign language lab, 1920s.*

LEFT: *Architecture students, 1920s.*

ABOVE: *WSC's "Orchesis Society" posing alongside Silver Lake.*

OPPOSITE: *Silver Lake scene. Dancing as an art form for young women began at the University of Wisconsin in 1918, and quickly spread to other campuses. Orchesis founder, Margaret H'Doubler, encouraged participants to "overcome needless inhibitions of shyness and self-consciousness" to achieve "emotional self-expression through rythmical movement."*

An early twentieth-century view of a chemistry laboratory in Morrill Hall.

ABOVE: *Trainer and horse.*

LEFT: *Finish line women's track, 1927.*

Nov. 8, 1945
To Pr. E.O. Holland
With Greatest admiration
Mike Barrett

GI Joe and GI Bill

IF YOU WERE A STUDENT IN 1940 AND HAD A CLASS IN WILSON HALL, it seemed like a long way to go. From the busy campus center below Bryan Hall, you walked to Wilson Road, a narrow, tree-lined street heading over Campus Hill to the college farms. Then you passed by a lush elm shading a grassy knoll—the location, ten years later, of Holland Library and the Women's Gym, a lonely pile of bricks and arches surrounded by tall grass. In just five years this structure would become the center of student social life as the "Temporary Union Building." Beyond the Women's Gym was the rim overlooking the football field, occupied only by a water tank and reservoir. By 1952 that would be the site of a sprawling new student center, Compton Union Building. Across from the water tank sat Wilson Hall.

When completed in the 1950s, this "new campus" had a different look than the more traditional lower campus. The tone was set by Holland Library (1949), a building of clean, straight lines, trim and efficient, like a book lying on its side. President Holland himself would have preferred that his name go on something more like the smokey Gothic building that memorializes his old rival, Henry Suzzallo, at the University of Washington. But the no-frills library at WSC nonetheless captured something of a president that students remembered as "quiet," "scholarly," "reserved," and "dignified."

As the new campus took shape, the old one gradually became so quiet as to seem almost abandoned. So dramatic was the switch in focus of activity between the college's first and second half centuries that the term "campus" would likely conjure up differing images in the minds of students from the two eras.

The biggest difference between the campus before and after World War II was not in the arrangement of its buildings, but in its relationship with the wider world. In 1940, the Washington State College was exactly a half-century old and in all that time it had been a world unto itself. In contrast, the story of the school's second half century would be filled with accounts of outside influences: war, the automobile, television, world politics, and a tremendous growth and diversification of the student body.

OPPOSITE: *Lieutenant Miles Barrett, U. S. Marines, a 1940 WSC graduate.*

Phillip R. Nalder, class of 1933.

To the students participating in football rallies and college politics in the 1930s, the dramatic events taking place in Europe and the Far East seemed remote to their lives. That is not to say that they were ignorant of these events. As early as 1934, the debate team argued against the proposition that "Hitler is a Charlatan." In the crisis year of 1935, a former secretary to Winston Churchill spoke on campus. Nevertheless, a poll by the *Evergreen* showed that, in case of war in Europe, most students wanted the U.S. to remain neutral. History professor Herman Deutsch told the *Evergreen* that he doubted there would be a war because "Germany and Italy will be somewhat reluctant about arming the working men," but sociology professor Fred R. Yoder believed "the thing has grown so complex and out of control of everybody, that it will be a miracle if conflict can be avoided." That year, too, an *Evergreen* editorial made an argument against ROTC that would be repeated on campuses in the 1960s: "To make peace a possibility we must think in terms of peace . . . [A]s long as the students are meeting in classrooms to learn how to go to war 'just in case,' there will be a case."

When the European war finally broke out in September 1939, an antiwar movement sprouted on the campus. In *Upstream: a Journal of Student Opinion* this group made a case for pacifism and staying out of Europe's squabbles. The January 1941 issue carried one student's declaration of resistance to the draft on the grounds that: "An Army of five million men is great enough to invade another country. What is there that will prevent our politicians from taking such action?" In any case, the article said, the side we would be fighting for is hardly superior to the Germans. "Churchill . . . is a notorious reactionary, who has made every effort in the past to destroy democracy—economic and political—in England. England isn't fighting to make the world safe for democracy. She's fighting for England and the vested power of the British people."

The Student Peace Committee presented a petition to President Holland in April 1941 declaring that "the time has come when we should take a definite stand against our involvement in the world crisis." Another committee, meanwhile, threw an all-campus dance to raise money for British and Chinese war victims. The *Evergreen* invited students on both sides of the isolationist-interventionist debate to write editorials. The pro-interventionists argued, correctly, that the U.S. could not hope to live peacefully in a world dominated by dictators. The isolationists argued, correctly, that entry into a world war would change American society irreparably.

This vehement debate over events beyond the confines of Washington State College was something new, a harbinger of future issues that would pull students, intellectually, away from college life and into the concerns of a wider world. In this case, international events settled the argument with unusual finality.

With the bombing of Pearl Harbor shortly before Christmas break in 1941, the outside world came crashing through WSC's shell of isolation. Instead of enjoying their traditional dispensation from the cares of the world, students found they were among the first to be

"Hello Walk" and Bryan Hall.

THE EVERGREEN

B. J. Hall, first semester managing editor, and long-time devotee of the Evergreen . . . . hails from the Alpha Chi house . . . . took over desk editor's job for second semester. Staff changes for the second half of the year brought not one but three managing editors . . . . Beth Pilkey of the Pi Phi's . . . . Kappa Luan Travis and AGD June Johnston . . . . this trio played triple-strength right hand to the editor . . . . especially in those times of crises . . . . The new plan not only proved the ability for working together . . . . but boosted chances for giving credit where credit is due.

Pilkey, Travis, Johnston

SECOND SEMESTER

Editor	Beverly Gregory	Sports Editor	Tommie Thompson
	Beth Pilkey	Art, Drama, Music Editor	Millie Swales
Managing Editors	Luan Travis	Servicemen's Editor	Mary German
	June Johnston		Verle Schoeff
News Editor	Alice Earl		Nina Howell
Asst. News Editor	Peggy Israel	Desk Editors	B. J. Hall
	Nancy Jamieson		Beth Fortnum
Society Editors	Honey Nicholson		Lucille Laws
Feature Editor	Barbara Meredith	Copy Editors	Sammie Harrison
Asst. Feature Editor	Lois French		Meg Gibson

Feature Editors Lois French and Barbara Meredith.　Sports Editor Tommie Thompson.　Servicemen's Editor Mary German.　News Editor Alice Earl.

Evergreen *editors, spring 1945. Women took over campus duties by the end of World War II.*

affected. "It was a sobering thing," recalled Jennie May Thomas Harold, '44, of Stevens Hall. "You had to sit down and try to decide what you should do." Some women wondered if they should just pack up and go home to be with their families. Others swore they would become ambulance drivers. Some men joined the immediate patriotic lineup outside the recruiting offices.

For those who remained at school, a strange interlude followed in which daily life continued as always, while everyone knew that unimaginable change lay ahead. Each month the campus lost more men to recruiting offices and draft boards. But as late as the fall of 1942 fraternities and dorms were still full.

During the 1942-1943 academic year, the war's impact became obvious. Stripped beds and suitcases lined up at the door were a daily sight in fraternities and men's dorms. Good-bye gatherings replaced football rallies at Pullman train stations. A lot of men quit studying on the grounds that they probably wouldn't be around when grades came out anyway. Some applied themselves with renewed vigor, in hopes of qualifying for officer candidate school, pilot training, or technical school. By the end of spring semester, men's dorms and fraternities were almost vacant.

They were soon filled by military personnel sent to WSC for special training. During the months following the Japanese attack on Pearl Harbor, the college contracted with the War Department to conduct Army Signal Corps instruction, Army veterinary education, Japanese language training, and a preflight school for bomber pilots and crews. At one point there were 1,900 military trainees on campus. They took over Ferry, Stimson, and McCroskey halls and several fraternity houses. With them came a whole different pace of life. The squadrons of future bomber crews arrived on campus, formed intramural teams to compete in campus sports, learned how to operate radios and other technical equipment and fly small aircraft, met girls, threw big farewell dances, and were gone within four months, to be replaced by a new unit. By the fall of 1944, nearly every college-aged male on campus marched to meals and classes. They even flirted in platoons when commanders of marching units spotted an attractive woman and ordered "eyes right!"

She smiled back because the attitude toward the soldiers on campus was that they were just another kind of college man. Surprisingly, given the mother superior attitude of the dean of women, this was the official policy of the college. Every Friday night the gym was opened for activities ranging from dancing to swimming, and women were encouraged to attend and boost the morale of the soldiers.

Boosting morale could be carried too far, as two women who needed escorts for a college dance found out. Since there were lots of men at the local USO (a servicemen's recreation organization) they went down and asked a couple of soldiers if they would be interested in a date. "What a catastrophe!" recalled Margaret Scull Pease, '44. "These small college seniors were not prepared for life in the fast lane." They were among many college women to find that the war

Unicyclist Leroy Bradbury, ASWSC President, 1942-1943.

ABOVE: *Army engineers training unit in Duncan Dunn dormitory (from the 1944 Chinook).*

RIGHT: *Stevens Hall party; only one male in sight.*

LEFT: *President Holland gets a shoe shine; campus women raised money through such projects for servicemen's organizations and the Red Cross.*

BELOW: *"Butch" in the 1945* Chinook.

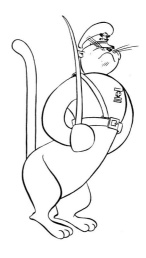

had begun to change social rules. The old pattern of dating, graduation, job, then marriage and sex, made less sense with a shipping-out date circled on a calendar—or so a lot of soldiers argued. It was during World War II that courting lost some of its leisurely pace and innocence.

One student said she could not recall ever hearing the war mentioned in a classroom. That was probably because professors didn't think it necessary; World War II pervaded college life. Six of the twelve convocation speakers for the 1943-1944 school year spoke on aspects of the war. Students on campus sold war bonds, rolled bandages, collected scrap metal, studied camouflage techniques, knitted sweaters for the British, and wrote letters to GIs they had never seen. Charlotte Snyder Carey, '44, of Community Hall remembered dressing up as a shoe-shine boy and, along with her classmates, shining shoes all afternoon to raise money for the USO.

The war changed coed fashions. Women gave up full skirts for the trimmer-cut, military look in blouses and suits that saved cloth for the war effort. For the first time, students considered news from the outside world a daily necessity.* Everybody had a brother, boyfriend,

---

* Often these reports came from Edward R. Murrow, '30.

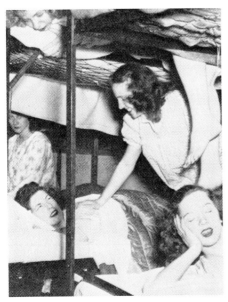

Waking up at Sigma Kappa (from the 1946 Chinook*).*

father, or other loved one to worry about. "I haunted the post office," recalled Marie Larson Rodkey, '44, who had a boyfriend overseas.

By early 1944, when fighting in the Pacific and in Europe reached full intensity, even the servicemen were gone from campus; "It was like a girls school,"one female student recalled. Women took over the campus, but they did so with no sense of "now we can do things our way." Instead, it was almost as a contribution to the war effort. Everyone had the idea that men should not come back to find that all the traditions that made college *college* had atrophied. "If I had a platform," said Jennie May Thomas Harold, '44, the first woman student body president, "it was keeping things going until the men came home." Women believed it was their duty to maintain as complete a college life as possible. They continued holding dances even though they mostly danced with each other. It seemed ridiculous at times, but the alternative, letting the treasured college traditions be forgotten, seemed worse. Irma Piovesan Rooney, '45, said: "I am sure that every one of us on the board of control felt that we were accomplishing our goal of contributing to the war effort by keeping a unified, strong, and proud school together until our men came home victorious."

In the meantime, women learned something about running political campaigns, student government, and the *Evergreen*. Campus leadership would never again be completely dominated by men.

WORLD WAR II ENDED IN AUGUST 1945, SHORTLY AFTER THE UNITED States dropped atomic bombs on the Japanese cities of Hiroshima and Nagasaki. As early as September, the first wave of discharged soldiers, sailors, and Marines arrived on the Washington State College campus. The "GI Bill of Rights," passed by Congress in 1944, guaranteed these veterans free college tuition and a minimal monthly living allowance. This legislation is considered one of the most successful federal programs in history. It solved the problem of what to do with millions of mustered-out troops and, at the same time, ensured that the United States would have an immense pool of educated citizens for decades to come.

The GI Bill made up the minds of millions of veterans about what to do after the war; they would go to college. Many who decided to attend WSC arrived on campus wearing uniform remnants—a warm sailor's peacoat, army tan pants, or unpolished government issue shoes. But you didn't need uniforms to identify them; a typical "GI Bill" was a twenty-two-year-old freshman or a twenty-five-year-old senior. He seemed a little more serious than other students. But whether that was the war experience or just a little more maturity was hard to tell. Women learned not to ask "What did you do in the war?" until they knew it was safe ground. Where vets gathered, however, it was the first question that came up. In the Kappa Sigma fraternity, ex-soldiers and sailors who had been in the European and Pacific theaters compared notes. In another fraternity, members were regu-

ABOVE: *Women's dormitory room; friends' signatures on the bedspreads, 1940s.*

LEFT: *Jennie May Thomas Harold, '44, the first female student body president. The picture was used on campaign posters; she led the "Fish Fans," a women's swim team.*

Temporary dorm in the TUB, about 1946. World War II veterans enrolling at WSC once again found themselves consigned to "barracks" life.

larly awakened in the middle of the night by screams of an ex-Marine who had nightmares. In one of the big barracks-like dormitories where many GIs lived, Bill Fitch, '50, went to the shower one morning to find an agitated ex-GI holding a revolver on several other students because, the veteran explained, he had been ordered to bring in German prisoners.

GIs did not feel sorry for themselves or flaunt their experiences. Though they were slightly suspicious of any young male who had not been in the service, the fact is nearly everyone had, so it was no great distinction. Some vets were genuine heros who could tell harrowing stories if they wanted to. Most, however, were the mechanics, medics, clerks, and deck hands who made up the bulk of the military. All had lost friends. But in most cases, war memories were of tedium and military bureaucracy. They were happy to leave it all behind and just be college students.

Ironically, what GIs saw when they got to WSC looked very much like what they had left. The veterans who arrived with the first major influx of September 1946 found themselves assigned bunks and hammocks set up in the Women's Gym at the top of Campus Hill. With military duffel bags propped against walls and stacked in piles, it looked for all the world like the interior of a troop ship.

President Wilson Compton, who had just replaced President Holland in early 1945, established a policy that no GI who could meet academic requirements should be turned away. To house the influx, Compton bought migrant worker housing located in Oregon and had the wooden structures shipped to the campus in sections. Eventually, he created four big GI dorms at the foot of Campus Hill: North House, where French Administration Building is now located; East House, adjacent to the east; South House, across Farm Way from North House; and West House, located in the little flat behind and below the present Fine Arts Building.

Each consisted of a long, two-story barrack enlarged by a series of wings. They were designed to accommodate 385 people, but at times they held nearly 500, as the college, which had a peak of 4,300 students in 1939, increased its enrollment to 6,700 in 1947. Two-thirds of the residents of these new dormitories were veterans who felt right at home with the springy floors, rattling windows, and assorted discomforts. The heating systems were so built that the rooms closest to the furnace got too hot, while those at the end of the wings were cold. Beds were thin-mattressed, military bunks, and roommates had to share dressers. Shower-room floors were cement

Campus view just after completion of Holland Library (top center), circa 1950. Note the hastily erected dormitory buildings on "Mud Flats" at center and lower right.

Starting a new semester at the Students Book Corporation.

and telephones were scarce. Worst of all, for GIs who had lived in temporary camps and fields all over the world, was the mud. The dorms were located on farm land and fresh fill, and when it rained the mud was inescapable. This housing area at the east side of Campus Hill became known as "Mud Flats," and it was said that you always could tell a guy lived there because the walk up to class left the back of his pant legs speckled with mud.

The college administration worked hard at pulling these makeshift dorms into the mainstream of campus life. Like other residence halls on campus, the dorms in Mud Flats had organizations to plan dances and "firesides." The occupants, who had much in common, developed an esprit and competed well in intramural sports and campus politics.

Yet, these residence halls, with two-thirds of their occupants veterans, took on a character that was different from the traditional dorm. As a report on South House, prepared for the college president in 1948, said: "The veteran element actively resents any action which might be construed as an attempt toward regimentation." Veterans had their fill of conformity and rules. When the men of South House were asked what the single thing they liked best about the dorm, thirty-five percent said its "friendliness," but forty percent said the independence it gave them. Nobody checked up on them or told them what to do.

This attitude posed a dilemma for upperclassmen. Training new freshmen in the etiquette of college life was the duty of every junior and senior, but ex-GIs were unlike eighteen-year-old high school graduates. The once awe-inspiring letterman with paddle in hand held no terror for a veteran of twenty bombing missions, or to someone who had experienced bar life in San Diego or Norfolk for that matter. A letterman's taunting "Come here, frosh!" too often resulted in a fist fight, so the freshman beanie requirement disappeared. So did mandatory attendance at pep rallies and rules governing Hello Walk and Senior Bench, all the things that had put seniors in control of the conduct of campus life. Veterans who joined fraternities naturally expected to put up with rules, but even there a line had to be drawn. Hazing and hacking became more perfunctory.

Veterans who had been in college before the war could see the difference in themselves. "In 1941," said Bob DeVleming, '48, "I never questioned the rules." When he returned to campus after serving in a tank crew in Europe, "you couldn't tell me anything.... We felt we were here to get educated, period. If we felt like smoking in the classroom in the meantime, we did."

For the first time, drinking was not considered wild behavior, but a regular part of campus life. The big water cabinets over toilets in the Mud Flats dorms made good coolers for beer. After class, students went to the American Legion Hall in Pullman for drinks. Carrying a

Classes bulged with returning GIs, late 1940s.

Bill and Barb Weaver with daughter Barbara Ann (from "Young marrieds" section, 1947 Chinook).

bottle of gin or vodka in a sack into the student union building to add to a Coke was common practice.

The other side of "GI Bill" is that there probably never was a generation of students more serious about its studies. Women whose college years started during the war found that classes suddenly became more interesting and more competitive when the veterans arrived. The teachers agreed. "It was a joy to teach them," recalled history professor Herbert Wood. He found that they came to class prepared and with a keen interest in how the world worked, born of a knowledge of how it could impinge on their lives. Political science professor Paul Castleberry said that it is possible to overemphasize the veteran's superiority—a lot of what they read and thought about on those ships and in those remote posts had little to do with academics. But there was no denying, he said, that they were more mature and had a clearer sense of what they wanted to accomplish. Margaret Davis Codding, who entered college in 1942, then dropped out and ultimately finished in 1949, was amazed by the changes wrought by veterans. "Their attitude was so impressive. All of us learned from them not to just accept somebody's word for it that that was the way it was, but to question."

Many things that happened on the Washington State College campus in this period blurred the traditional image of "college life." Veterans arrived with a feeling that they had wasted enough of their lives and wanted to get on with the serious business of family and career. They didn't shun the traditional feeling for the success of college athletic teams or interest in politics, but they gave only so much time and energy to them. The GIs, moreover, were a heterogeneous group; they were many different ages and came from many parts of the country, and so did not necessarily share a common view of what college life ought to be like. Finally, many vets came to WSC to finish interrupted college careers, and so were only on campus a year or two before graduating, again weakening the traditional cohesiveness of the student body. Lee Sahlin, '47, a returning vet, regretted that he knew only a few of even his graduating class in the short time it took him to finish his degree.

Perhaps the biggest change of all was the arrival of married students. Before World War II, there were only a handful of married students at WSC in any given year; after the war they were a fixture of campus life. The 1947 *Chinook* introduced a new yearbook section for "young marrieds." It featured student sweethearts sharing noodle casseroles in their tiny kitchenettes, families perusing Sunday papers together, fathers and mothers posing with wiggling babies or pushing buggies past Bryan Hall, and couples gathered for cards and conversation on a Friday night because there was no money to go out. Brooks Gunsul, '52, an architecture student who had little time or money to spare, remembers "social life" as driving with his wife and another couple to Moscow for a beer and conversation, or taking a Sunday drive to Boyer Park with a watermelon in the trunk. The young marrieds adapted to college life as best as circumstances would allow. Gunsul and his wife were poor, but they never missed a basketball game. Gunsul didn't have much time to spend on student politics, but on Sunday morning friends who were in student government showed up at their apartment door with a sack of donuts ready to participate in an updated version of the old dormitory bull session.

The college purchased and moved in surplus World War II government housing—boxlike structures that would continue to be used by married students for decades. But these complexes on the east side of campus called North, South, and East Fairways, didn't begin to meet postwar needs. Most married couples found tiny basement or upstairs apartments around campus. Clearing the kitchen table of the dinner dishes so they could type papers, or waiting for babies to fall asleep so they could open a textbook, wasn't an easy way to get through college. But the fact that there were so many who faced this situation after the war created a certain camaraderie. Bill and Alice Fitch (he '50, she '49) lived in an old house divided into five apartments. "If somebody made popcorn, it traveled in our common air ducts," recalled Alice. As soon as they figured out where it was coming from, "we were all having popcorn."

A vast trailer camp, called "Trailerville," was opened on the Palouse River at the foot of Campus Hill. The students used a "wash house" equipped with newly-invented Bendix automatic washers. There were no dryers yet, so laundry was hung on a half-acre of clotheslines. Row on row of diapers flapped in the wind—the pennant of this Cougar generation.

And they were Cougars. Many attended dances and football games as couples and made important contributions to campus life. Tom Matthews, student body president in 1947-1948, was a married student, as were *Evergreen* editors Andy Adams, '47, and Jacqueline Beard, '48. At the 1948 Homecoming rally, the Trailerville contingent carried a big sign reading: "Cougars Expecting A Cub." When, in February 1948, the South Fork of the Palouse River began to flood Trailerville, an appeal went out to Mud Flats, the dorms, and fraternities. "The college came to the rescue," recalled Joan Degerstrom, whose husband, Neal, '49, was an engineering student. The student volunteers first worked in gangs to sandbag the river's banks. When that failed, they carried the pets and children (and Joan, who was pregnant) through the water to safety; then the volunteers returned to help clean the muck out of trailers.

"Trailer Village" residents Norm and Ginny Majer, 1948.

Education majors, 1947.

THE VETERANS CHANGED THE LOOK OF STUDENT POLITICS. THE GREAT majority of them became "independents," so Greek Row, which began to lose control of student politics just before the war, found itself vastly outnumbered. Ex-GIs who did join fraternities didn't have either the social control or the dedication to campus politics to maintain the kind of elaborate political machine that kept fraternities in charge in the thirties. TNE was revived, but the most it accomplished, even its members admitted, was to influence the choice of candidates on some Greek tickets.

And independents had a new source of strength. For the first time there were "bread and butter" issues in student politics, including such things as the quality of food in the new dining halls, the scarcity of housing, and getting the administration to do something about the mud in Mud Flats. These issues applied more to independents than to Greeks, and politicians running independent tickets used them to get out the vote.

Independents swept nearly every election of the postwar years (the exception being 1949, when fraternity man Wes Foss was

Circa *1948 campus spoof of the "Dixiecrats," a Southern faction which had broken away from the national Democratic Party. Campus politics often modeled national politics or mocked it, as students are doing here.*

elected). But the battles were spirited. In 1947, the campus was awash in flyers and reverberated with messages broadcast from sound trucks. The independents formed a two-block-long parade, carrying torches and signs, and marched to the practice football field, where Greeks were already rallying. On election day, independents dispatched a "Paul Revere," riding a horse and wearing wig and triangular hat, to gallop through the campus to warn voters the Greeks were coming. Greeks hired a plane to drop leaflets on the campus (the pilot's flying license was later suspended for flying too low).

Between elections, however, more things drew students together than separated them. One of the college's improvisations to deal with the postwar influx was to convert the original campus gymnasium (1899), into the TUB, or Temporary Union Building. It was at least roomy. The main floor, a converted basketball court, had dozens of tables and singularly uncomfortable wooden booths. A more intimate setting was available in a basement room called "The Drain" (because it was at the bottom of the TUB), where a few booths surrounded a small dance floor and jukebox. The large cafeteria on the main floor was always alive with bull sessions, card games, and a jukebox belting out the popular songs of the era—Phil Harris's "That's What I Like about the South," Frank Sinatra's "I've Got a Crush on You," and "I Want To Be Loved" by the Andrews Sisters. Coffee was self-served from big metal urns and the grill sometimes had forty hamburgers frying at once. Dances were held every Friday and Saturday night and they were hugely popular. A survey in the spring of 1950 found that over fifty percent of the students said they attended the dances at least sometimes.

The TUB was not, however, adequate to the needs of nearly 7,000 students, and, since the end of the war, administrators and students sought legislative funding for a replacement. In 1949, a delegation of students, including student body president Joe Matsen, Phil Sorensen, '48, Betty Jo Lyon Sorensen, '49, and about a dozen others, went to Olympia. Testimony during the day was followed by customary lobbying in Olympia bars at night. It was the first time students had taken a direct hand in the politics of the school's financial support.

Naming the new student union building for President Wilson Compton meant it could become the Compton Union Building, thus the initialism "CUB." But it was entirely appropriate otherwise, for President Compton was peculiarly identified with this postwar generation. He arrived at WSC just before them, in early 1945, and guided the college through tumultuous years of adjustment to a larger student body and an expanded mission. Compton, who had a business background, was not exactly a "student's president," but he seemed to care about them. The Comptons threw big picnics for students and occasionally opened the president's mansion to students who were not able to find adequate housing.

People usually say "the Comptons," because it was a dual administration. Helen Compton served as an unofficial inspector general, constantly searching the campus for problems that needed to be fixed. A housewife in student housing might open her door, mop in hand, to find the president's wife "just saying hello." If the woman didn't watch it, Mrs. Compton was capable of grabbing the mop and starting in on the floor herself. The president's wife visited Todd Hall and ordered the walls repainted in bright pastels. She dropped in on Ferry Hall and sent orders that the antiquated urinals be replaced. She should be given much of the credit for the college's successful effort to keep up with rapid student population growth. But she was too energetic to be popular and her enthusiasm was one of the things that accounted for President Compton's short tenure at the college.

Among the others were his reforms in faculty governance and evaluation, which stirred faculty up; drastic changes in college organization, which stirred up deans; his meddling in sports, which stirred up the alumni; and finally his habit of giving interminable speeches to all of them. Charles McAllister, president of the Board of Regents from 1942 to 1952, believed that he knew how to run WSC. He had, after all, visited a lot of campuses and had written a book on campus governance. Eventually, McAllister gathered his board behind him to force Compton out.

ABOVE: *Dancing at the TUB.*

LEFT: *Ground breaking ceremony for the future Compton Union Building. Student body president Wes Foss (second from left) poses with President Compton and members of the Board of Regents. In this period, Compton (second from right) was squabbling with the regents. Charles E. McAllister, looking at Compton over Compton's right shoulder, led the drive to fire the president soon after the picture was taken.*

The annual "Turkey Trot" run has long been a campus tradition.

Compton was away from campus that day in May 1951 when the announcement came that he had been fired. A contingent of student leaders, led by Student Body President Dave Nordquist, '52, drove to Spokane to meet Compton at the airport and escort him to campus. In Pullman, several hundred sympathetic students waited on Rogers Field to greet their recently deposed president. The situation was remarkably similar to the scene in 1892, the first time the college's chief executive officer had been fired. The white-haired, hollow-eyed Compton mounted a platform to address angry students, as President Lilley had done fifty-nine years earlier. But this time the outcome was different. Compton was wiser than Lilley in what he said to students (basically "what is done is done."). The students, while feeling sympathy for their president, were aware of the many controversies surrounding him, and did not misconstrue the firing as an attack on the college itself, as the 1892 students had. They cheered Compton to show support, and then dispersed.

Life, a top weekly magazine in the country at the time, ran an article titled "Picture of a Good Man Who is Getting the Ax," which cited Compton's accomplishments at WSC and discussed his family's tradition in higher education (his father and two brothers were also college presidents; brother Karl was president of Massachusetts Institute of Technology, while brother Arthur was president of Washington University in St. Louis and winner of a Nobel Prize in physics). *Life* later printed a letter from two student leaders, George Goudy, president of the class of '52, and Keith Jackson, president of the class of '54*, applauding the article. "However," the students wrote, "we differ with you on Compton's 'greatest achievement.' It is not the tech building but the personal fatherly touch he has maintained with the students."

THE GI GENERATION WAS A SINGULAR CASE; A GENERATION OF STUDENTS that brought to the classroom more experience than many people ever know, students who represented, not "promise," but promises kept. They hurried through school, reared families along the way, impressed their teachers, and yet never abandoned the football team.

One vet, Wes McCabe, '46, offered the interesting thought that "the 1940s was the beginning of the 1960s." This idea might shock many forties graduates, the parents of the sixties "radicals." But there is a certain amount of sense in it. The GI generation tossed aside sacred social rules, questioned teachers, and did not hesitate to pursue their interests to the administration and beyond. They had, like the generation of the sixties, a sense of being special, and possessing a special insight into the workings of the world.

By 1952, the grizzled vet, with a service jacket and stories of remote locales, was a campus anachronism. "The old guys didn't have the same attitude," said Walter Trefry, '53, who, as a freshman, lived with vets in mud flats. "Most had been through their own private hell and the fun of school wasn't there. They were a great bunch and helped their 'little brothers and sisters,' but they were a more mature, less fun-loving group." In 1947 everyone on campus, it seemed, was home from the war. By 1952, one vet who was still wearing old combat boots to cope with winter snow remembers feeling alone and out of place. ■

---

* He was later to become one of America's most distinguished television sports broadcasters.

GI Joe and GI Bill

*View from Bryan Hall tower; the TUB (old gymnasium) at right, circa 1940s.
Holland Library later was built in the open area in the foreground.*

KWSC announcer Stanley "Googie" Locke, '46. Broadcasting was popular on campus, partly due to Edward R. Murrow's fame. Murrow, in fact, later made a promotional film for WSC.

Free coffee day at the bookstore, December 1946.

Fountain area in the Temporary Union Building (TUB).

ABOVE: *From the left: old post office, old music building, Van Doren Hall, and recently constructed Holland Library, circa 1950.*

RIGHT: *Jam session, 1949.*

OPPOSITE: *Students led the campaign to replace the old "TUB" with a new student union building.*

The Last Panty Raid

STUDENTS GOING TO WSC IN THE 1950s ARRIVED IN THEIR OWN CARS. The campus police said that there were 2,800 student-owned automobiles registered on campus in the 1955-1956 academic year, or almost one for every two students on campus; the following year there were 350 more. Police chief Ernest Schrenk said: "The parking facilities have become so saturated that the problem has reached the point where it is almost uncontrollable." Wilson Road in front of the library and the CUB was snarled with traffic between classes. Nearly every bit of vacant real estate near the campus was turned into parking lots; the spot where the college was founded in 1892, between the modern Holland Library and the Compton Union Building, became a storage pen for student automobiles in 1954. The first parking meters went in, around the CUB, in 1959.

Most cars (or "rods," as they were often called) were merely transportation, stalwart Model As or the more shapely varieties from the late forties with their long hoods and billowing fenders. Some "hot rods," however, were rolling personal works of art, chariots of gleaming candy-apple red, cobalt blue, or lime green, often with dramatic names neatly painted on fenders—"The Plum" for a purple humpbacked Hudson, or "White Lightning" for a white Chrysler with flared tail fins. Inside, they were luxurious apartments, with wide, couch-like seats, dashboards studded with gleaming chrome knobs and, dangling from rear view mirrors, dashes of personality in the form of oversized dice or stuffed cougars. These cars were more than transportation, they were personal signatures. In the fifties you could be known all over campus for your car.

Cars did as much as anything to kill "Dean Annie-ism," the college administrator's doctrine that one could compel students to be moral by not giving them the chance to be otherwise. Curfews, chaperones, and crisp Pullman nights were the main tools of the dean of women. But what could she do in an era of drive-in movies and cars with heaters? She was forced to trust the students themselves.

The ultimate expression of freedom from parietal control, the unchaperoned spring-break journey to Oregon or California beaches, became a college tradition in the 1950s. During the 1960 spring break, four men and five women took off for California in a dark blue 1954 Rambler and an oil-spewing 1950 Chevy pickup loaded with sleeping bags and tents. Their parents had said yes, "because they knew we were good kids," said Monita Engvall Horn, '60.

OPPOSITE: *Dad's Day rally, 1958.*

Only one member of the group, Nancy Pittenger, had been refused permission to go along, so she accompanied the rest as far as Portland, there to board a train for home, as ordered. Before doing so, though, her friends took Nancy to a phone booth to call her parents and make one final plea. "The rest of us hovered outside watching her face through the finger-smudged glass," Mimi Jeswine Kissler, '60, recalls. After an agonizing wait, during which the small crowd tried in vain to follow the pantomime in the booth, "she came out smiling." Nancy and her friends hit the road.

Cars had begun to make college students more responsible for their lives, whether or not society was ready to accept the fact. When in possession of a motor vehicle, they could do what they wanted. Automobiles also made traditional student recklessness potentially lethal. During the first three months of fall semester in 1955, for example, automobile accidents involving students attending WSC resulted in nineteen injuries and two deaths. From that time forward, campaigns for driving safety were a mainstay of the campus scene.

Cars changed campus life by dispersing it. For the first time, students could escape the island-like setting of the Pullman school that had always forced interaction and innovative recreation.

Football Queen Donna Jacobson and Bob Gambold, 1951.

COUNTERBALANCING THE TENDENCY OF AUTOMOBILES TO FRAGMENT THE student body was the unifying effect of the new CUB, opened in 1952. WSC students had never had anything like this vast three-story building, with its complex of ballrooms, bowling alley, lounges, and food dispensaries. By its mere existence, the CUB altered campus life. The facility demanded programming and the activities held there formed an important part of fifties students' college memories. The weekly "Popcorn Forum" in the CUB became one of the intellectual events of college life. Invited speakers discussed and answered questions on issues of the fifties, ranging from school desegregation in the South, to the Soviet invasion of Hungary, or the legitimacy of hypnotism. "Friday at Four," held in the same room, featured campus musicians, especially jazz trios and male singing quartets that were the fashion. Among the more popular were Gordon Sanders's Four Chords and John "Tex" Sandifer's "Uncalled Four." Friday and Saturday night dances in the ballroom were usually so crowded that couples could hardly move. On Sunday afternoons there were "Battles of the Bands" in the CUB ballroom, open to instrumental groups of all types.

The most important activity at the CUB was "CUB Lab." Between classes, "CUB Rats" flocked to the Lair, the low-ceilinged room crowded with tables and rows of back-to-back, vinyl-cushioned booths. They would play cards, "check out the talent" (observe the opposite sex), sometimes study, or just sip a Coke and gaze out the window. The CUB was the place for "Coke dates," minimum-cost and minimum-risk boy-girl meetings that might have been quickly arranged with someone just met in class, or by a roommate trying to get something started.

A big topic of conversation in the CUB was the new music of the day, rock and roll. Every generation of young people chooses its own music, and elders rather predictably sniff and proclaim it to be so much racket. But rock and roll aroused more than the normal generational dissonance. Partly this was because of the state of technology. Fifties students were the first to have record players in their rooms and the first to have access to cheap transistor radios that could be carried anywhere and listened to at any time. Thus, they were members of the first generation to have direct access to music uncensored by those in authority. When the resulting "teen market" had grown sufficiently, "top forty" stations broadcasted rock and roll in unlimited volume (in both senses), reaching youth everywhere. Music made for, and beamed exclusively to, young people had a role in creating what, in the next decade, would be termed the "generation gap."

The other thing that made rock and roll a special case was the nature of the music itself. Big Band era teen idols like Bing Crosby and Frank Sinatra became controversial for serving up saucier versions of mainstream American music. Rock and roll performers like Little Richard, Ruth Brown, Fats Domino, Buddy Holly, the Drifters, Jerry Lee Lewis, the Platters, Chuck Berry, and Elvis Presley did not come from the mainstream. Their music was a volatile mixture of black Southern blues, white country-western, and ghetto melodies from America's large cities. Elders were right to suspect that rock and roll introduced something irreverent and combustible into the homogeneous, isolated culture of the Palouse.

Holland Library and the Compton Union Building flank the old TUB in this 1954 view. Note the bumper-to-bumper parking along Wilson road. The TUB soon would be demolished, providing additional parking space.

As they sat in the CUB listening to rock and roll on the jukebox, students were trying out all sorts of new ideas. "The latest subject for several CUB Labbers was Zen Buddhism, no less," Carole Eardley reported in her *Evergreen* society column in 1956. "Some of us," recalls Nancy Gale Compau, '57, "would meet at the CUB and drink coffee, discussing the woes of the world and how we would solve them. We got into a period of talking about H. L. Mencken and reading his works, and that sort of thing. We'd discuss communism and existentialism, etc. We thought we were terribly sophisticated."

Students of the fifties have been called "the Silent Generation." Perhaps they were silent because they were listening. It was a time when students were challenged, more than ever before, to consider matters in the larger world. No previous generation of WSC students heard more controversial speakers, wrote more editorials and letters-to-the-editor addressing social concerns, or started more organizations. And one of the most popular events at the CUB was the aforementioned weekly "Popcorn Forum" where issues of the moment were discussed.

This was the era of the Red Scare, a time when millions of citizens became convinced that communists, socialists, and subversives were destroying America's social institutions and loosening its moral fiber. An unscrupulous senator from Wisconsin, Joseph McCarthy, exploited this fear and apprehensiveness for political ends, creating a national panic. In the early fifties, McCarthy's senate hearings were broadcast almost daily on network television. Thousands of Americans had careers destroyed and lives ruined by false charges made

"Friday at Four" in the CUB.

ABOVE: *Compton Union Building dance.*

LEFT: *"CUB Lab," 1960. Male student at center, opening a book, is John Chaplin, who later in 1973 became head coach of WSU's track program.*

Service counter in the CUB.

Mary Davis, 1962 Junior Prom Queen, with Don Olson.

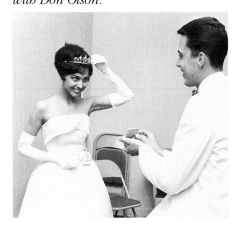

against them. Anticommunists also paid a good deal of attention to college campuses. Members of a Washington legislative committee arrived at WSC to survey books in the library and to scrutinize professors; they were looking for anyone who might be spreading dangerous ideas.

One WSC professor scolded students, in letters to the *Evergreen*, for being apathetic in the face of this threat to academic freedom. But it's clear that a large number of students (in contrast to the population at large) abhorred McCarthy and weren't afraid to let it show. When a defender of McCarthyism appeared on campus, he was roundly booed by students (leading conservative students to charge that anti-McCarthyites wanted freedom of speech only for their own side). The professor who berated students for their apathy toward McCarthyism was instantly backed up by supporting letters written by students. "I say 'hurrah' for the professors and students who never tire of trying to keep what little freedom we have," Betty Hooper wrote to the *Evergreen* on May 13, 1955, at the high tide of McCarthyism. "I would like to hear a Marxist or a supporter of Russian communism speak," wrote Russell McCormmach, '55,* on the same page—a radical

* One of WSC's Rhodes scholars.

Campus voting booths.

statement at a time when careers might be ended for saying such things.

Despite those weighty discussions at the CUB, Nancy Gale Compau admitted, "We were not really all that concerned with the world situation. We were concerned with having a date for Saturday night." This was, no doubt, a fair generalization about the attitude of fifties students. But it would be no less true of any previous generation, with the possible exception of those in school during the world wars. The Great Depression of the 1930s was a national emergency, but students at the time were assured that events were out of their hands and that the best thing they could do was survive as best they could and go on with college activities. For behaving the same way, fifties students were called "silent." It's almost as if the rest of the world had begun to judge 1950s college students by a new standard, even before college students were ready to consent.

Students of the 1950s were aware of their dilemma and were able to analyze it. The debate over Senator McCarthy's threat to academic freedom in 1955 spawned an exchange in the letters column of the *Evergreen* about what was making students so "blah," as critics put it. One letter writer declared that it was a bland generation because it was given no freedom of maneuver; specifically, it could not even choose its own curriculum of studies. Sophomore Jack Pemberton wrote that his fellow students' political disinterest was a response to frustration with the times. "A defense mechanism, psychologists call it. Problems are tough to face, so we decide not to face them at all, and sleep."

IN HIS ANALYSIS, PEMBERTON ADDED THE THOUGHT THAT, "HUMAN society seems to contain a certain amount of energy; what is not spent at work is spent on play." Perhaps that explains why the "Silent Generation" was one of the noisiest Pullman remembers. Before football games they held "noise rallies" (around bonfires where Streit-Perham Hall is now located) attended by 3,000 to 4,000 students, and then linked hands and went running through campus in a wild "serpentine." Every spring, water fights began at one location and spread from dorm to dorm area until they engulfed the whole campus. Another favorite pastime of a certain segment of school-spirited Cougars was to drive to Moscow bars and bait Vandals. "You from the UI? Who's your toughest guy? That cross-eyed ape? Ha!" The Moscow police did not think of this as the Silent Generation.

The rivalry between WSC and the University of Idaho, a tradition that started the year WSC opened, was alive and well in the fifties. It got national attention in 1954 when WSC lost a football game to the University of Idaho and 500 WSC students, led by student body president Dale Boose and accompanied by the Cougar Band, paid off a bet by walking the nine miles to the Vandal campus. The annual tradition of walking to the victor's campus had been established twenty-eight years earlier, and in every instance during that time Vandals had walked. *Life* magazine carried a photograph of the precedent-breaking walk by WSC students. In 1957, the rivalry between the two schools again made news when a brawl involving a thousand students from both schools broke out after the annual football game.

Fifties students went to dances, casual "hops," and "formals" in tuxedos and strapless gowns. They elected Homecoming Queens,

Water fight, 1958.

Harvest Ball Queens, Winter Kings, Independent Queens, Junior Prom Queens, and May Queens. They sponsored all-campus carnivals, all-campus talent shows, and mock political conventions that involved a large portion of the student body. Every residence hall, fraternity, and sorority put up elaborate decorations for Homecoming and entered the annual snow sculpture contest.

An *Evergreen* editorial explained, for the benefit of alums returning for Homecoming, what was "in" and what was "out" with students in 1958:

> Smoking on campus is *in* . . . Filter tip cigarettes are *in* . . . Jig saw puzzles are *out* . . . Flagpole sitting is *out* . . . Dates for basketball games are *in* . . . Playing bridge in the CUB is *in* . . . Pinochle in the CUB is *out* . . . Frisbies and hula hoops are *in* . . . Fez caps and Vigilance committees are *out* . . . Publications Ball is *out* . . . Baggy sweaters, leotards and head-ache-bands are *in* . . . Car coats are *in* . . . Raccoon coats are almost *out* . . . Queen contests are *in* . . . Getting good grades is *in* . . . Married students are *in* . . . Long engagements are *out* . . . Beating the University of Idaho is still *in* . . . Going home week-ends is *out* . . . Pizza Pie is *in* . . . Dirty, baggy cords are *out.*

The collegiate cords of the twenties and thirties had been replaced by jeans and cotton slacks. "Ivy League" dress began to take hold in 1956: for men, small-patterned plaid shirts with button-

Governor Albert Rosellini crowns Homecoming Queen Kathy Krogue, as President French (at left) looks on, 1961.

*University of Idaho's TKE cannon—
a trophy on the Holland Library lawn.*

down collars, slacks without pleats but with a little belt across the back, and pullover sweaters, either with traditional vee-neck or new rounded collars. For women, cashmere sweaters, with matching scarfs, were still popular. Skirts could be billowing out over petticoats or the Ivy League pleated plaids. Men wore their hair waxed into a bristle, or short and combed to one side in a "crew cut." Women wore hair short and brushed back, or longer with a ribbon holding a ponytail or a beret over one temple. Both men and women wore saddle shoes and penny loafers. Modified low-cut tennis shoes were just catching on for common wear. Knee-length Bermuda shorts were first seen on campus in the spring of 1957.

WHAT WAS REALLY *IN* IN THE FIFTIES WAS PRANKS. THE CONCEPTION AND execution of such pranks as stacking bottles across a dorm neighbor's doorway so that he dare not move one lest they bring the whole thing crashing down, or filling the entire room with wadded newspaper, required immense amounts of ingenuity and time. A favorite trick on a roommate was to remove bureau drawers, turn the bureau upside down, replace the drawers, then right the bureau. As the owner pulled open each drawer, the contents would empty on the floor.

Maecel Johnson Foote, '58, of Stevens Hall kept a list of thirty-nine such tricks to play on others in the dorm, including: (1) short-sheet bed, (2) remove bed slats, (5) vaseline on doorknob, (11) swipe robe and towel while in shower, (14) scotch tape over water faucet, (16) take pins out of door hinges, (17) take pins out of door hinges and re-hang door upside down, (20) pepper under pillow, (21) wet macaroni in the bed, (25) paint soap with clear fingernail polish, (28) if two rooms are the same shape, change furniture etc., so person thinks she is in the wrong room, (30) skunk cabbage leaves behind heater or by light bulb, (37) trade doors with two rooms.

Unknown groups of fifties students assembled a Model A on the roof of the CUB; attached a giant face and hands to one of Bryan Tower's clocks to turn it into a massive Mickey Mouse watch; somehow reached "Nature Boy," the giant relief of a reading student attached to the outer wall of Holland Library, to label the book he peers into "Playboy Magazine."

Stealing a rival living unit's pennants, trophies, and such other possessions as the Stimson Hall fountain's Minerva was commonplace. Many a morning, students walking to class saw captured University of Idaho statues, flags, or signs displayed on the roof of the CUB or Holland Library. The College of Agriculture's pigs and cows routinely found their way into rival dorms, sororities, and fraternities.

An organization known as the Effervescent Order of the Yellow Dogs, mainly a drinking organization, learned that a Pullman car lot was selling a used university pickup truck, complete with official markings of a campus work crew. The students arranged to lease the truck for a day and then "midnight requisitioned" several barricades and workers coveralls from a college shop. The next day, E.O.Y.D.

members, dressed in coveralls, arrived at Holland Library in the truck, blocked off the sidewalk, and proceeded to spend the day digging an immense crater next to the library entrance. At the end of the day they got in the truck and drove away "unquestioned and unmolested," recalled E.O.Y.D. member (and 1957-1958 student body president) Bill Stuart.

Few students could match the subtlety of a classroom gag concocted by two graduate students in the College of Education. The instructor announced that everyone should come prepared to discuss the behaviorist and psychoanalytical approaches to counseling in the next session. "Merle [Meacham] and I decided to have some fun," recalled Dr. Laurence Peter, author of the famous book and social theory *The Peter Principle*. When the discussion began:

> I took the behaviorist position and argued as convincingly as possible that it was the basis of all successful counseling. Merle took the psychoanalyst position and defended it with all his might. I pretended to be swayed by his argument and gradually moved to his position, while he moved toward mine.

From the left: Jody Craft, Dot Cameron, and Harriet Galber, soaking wet after a campus prank, March 17, 1957.

As other students took one side or the other, only to find their arguments refuted by people they thought they were agreeing with, the discussion became "zestful," Dr. Peter recalls. "As we left the room the professor, who saw through our little act, winked at us, but some classmates were still trying to pin us down to one position or the other and we changed positions with each question."

While the fifties generation never talked of "destroying the existing order," as many of their successors would, they managed to destroy some existing orderliness.

Why? Keith Lincoln, '61, a football star and later director of the WSU Alumni Association, thought it was partly the old idea that entertainment was mostly do-it-yourself. "We didn't have VCRs in our apartments. If you wanted some laughs, you had to make them." That was the only reason he could think that one Saturday night he and some friends, standing in front of the Cougar Cottage on Colorado Street, watching cars stream back from dates, decided to conduct a "border check." They stepped out into the street and began halting vehicles, asking drivers where they were going and if they had a good time and saying things like, "Say, I didn't know you and Sue were dating!" while an ever-growing line of backed-up cars started sounding their horns.

The campus was small then, Lincoln said, "like a big family." You could pull a trick like that, knowing you would irritate people enough for a joke, but not make them sore. You don't pull pranks on strangers.

THE BIGGEST COLLEGE PRANK OF ALL WAS THE PANTY RAID. IT HAD everything: rowdiness, sex, and defiance of the administration's most sacred rules. One early student told his daughter that he participated in a panty raid in 1902. If true, it would mean that panty raids have a long tradition at WSC, in more ways than one. President Bryan, in his history of the college's early years, reports dourly that the first "Founder's Day" in 1911 was "sadly marred by an inexcusable invasion of Stevens Hall, undertaken in a spirit of prankishness, but leading to distressing results and criticism and unpleasant notoriety for the college."

The one that fifties students remember most was the big panty raid of 1956. It started with a water fight on a warm May Day and by evening had evolved into the annual panty raid. Men came flocking to the excitement until hundreds were swarming around Wilmer, Davis, Duncan Dunn, and Community halls, and the sororities.

The scene resembled a sixties "student riot": people shouting, chanting, and running about, spotlights playing across the fluid mob, a sense of volatility in the air arising from the fact that no one was in charge. "They got so wound up it was almost scary," recalled Nancy Gale Compau, who watched from the Pi Phi house. "They chased all over the campus, demanding panties. Our housemother locked all the doors and windows, then went upstairs and called down to them to go home. Someone threw down a pair of underpants, and they left."

At Wilmer Hall, the housemother ordered all the women to the first floor "partly because some of the girls had their windows open and were showing too much interest," said Chellis Smith Swensen, '57. Most women seemed to be amused, as long as the men didn't actually get into their buildings. Residents at Regents Hill tied sheets together and lowered them out the window to the men as a joke.

Eventually student leaders arrived and went through the crowds trying to calm everyone down even as police tried to intimidate them. The combined efforts had the whole thing broken up by about 11:30 that evening.

Student opinion on such activity was divided. The editor of the *Evergreen* wrote: "Just when it looks like the students at WSC are making some material progress toward gaining more responsibility and becoming mature, a group of idiots foul up the works." But a letter writer argued that the American males who had won so many past wars owed their fearlessness and boldness to the training of campus panty raids.

The administration had no doubts about the seriousness of the whole thing. Both President French and Dean of Students Jack Clevenger issued blazing denunciations of the mob behavior, particularly since someone had thrown a military smoke bomb into Wilmer Hall, doing considerable damage to a room and endangering residents. Two men caught on the fire escape of Duncan Dunn were immediately expelled from college.

In such cases the inclination of the French Administration, as with previous administrations, was to apply these regulations with intimi-

President C. Clement French.

dating force. Administrators generally believed that a show of weakness when dealing with students could be fatal.

Tom Tiede, '59, later an award-winning columnist for the Newspaper Enterprise Association and author of five books, but then a columnist for the *Evergreen*, offered as a typical example his discovery that the steps around Holland Library had been worn smooth and became dangerous in wet or snowy weather. In his column, Tiede enumerated pratfalls he had witnessed on the steps and *demanded* the administration take action. Tiede always believed that his column guaranteed the steps would remain as they were. "I believe they would have been fixed routinely had I not gotten into the act," Tiede said thirty years later. "The administration did not appreciate student demands, you see, and the custodians did not like squirts setting their agenda."

WHAT MADE WOMEN'S DORMS AND SORORITIES IRRESISTIBLE WHEN A mob of male students formed was not merely sex, but the fact that these were official citadels, with curfews as drawbridges and housemothers as sentinels. When lines are drawn in the dust before college men, they try to cross them. It is no coincidence that panty raids

Ada Bevaart, Regents Hill dormitory, 1958.

disappeared as the college's parietal rules designed to protect female students disappeared.

A major campus issue in the fifties was "segregation"—not just of blacks and whites but of males and females, as well. Students noticed that as the campus became larger, men's and women's residence halls were being placed farther and farther apart. As new dining halls opened, the men of Stimson and Waller halls found themselves eating alone in the old Commons. The situation was the same in the Stadium Commons, where the men of Mud Flats ate their meals.

Starting in 1955, students called upon the administration to reorganize dormitories—put women in Waller Hall, for example, and men in a wing of Regents Hill—so that men and women could live closer together. It was argued that "added female influence in dining rooms now used by men would improve table manners and the quality of dress," as one male student put it in a letter to the *Evergreen*.

The integration movement was incidentally spearheaded by the Alpha Phi sorority, which was building a new house and so took up temporary residence in East House, one of the former GI dorms of Mud Flats. The women ate their meals in the once totally male Stadium Commons. One of the Alpha Phis wrote to the *Evergreen* to assure that integration worked. "Both boys and girls have gained confidence in their ability to carry on conversation with each other," she testified.

"They have a worthwhile cause," an *Evergreen* editorialist wrote of dorm integrationists in 1955,

> there is no doubt about that. Anyone who has been down in the Stadium Commons when the Alpha Phis walked in is convinced of that—400 heads all swiveling toward the door at the same time tell of the quiet desperation of the "isolated independents."

The students thought of "integration" as a means of honing social skills and increasing social opportunities. But inadvertently they had begun talking about one of the main issues of campus life. "Coed" was a term like "separate but equal," ostensibly neutral, but in fact covering profound distinctions in treatment. Curfews and other rules applied almost exclusively to women. The penalties and social opprobrium for sexual misconduct was more serious for women than for men. A "Women's Career Day" in 1958 had exhibits on only four professions: teaching, nursing, home economics, and secretarial science. Most women believed that those were their choices and selected one of them. Most didn't expect to have a career in any case because the presumption was that they would get married and set up housekeeping immediately upon graduation. "Heaven help the girl who graduated and wasn't engaged," said fifties student Nancy Gale Compau.

To see the situation from the point of view of college men, an observation of a woman student twenty years earlier is instructive. Genevieve Thornton Esplin, whose mother ran a boardinghouse in the 1930s, said the rule of the house was that the two college-aged daughters must be treated as sisters by male boarders and not potential dates. The women found that men who had grown up with sisters had no problem relating to the women as just people, while men who hadn't had sisters seemed hard put to relate to the women as anything but potential girl friends.

To the typical college man, college women were objects of mystery and wonder. "Between the innocence of bobby sox and the sophistication of mink there lies a curious carefree creature called a coed," a male editorial writer for the *Evergreen* tried to explain in 1956. "Teachers fluster them, mothers protect them, little sisters idolize them and boys worship them. . . . She is pride with a pony tail. . . . She has the eating habits of a canary and displays the energy of a mountain trout. . . . The coed loves weekends, formal dances and cashmere sweaters and red convertibles and men."

College men spent much of their day thinking about coeds and still didn't know a lot about them. It was hard to get to know a woman as a person when you were blinded by her beauty in the first instance, and then in later instances (in dorm lounges or athletic competitions) were severely limited by custom and campus rules. Among the many

SDX "calendar girl"; setting is the landscaped backyard of the President's residence, May 27, 1959.

ABOVE: *Smoking in the living room after hours.*

RIGHT: *Sleeping on the sun porch, June 1957.*

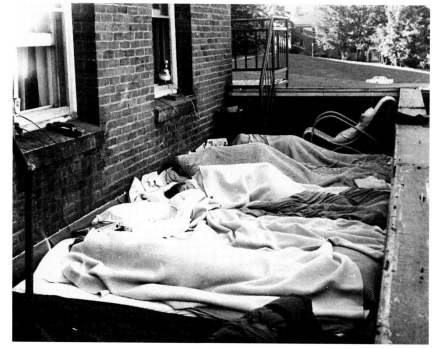

primal motives behind panty raids and the telescopes that men constantly trained on women's dorms was a certain amount of honest sociological curiosity. What goes on in the carefully guarded sanctums of women's dorms?

Actually, dorm life of the women was much like the dorm life of men. Some of them swore, many (perhaps most) of them smoked, all of them knew there were ways to sneak out of the dorm after hours if they wanted to.* They roughhoused, much as the men did. "Sunday night was a madhouse," Maecel Johnson Foote, '58, of Stevens Hall wrote to her parents. It seems people on the first floor were throwing everyone in the showers. "They started out by throwing in everyone who was engaged or going steady, then they threw in Jody because she used to be sponsor, then they started throwing in everybody they could get their hands on."

Chellis Smith Swensen's description of life in the dorm in the late 1950s would fit almost any dorm in almost any era: "the smell of popcorn or homemade fudge cooking; the hall phone that nobody ever wanted to answer unless they thought the call was for them; serenades after hours from the courtyard; the pileup of couples on the front porch shortly before the doors were locked at night." When someone did answer the hall phone, Monita Engvall Horn of Wilmer recalled, "Most people remembered to use the code words 'telephone' if it was a girl on the line and 'phone' if it was a boy."

The WSU archives preserves a single copy of the minutes for one dorm meeting—that for Wilmer Hall on the evening of February 11, 1957—but it pretty well sums up all dorm meetings:

> The meeting was called to order by the president, Bobbie Martin, at 6:30 in the evening. The minutes were read and corrected.
>
> Bobby requested that we follow parliamentary procedure during the house meetings. She explained that this would make the meetings move faster and asked the women if they were willing to follow Roberts' Rules of Order. There being no objections, Bobbie also asked that the girls pay attention during the meetings and not write letters.
>
> This week is "Winter Week" and Sandy White and Joyce Asimus are co-chairmen of the snow sculpture contest in the dorm. Because of the lack of snow, Sandy asked for help in making a door decoration in the place of the snow sculpture.
>
> Mary Darland explained the function of the dining hall committee and its place in the committee system of the dorm. She said, [etc.]. . . .
>
> Janis Brake reprimanded the women for necking in the beau parlor and drawing room, and asked their cooperation in solving the problem [etc.]. . . .

---

* At Regents Hill, for example, all you had to know was that the exit in the formal lounge was not connected to the alarm system.

Letters home contained more discussion of relationships with roommates and girl friends than classes or boys. In a letter to her parents Sandy Wilson Barrett, ' 62, of Regents Hill recounted at great length an afternoon trip to the library, the CUB for a Coke, then a movie, then back to the CUB. "We sat and just talked for a long while, and I finally got to my room at about 8:30. What a day!"

The dorm was a social life within a social life. When anyone received a cake or cookies from home there was an ad hoc party in her room. When anyone got engaged there was a party. When anyone won an award, an office, or a bet there was a party.

To make life interesting there was the rub of many personalities living in close quarters. One dorm resident arrived in the fall to find she had two roommates, one "really nice and doesn't smoke and we both like to sleep with the window open," she wrote her mother. "The other girl . . . keeps the window closed, heat on and her room is like an oven. . . . Also she smokes all the time, swears quite a bit, and is always griping and complaining about anything and everything." In a letter home at the end of the semester, after reiterating the complaints for the fourth or fifth time, the letter writer added, "Not that we don't get along, because we do."

The same close living that created conflict also inspired friendship. "In high school," one woman recalled, "I had been a loner and lonely. . . . In college I discovered other people like myself. I bloomed. I became lively and learned how to be a friend and had friends."

Nothing is so clear in the letters home of college women as the affection they developed for their dorm mates. One woman wrote to her younger sister, who had recently visited the dormitory:

> Remember_____? Small gal, long hair, kind of plain?
> Well, she went to the Military Ball Saturday night. It
> was her first formal dance and she had to borrow a
> formal and all. She sure was excited and looked real
> nice. Everybody was coming down to watch her get
> dressed and to see how she looked and everybody
> was real happy to see her go to the dance because
> she hardly ever goes out at all. Well, after she left, the
> excitement died down.

Life in sororities and women's dorms was much more structured than in fraternities and men's dorms. There was a dress code for meals. Also, in most dorms there were two "dress nights" in which residents dressed in their best clothes. They dined family-style around small tables and everyone remained seated until the housemother rose and left.

In sororities, specific procedures were often more rigid. A Pi Beta Phi recalled that a bell called the women to dinner every night:

> The housemother, the house president and one other
> officer would enter the room and walk over to the
> three chairs that were in the corner. We would line
> up and file by them, shaking hands and saying,

Sunday morning at Stevens Hall, 1957.

'Good evening.' Then we sat and chatted until the houseboy opened the French doors between the living room and dining room and announced, 'Dinner is served.' We filed in behind the president and housemother, and remained standing behind our chairs until Grace was said.

These rules did not, of course, turn girls into angels. Dorm residents and sorority members chaffed under them and often violated them. But, with all the safeguards, it was easy to get caught. Nancy Gale Compau recalled a rare trip into the wheat fields on a Friday afternoon to drink a few beers with some other women from the sorority. When they returned, others smelled the alcohol. "We had a severe talking to by the morals committee, or whatever it was. You simply had to mind, or you got into trouble with everyone. That generation was so conditioned to minding parents, teachers, and anyone else in authority that it seldom occurred to us to revolt."

In 1959, Tom Tiede used but little exaggeration when he wrote a poem for his *Evergreen* column entitled "Plight of the Coed":

> They sign in and they sign out
> They cannot think, they cannot doubt
> They can't wear this, they can't wear that
> To every tea they must wear a hat.
> They're not to drink and they're not to smoke
> They're not to know an off-color joke.
> They study hard, they study late
> They must conform, and they must date
> And when for equal rights they bid
> Their answer: "Shut up babe, you're just a kid.

Dormitory construction accelerated with the arrival of the "baby boom" generation.

THE SUDDEN DISSOLUTION OF SPECIAL RULES THAT ONCE DEFINED NEARLY every aspect of the lives of women students was the single greatest change in a century of campus life at Washington State University. It took about a decade, roughly from 1959 to 1969.

One of the many things that made the fifties into the sixties was the arrival in college of the World War II "baby boom." Sandy Wilson Barrett wrote home from Regents Hill in 1959 that bunks were being crowded into every corner of the dorm to accommodate the influx. Because of the crowding, "we will have no seated service—all cafeteria style, even Sunday dinner," she wrote. Such practical adjustments undoubtedly had a role in altering the student's view in how he or she related to the university. This change was suggested in the mid-1980s by WSU anthropologists who turned a professional eye on campus life as a part of studies done in preparation for the university's 1990 centennial:

> When we look at pictures of meals served at Commons during the 1930s, we see small groups of individuals at tables, waiters who brought serving bowls and platters of food to each table, and other details which generally give an aura of domesticity. Today, food is served cafeteria style, which is the ultimate in institutionalization.*

*Darby Stapp and Julia Longenecker, *Washington State University Centennial Digs* (1986).

Could *in loco parentis* survive when college authorities were no longer parental figures, but merely "administrators" arranging room space and meal service?

After 1957 larger dorms (such as Kruegel, Neill, McAllister, Gannon, and Goldsworthy) were completed. The first "skyscraper dorms," Orton and Rogers, handling over 1,000 students between them, opened in 1964. Out of necessity the university* began to permit more female students to live off campus in apartments. Giving this freedom to some women made it difficult for the the school to argue that *in loco parentis* was indispensable.

The new freedom from university supervision also coincided with the arrival of new ideas. When Nancy Gale Compau was a student in the mid-fifties, the main moral question seemed to be "whether or not you could marry someone outside of your 'own faith.'" Sex was discussed only with great circumspection. "We spent countless hours wondering if anyone had ever 'done it,' but we would never talk about it unless you whispered about it among friends."

By the late fifties, national writers had succeeded in making society's rules about sex a proper issue for discussion. Nearly everyone was against "free sex," but if you were just a little daring and determined to be open-minded you could at least discuss it. This radical new idea was spread with uncommon speed among college students by *Playboy* magazine, which was for various reasons a bestseller on campus. By the late fifties, photographs that would have

---

* Washington State College became Washington State University in 1959.

ABOVE: *Checking into the "super-dorm" Rogers Hall, completed in 1964.*

LEFT: Playboy *magazine was more than entertainment in 1959; it was a source of provocative social and political ideas.*

been contraband a few years earlier were hanging openly on men's dormitory walls, and administrators were happy just to get them down or hidden for Mother's Weekend. The magazine's influence went beyond the photos. "We all read *Playboy*," said Barbara Lof DeMichele, '66, who lived in Streit Hall. "The amazing thing to me now is that we women were as influenced by the *Playboy* philosophy as were the men. The country was at least two years away from women's lib and an awareness of the exploitation of women's bodies. So the *Playboy* philosophy seemed about as liberated as you could get."

The combination of the growing student population—too many for the administration to keep track of—and these new ideas revolutionized within a few years assumptions about the proper behavior for women. Barbara Lof DeMichele said:

> In 1962, the continuing agreement was that 'good girls don't do it.' By 1966, sex was considered 'healthy,' 'an expression of love'—in short, the *Playboy* and hippie philosophy that anything was okay, 'as long as you don't hurt anyone else.'
>
> We were definitely debating and thinking about and sometimes experiencing the so-called 'sexual revolution,' we all knew it was possible to get abortions [that were still illegal], we all knew more people who 'had to get married' and didn't think of it as a moral shame. . . . Men and women were beginning to live together openly.
>
> No matter what your personal decision, the important thing for women was that you could make a decision. That's the reason that I see the 'sexual revolution' as one precursor of 'women's liberation.' For the first time, women couldn't just fall back on 'what my mother says,' or 'what the church says.' You had to make a choice.

The new behavior was not a result of a relaxation of *in loco parentis*, as many parents thought. In fact, the rules remained in effect long after they were really tenable. They were nearly impossible to justify as the questioning students of the sixties asked what right those who contract to educate have to supervise personal lives. In 1963 Vicki Bridge wrote to the *Evergreen* that checking in by a certain hour, "because ultra-moma says it is the right thing to do" stunted student moral growth by leaving important behavior decisions to others. Another problem was that the rules did not apply to men. The university would have found it difficult to extend them to men, yet maintaining a separate standard for women was more and more difficult as feminist ideas took hold.

By the time students managed to negotiate away the last of the parietal restrictions on women in 1968, Dean of Women Catherine M. Northrup was working as hard as students toward that goal. The only difficulty, recalled Johanna Slind '68, a representative of Associated Women Students who served on the committee that rewrote the rules, was in disposing of the rules in a manner that would not give the general public the impression that the university was thereby endorsing licentious behavior.

The argument against different treatment for women in the matter of living rules was naturally extended to other aspects of campus life. In the matter of including women in campus leadership, the college, with its democratic and coeducational origins, was as progressive as any in the country. Women always played roles in student government, the student newspaper, and in other student organizations. But it was the Big Men On Campus who ran things. That began to change after World War II turned things upside down. While a woman *Evergreen* editor or top student government officer was almost unheard of before the war, in the fifteen years after 1945, about one of three *Evergreen* editors and one of three student body vice presidents were female. Change was slow, however. After the era of female student body presidents during World War II, another woman would not be elected to the position for thirty years, until Linda Carlisle in 1975-1976. Even the radical organizations of the sixties were dominated by men. (Some of the first active feminists on campus were women who broke away from the radical Students for a Democratic Society because male leaders wanted to assign women all the clerical work). In the 1970s, female top editors of the *Evergreen* were as common as male editors. In 1986-1987 Barbara Gorum was student body president; she was followed in that position by Kristi Phillips. Neither believed that being a woman had any significance in their candidacies or tenure in office.

As the existence of the special term for women students, "coed," suggests, they were a special category of college student. They were expected to have higher standards and lower ambitions than men. As limitations on the careers, campus offices, and social behavior of women students disappeared, so did the term "coed." ■

The Last Panty Raid

ABOVE: *Butch and the Yell Squad.*

RIGHT: *Students lock hands in a serpentine following a nighttime pre-game rally.*

ABOVE: *Student-owned automobiles swamped parking facilities in the 1950s and early 1960s.*

LEFT: *Kruegel Hall, one of the new large campus dormitories.*

OPPOSITE, ABOVE: *The Sophomore Tolo theme, "hungry i," was the name for a nationally famous late-1950s bohemian hangout in San Francisco. The "i" in "hungry i" stood for "intellectual."*

OPPOSITE, BELOW: *Campus election "watch night"* circa 1961.

ABOVE: *Harriet Galber and Dorothy Cummings, ready for the "big dance," 1956.*

RIGHT: *Congratulations for the Harvest Ball Queen.*

ABOVE: *Dancing in the CUB, early 1960s.*

RIGHT: *The annual CUB Carnival featured games, contests, and entertainment.*

WSU student Sandy Wilson and Bob Barrett, of Idaho's Navy ROTC program,
at the Military Ball, March 25, 1960.

he Sixties

THE MOST DISRUPTIVE DEMONSTRATION IN THE HISTORY OF WASHINGTON State University, involving the largest proportion of the student body, and the one that most threatened the use of violence, was staged by the school's first students in 1892. Albeit the student body was small in numbers, but when they armed themselves with fresh eggs and vegetables from the college farm and chased the college president and a member of the Board of Regents off campus, they set a standard that subsequent generations found hard to top.

Students have always been "disruptive" with their pranks, panty raids, and annual fist-swinging melees that broke out at football games with the University of Idaho. Unruly behavior was by no means an invention of the 1960s generation. Edythe Greenawalt Roberts, '24, who grew up in Pullman, remembered as a small girl being scooted off a downtown street about 1910 because students were marching down Campus Hill toward the business district. They were miffed at some insult by townspeople. A 1938 graduate, who had often regaled his children with stories of the glorious student strike of 1936, remembered his son's defending campus unrest in the sixties by declaring: "*You* went on strike." The best answer the older alumnus could come up with was, "Yes, but we were right."

Even in the "silent fifties" protests were common. Tom Tiede, '59, recalled "platoons of students . . . shouting and making merry" on Dean of Students Jack Clevenger's lawn. Pat Caraher, '62, remembered a hundred students chanting in front of President French's house to protest the assignment of all the parking spaces between Holland Library and Compton Union Building exclusively to faculty. It turned out the president was gone. When Mrs. French emerged to announce the fact, the young demonstrators, with typical delicacy, began to chant, "Feed her to Butch!"

Students of all generations have been prone to act impulsively on whatever notion might strike them. No doubt, this tendency is due partly to a youthful excess of energy, and partly to a lack of social constraint to keep a job or to answer to one's parents. But some social critics have suggested that the "generation of the sixties" was a special case. Perhaps they were spoiled by post-World War II affluence. Perhaps their attitudes were the result of tolerant child rearing practices preached by the influential Doctor Benjamin Spock. No doubt, their actions were partly attributable to the fact that students seldom have alternatives to "demonstrating" their feelings, since few

OPPOSITE: *Rally outside the CUB following the shooting deaths of four students at Kent State University, May 1970.*

college administrators have ever solicited memos from them. What-ever the cause, action has always been a student response. Admin-istrators meet, professors write, students act.

On December 8, 1961, the *Evergreen* carried a front-page story that began: "Angry Student Mob Marches on French."

> Some 1,500 students chanting 'We want French, we want French,' thronged over the WSU campus last night in protest of the no early vacation ruling made by President C. Clement French Wednesday.

That same day, a second protest, a "peace march," took place on campus—perhaps the first of the sixties. It was led, not by students, but women faculty, faculty wives, and women from the Pullman area objecting to the nation's nuclear weapons policy and "the wanton disregard for the welfare and safety of the human race." When the ardor shown by 1,500 students asking for an early Christmas vacation was combined with volatile political issues, like arms control, you had *the sixties*.

CUB, pre-radical period, 1963. Basket-ball players Jim Lemery (far left) and Alan Thompson (far right) talk with two friends. The wall poster was a harbinger of the future; U.S. Senator Paul Douglas was an early critic of America's Vietnam policy.

AS EARLY AS THE LATE 1950S, STUDENTS BEGAN TO WONDER ABOUT
THEIR role in resolving political questions. In a November 7, 1958
editorial entitled "Beatniks? Nix" an *Evergreen* writer did a good job
defining fifties student attitudes:

> Crowded conditions, increased enrollments, a
> shaky world condition, nuclear weapons, and the like
> have put a cloud over the head of our generation.
> Whether the full impact of these things is evident in
> our daily living may be questioned, but they have
> had their effect. We aren't the carefree, devil-may-
> care college students. But, for that matter, we aren't
> 'angry,' 'beat' or necessarily 'silent' either.
>
> We're concerned with getting out in the world and
> 'making our own'; we expect to work and work hard;
> we want some enjoyment from our college days, but
> generally it is the organized, 'clean' kind of fun.
> We're interested in good grades, high GPAs, good
> records, and not much intellectual development (in
> spite of high GPAs).

CUB ballroom, circa *1965.*

Card stunts at football games in the 1950s and 1960s required careful organization of student body rooters.

Some people might call us 'Blobs,' but others will call us well-adjusted and typical. This latter group will be happy with the products of education that WSC is producing. They will be pleased to hire and promote us and we'll be glad to work for them.

A week later, a reader responded to the editorial in a letter to the editor:

Far be it from me to deny their [beatniks'] absence here—nor do I defend their attitude. They have carried their rebellion from society past the end.

However, the Beatniks are at least aware that this country is somewhat 'sick.' They realize that America is far from having all her ailments cured, diagnosed or even detected. . . .

A healthy society must be dynamic if it is to persist. The role of the student as a member of a society is not that of one 'well adjusted' to existing conditions. He should, rather, examine these conditions with the intellect that college should have developed. He should then decide whether to accept, modify, or reject them. . . .

Would you turn WSC into a finishing school for the outer world? Would you make it a four year course in molding the social man, with lessons in 'How to Choose the Right Religion,' [and] 'How to avoid Major Issues Without Half Trying?'

This was the contrast between the fifties and the sixties. The story of the radical student era of the 1960s is the story of what caused a substantial portion of those attending college to adopt the latter view—that students have a duty to "decide whether to accept, modify or reject" the world as they saw it.

Studying in Holland Library.

Sally Cave Meyer, '59, believed much of the impetus came from faculty members who attacked student complacency and taught critical thinking. She remembered that her own college reading program included works by Chinese revolutionary leader Mao Tse-Tung, Beat Generation novelist Norman Mailer, and a whole range of provocative psychologists. Students openly discussed the civil rights movement and its impact on the South in political science classes; sociology teachers raised issues of poverty and race. There were even a few people around who had direct experience with these otherwise abstract concerns. Meyer remembered one bearded graduate student who displayed scars acquired in a civil rights demonstration in the South. Reflecting on what happened after she left WSC, Meyer declared: "The 'movement' had begun, and we took it with us into the college classes we were teaching within the next few years."

In the late 1950s and early 1960s, the federal government began to play a more active role in matters of social and economic welfare. In civil rights, for example, the Department of Justice started to enforce a rigorous desegregation program in the South, an area then thought to be the last bastion of race prejudice and discrimination in the country. On the international scene, the Nuclear Test Ban Treaty of 1963 held out hope to those worried about nuclear war. Government-sponsored programs like the Peace Corps offered thousands of students opportunities to exercise their idealism and change the world *through* government service.

John F. Kennedy, the thirty-fifth American president, was the driving force behind many of these changes; he was also a leader whose personal attraction was irresistible to many college students. Kennedy's appeal was apparent when he visited the WSU campus

Presidential candidate John F. Kennedy speaking on campus, February 11, 1960.

during his bid for the Democratic presidential nomination on February 11, 1960. Students packed both Bryan Auditorium, where Kennedy spoke, and the CUB, where the candidate's voice was carried over an intercom system. Kennedy was young, sophisticated, and managed to wield power without appearing to take life too seriously.

In his Bryan Hall speech the future president emphasized higher education's importance. He told students that in nineteenth-century Belgium each college graduate was allowed to cast three votes. "I am not advocating this in America," Kennedy said, flashing his famous smile, "at least not until more Democrats go to college." One of those who squeezed into Bryan Hall to hear Kennedy was Sandy Wilson Barrett, '62. "It was well worth the discomfort," she wrote to her parents. "Kennedy is a most interesting speaker, and a very impressive person." It's likely that no president ever commanded respect on college campuses the way John F. Kennedy did.

When news of Kennedy's assassination reached WSU on the morning of November 22, 1963, the shock was so great that many students look back on it as the moment when an era of turmoil and alienation began. Barbara Lof DeMichele, '66, recalled walking from Campus Hill back to Streit Hall, when another woman ran up to her and said that Kennedy had been shot. DeMichele immediately assumed it was a wild rumor. "I *couldn't believe* that an assassination could actually happen in this country." The insult to a student's well-ordered world was particularly acute because Kennedy had led college-aged people to believe they would help shape America's "New Frontier" and that the future was uniquely theirs. Twenty-five years later Barbara DeMichele wrote:

> It's hard to remember how much young people were involved in political thought in those days—partly *because* Kennedy had made it so attractive. I remember my roommate Gail [Inkpen Trimble, '66] remarked during our senior year that Kennedy was the last politician who we would ever believe in. I think she was right.

THE "GET INVOLVED" MESSAGE TO COLLEGE STUDENTS, WHICH KENnedy's charm and the Peace Corps highlighted, came to students from many other sources as well. An important wellspring of this opinion was an organization called the National Student Association, the NSA for short. Representing 1.2 million students on 300 college campuses, NSA held gigantic conventions every summer. These assemblies were dominated by delegates from schools where student activism and radicalism were rapidly taking hold. Thus, when classes began each fall, student representatives brought back to WSU resolutions that had been passed at national meetings; almost invariably, student government rejected these proposals as being too radical. In 1965, for example, the NSA convention called for an end to the American "offensive role" in Vietnam, endorsed the student "free speech" strikes on the Berkeley campus of the University of California, and called for sit-ins and other desegregation movement measures to be applied to protest northern slum conditions. These suggestions proved so controversial in Pullman that students voted in the spring of 1966 to sever relations with NSA. But in the meantime, "radical" politics were introduced directly into the campus debate.

The WSU student body might end its affiliation with NSA, but issues of poverty, racism, and war would not go away. In particular, America's involvement in Vietnam inspired increasingly negative reactions on college campuses. As time passed, this antiwar sentiment became radical and was introduced directly into the discussion about how college students might build a better world.

Traditional football rally "serpentine;" within a few years, however, student gatherings were as likely to be for a protest march as a sanctioned campus event.

It was still an academic debate in 1965. Vietnam was far away and, in the minds of most WSU students, the Southeast Asian war remained an abstraction. Outwardly, the campus in 1965 looked very much like it did in 1955. The fad that fall was a television program called "Batman," in which the hero drove a "Batmobile," wore a mask and cape, and engaged villains in badly staged fistfights while comic-book words, "Bam," "Womp," and "Pow," exploded on the screen. Students packed into Butch's Den in the CUB to watch the spectacle on a real color television, the first many of them had seen. When the *Evergreen* ran an editorial decrying the frivolity of it all, one group of students replied: "Biff! Zonk! Ooof! Zloop! for the *Evergreen*." They were right; you can't have a *serious* college fad.

It is more than symbolic that the Batman craze came to WSU by way of television. One of the motifs of life on the Pullman campus prior to the 1960s had been isolation; the school was like an academic island, a world unto itself. But little by little, students came to interact with the wider world. Wars, movies, then radios and automobiles, interrupted but did not destroy the pristine isolation. With television's arrival the outside world became at least as important in determining campus attitudes as student interaction. Every part of college life came to be profoundly influenced by television. The *Evergreen* was no longer the most important source of news. Campus theater, dances, and other forms of live entertainment became less significant. Student leaders found their ability to shape campus attitudes eroded by television's influence. By the late 1960s, shows like "Rowan and Martin's Laugh-In" and "The Smothers Brothers" openly satirized "establishment values" and ridiculed American domestic and international policies.

Television brought the outside world to Pullman in other ways, as well. Night after night CBS, NBC, and ABC evening news broadcasts showed footage of bloody fighting in Vietnam. By the late sixties,

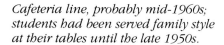

Cafeteria line, probably mid-1960s; students had been served family style at their tables until the late 1950s.

"Power to the people." Military fatigue jackets were worn by counterculture activists as well as ex-servicemen enrolling at WSU in the late 1960s and early 1970s.

viewers routinely watched rioting in black ghettos, the effects of terrorist bombings, sit-ins, and massive campus protests. Each night CBS News anchorman Walter Cronkite tallied the number of American military men and women killed in Southeast Asia. In 1968, television networks broadcast stories of the brutal assassinations of civil rights leader Martin Luther King and presidential candidate Robert F. Kennedy. Television also showed the smoking wreckage left by the riots that followed in more than 130 American cities. Television brought to Pullman images of police violence, citizen protest, and rioting associated with Mayor Richard J. Daley's stage managed, 1968 Democratic National Convention in Chicago. It was hard to concentrate on the fortunes of Cougar football when the nation's social and political structure appeared in ruin every night on CBS.

THE MAJOR STORY OF THE 1960S WAS, OF COURSE, VIETNAM. FOR MOST college-aged students from 1965 to about 1973, the war had a major impact on their lives. Many dropped out of school and joined the service. During the period from 1965 to 1975 Army and Air Force ROTC programs at WSU graduated over 800 second lieutenants. Many other students on campus were recruited and joined officer training programs on graduation.

Other students supported national policy, but, all things being equal, would rather not have been bothered with the prospect of a distasteful detour from their careers. That was a big difference between World War II and the Vietnam War. With Vietnam, there was no sense of national emergency. The government itself did not claim to be in trouble or request a national sacrifice. Young men about to be drafted were given no clue that their sacrifice made any difference to anyone else.

During the early years of the war, student deferments from the draft allowed many men to go to school in the hope that the war would end before they graduated. But the deferments themselves were a source of consternation. The rules were set up so that men could be drafted if they did not maintain a sufficient number of college credits. Nor could male students temporarily drop out of school and not escape conscription. Whatever the reasons for establishing such a system, the general message seemed to be that if you didn't have the grades or the money to go to college you went to Vietnam. And it seemed to follow that if you went to Vietnam you were just unlucky—hardly a spur to patriotic service. Later, the system was switched to a "fairer" lottery system. A poignant college memory for Vietnam-era males is listening to the radio and searching the papers to see if, literally, their "number was up."

Many students, including those with good academic standing or safe draft numbers, nevertheless felt a nagging guilt about sitting in dorm rooms or apartments watching the Vietnam conflict play itself out on television. About the only way to square one's conscience was to look upon the war as one that no one should have to fight. As time passed, more and more students began to think this way and came to oppose the war openly and with vigor.

"I was constantly aware of being thrust into a lot of ethical questions at a very young age," recalled Scott Hendrickson, '71, an honors student and vice president of the student body. Harlan E. Jones, who entered WSU in 1966 and became active in student government before quitting to join the federal government's Volunteers in Service to America, or VISTA program, had the same feeling. "When I came to college I felt the country should fight communism; somebody had to stop those bullies." But as Jones listened to the growing debate over Vietnam it began to appear to him that the war "just wasn't what it was said to be. It probably was a civil war in Vietnam. It all began to look very suspicious." The worst thing was: "It was not an abstract question." Jones had to decide, "is it all right for me to go out and kill people? That question hung over me from 1967 to 1972."

Anti-Vietnam activity at WSU, which began with small marches in 1965, was modest when compared to the often violent clashes that occurred on other campuses across the country. Once antiwar protestors towed an old car onto the mall and then proceeded to smash it with sledgehammers as a symbolic protest against violence. On another occasion, demonstrators wrapped animal entrails from a butcher shop in a sheet and spread them out before a formation of cadets at an annual spring ROTC review. Another time, when the *Evergreen* ran an editorial in support of the war, dissidents gathered up all the copies of the paper they could find and burned them on the mall.

Protest parades of one to two hundred students were common, and occasionally groups would go further, calling for nonviolent sit-ins at buildings where military recruiters set up on campus. In one typical demonstration, the local chapter of the Students for a Democratic Society (SDS) gathered in front of the CUB in October 1969. About fifty ralliers then marched to the campus recruiting office, where Marine representatives were scheduled to recruit officer candidates. The protesters, including WSU faculty members, sat down in the office but did not try to prevent those who arrived for interviews from entering. The recruiting went on as scheduled and the protesters eventually dispersed peacefully. Another instance, in

Guerrilla theater on the CUB Mall, October 1969; activists staged farcical skits protesting U.S. foreign and domestic policies.

which two students were arrested for forcing their way into the recruiting office, was an exception.

By the late sixties, each new WSU semester witnessed antiwar groups sponsoring Vietnam moratoriums at which faculty members and other interested parties discussed the conflict in open forums. Most of the few hundred who showed up were already converted.

An outspoken opponent of the war, Nola Hitchcock Cross, '70, became *Evergreen* editor in the fall semester of 1969. She was controversial for her downplaying conventional campus news about sports and social life and, instead, devoting large portions of her paper to Vietnam and other social issues. She drew so many complaints that when she was invited to defend her actions at a CUB forum, the session was billed as "Who the Hell's Nola Cross?" Yet, the *Evergreen* never became the polemical antiwar organ that many student newspapers did. Cross's editorials against the war were calm and cogent. Alongside her anti-Vietnam essays, she printed editorials by assistant editor, Gary Eliassen, who was in favor of the U.S. commitment to Vietnam.

If America's active involvement in Vietnam had lasted only as long as our participation in World War II, American military forces would have left the country in early 1969. But it wore on. Students who came to WSU as freshmen just weeks after the United States made its first major troop commitment to Vietnam were graduating in 1969 and many were surprised to find themselves headed for Southeast Asia as members of the armed services. It was a war without end, and that prospect finally won over many students to the antiwar movement. One said, "Even if it was right at one time, at some point there were just too many lives being lost and it stopped being moral." Even students who were inclined to trust the U.S. government before couldn't escape a feeling that there must be *something* wrong; either the war was wrong to begin with or it was being run badly. Bill Walker, '73, said:

> I guess you could say I was a naive conservative. I supported Vietnam as a concept; that is America had an enemy, which in one way or another threatened us, and therefore, as in all wars, needed to be defeated. The details of the war I chose to ignore. But one thing I firmly believed then and now was that once we are in a war we should fight it out full-out and not play games with it as we did in Vietnam.

That was one of the common views.

Exactly how student opinion on the war divided up at any given moment is impossible to know; some vacillated, others changed their opinions over time. In the climactic month of May 1970, the *Evergreen* published a ballot that asked students whether or not the United States should withdraw immediately from Vietnam. Only a small percentage of the student body responded—602 opposed immediate withdrawal and 392 approved. The conservative Evergreen editor supporting the poll said there was "the possibility that someone could 'stuff' the ballot box." Most of the 3,000 or more students actively protesting the war at that time did not bother to respond to the poll, but instead voted with their feet by attending a rally on the CUB Mall. That same spring, about 250 people showed up for a pro-war counter rally. Earlier in the school year, the Associated Women Students polled living groups on their support of the Vietnam Moratorium. Seven were opposed and eight were in favor.

THE SIXTIES WERE MORE THAN JUST DEBATE OVER AMERICAN INVOLVE-ment in the Vietnam War. For most students, weekends were still important opportunities to have fun. The decade also proved to be a second "golden era" for rock and roll and practically everyone, from ROTC Special Forces candidates to SDS radicals, listened to the same radio stations. But as the sixties progressed popular music became an increasingly important vehicle for social criticism. This "protest music," ranged from the poetic, like Bob Dylan's "The Times They

Night dance, circa 1968; Wilson Road had just been closed off to construct the new CUB Mall.

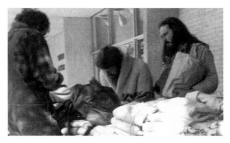

Hippies frequently sold goods in front of the bookstore; overalls, work shirts, and hand knit sweaters and ponchos from Latin American countries were commonly worn by students in the early 1970s.

Are A-Changin', to ballads that were anthems of the era. Country Joe and the Fish sang:

And it's one, two, three,
What are we fightin' for.
Don't ask me, I don't give a damn,
Next stop is Vietnam.
And it's five, six, seven,
Open up the Pearly Gates.
Don't stop to wonder why,
We're all gonna die.

One thing that these songs had in common was that they were opposed to war. There was little pro-war popular music during the Vietnam era, just as there was no antiwar music during World War II.

When the music was not antiwar, it seemed opposed to conventional American society. It was deeply introspective at least, and often advertised the virtues of mind-altering drugs. The Beatles turned from "I Want to Hold Your Hand" (1964) to "Lucy in the Sky with Diamonds" (1967). Drugs were seriously preached as a philosophy of life from campus to campus by ex-Harvard professor Timothy Leary.* By 1970, many WSU students were using a variety of drugs that included cocaine, LSD, and marijuana, though it is impossible to know how widespread this use was.

THE TRADITIONAL, "CAREFREE" FEELING OF THE WSU CAMPUS EVAPO- rated after the middle 1960s. Everything, it seemed, was tinged with controversy. The speakers and entertainers featured during the academic year of 1969-70 included: Frank Mankiewicz, former press secretary to Robert F. Kennedy; black Congressman Adam Clayton Powell; David Schoenbrun, correspondent and critic of U.S. involvement in Vietnam; Morris Udall, a Congressman who spoke on the dangers of overpopulation; Tom Gunn, the radical student body president from the University of Washington; an advisor to the House of Representatives Committee on Un-American Activities; an executive of *Playboy* magazine speaking about the sexual revolution; and Allen Ginsberg, poet and one of the founders of the Beat Movement in the 1950s.

The university administration and faculty, afraid to give students a *casus belli*, abandoned their traditional roles as censors and arbiters of taste. Student posters, pamphlets, movies, art exhibits, and graffiti were designed to stun anyone who came into range. People wanted to shock and to be shocked. In the fall of 1969, the *Evergreen* ran a movie review written by film critic Judith Crist: "Some may find it

---

*Leary received a Master of Arts degree in psychology from Washington State College in 1947.

'sick' in its negativism, its concentration on the sensuous and erotic for its own sake." It was a movie in tune with the times.

By the last years of the decade, button-down shirts had given way to sweatshirts, ragged at the arms where the sleeves had been sheered off, or to T-shirts with political statements, pictures of Che Guevara, or beer labels. Women switched from knee-length pleated skirts to faded jeans or to body-hugging miniskirts that were cut several inches above the knee. Women also grew their hair long and let it hang down their backs. Men, even conservatives, grew their hair longer and added mustaches and beards as fashion statements. These changes supplied topics for many a heated family conversation at Christmas and spring breaks.*

* This was not, however, the first time hair was an issue on campus. In the early 1920s, the college administration became upset when women started "bobbing" or cutting their hair. Trendsetters in sororities were entreated by administrators to stop the fad. Like the long hair of the sixties, the short hair of the twenties seemed like a deliberate flouting of society's values.

Ceramics class in the new Fine Arts Building, 1971; arts and handcrafts became increasingly popular in this era.

Y'ALL   KILL

By the end of the decade, the WSU campus was a curious amalgam of movements, ideas, ideals, and ideologies. Hippies with garish beads, beards, headbands, and flowing skirts, lounged about the Mall, petting dogs, spreading messages of love, espousing the virtues of LSD and marijuana, selling handmade jewelry, pottery, incense (Patchouli), and leather goods, and taking pride in being called "freaks." Members of the Black Student Union, the Radical Union, and other groups could be heard giving speeches on the Mall. Radicals handed out or sold copies of locally produced tracts, including *Burgerville Blues*, *'Sblood*, and *Spark* ("a radical union compendium of Lies, Sex and Cheap Thrills," as it explained itself). These publications, adorned with evocative photos and intricate illustrations, were written in the special sixties argot that became a trademark of the genre. When there was a shortage of dorm rooms on campus, the *Burgerville Blues* intoned, "That old Wizard Glen T. [President Glenn Terrell] and his band of liberal apologists have overextended themselves again." Pullman landlords "could only slobber over their jowls in anticipation of huge profits. . . . There is an alternative, but it cannot and will not come from the administration. It must come from us, the students, the people. We must organize collectively and demand fair priced adequate housing for all." The article ended by calling a meeting to form a tenants' union.

Life for students in the sixties tended to play itself out as a series of "issues" that had to be addressed and "intolerable conditions" for which redress was demanded. When activists wrote about drinking at WSU, it was not done as a half-serious joke, as it would have been in earlier decades, but as an investigative article seeking to reveal the extent of alcoholism on campus. One group marched through downtown Pullman, signs in hand, to protest high prices. In May 1969, eighteen "straight" (non-radical) student government and dormitory officers published an open letter in the *Evergreen* addressed to the dean of students. The complaint, restrictions on students, was an ancient one, but the tone was strictly from the sixties: public and accusatory. They listed recent reforms in dorm life. After each, they asked the dean of students, "What was your role in this?" Then they answered: "Zero. . . . After an examination of these six items, we hope you will forgive us for asking personal questions. But what *do* you do in French Administration Building?"

In previous generations, the welcome-to-school issue of the *Evergreen* advised freshmen on how to "fit in" on campus. The welcome back issue in the fall of 1969 implored freshmen to "Ask why. . . . Ask why to the ROTC. Ask why to your landlord. . . . Ask why to the campus police that carry guns. . . . Ask your teachers why."

Everyone, it seems, had a cause. The 1970 *Chinook* was dedicated, not to a beloved professor or to general good times in school, but to the threat of pollution. The opening essay contained illustrations of ugly dams and freeways, and said:

What has our education done for us? The USA
represents six percent of the world population and

IF ALLOWED TO SURVIVE
THIS GRASS WILL PRODUCE
ENOUGH OXYGEN FOR TWO
STUDENTS TO BREATHE FOR
ONE SEMESTER

Ecology, environmental awareness, and wilderness preservation were new concepts; typically, students were among the first to take up the cause.

controls fifty percent of the income. We are responsible for the greatest exploitation and pillage of natural resources in world history. Our affluence is digging its own grave. We are a cancer within the environment, and soon the organism must perish. People forget what a blue lake used to look like. What did you do today to help clean up the world?

This was the sixties counterpart to the call to "school spirit." Apathy, that ancient college sin, was still around, but was equated with failing to attend debates about pressing issues.

IT WAS DIFFICULT TO AVOID THE PROLIFERATING CONTROVERSIES OF THE era. Campus Christians were drawn into a polemical debate when they opposed a "group" called the League for the Promotion of Militant Atheism. The League's origins explain something about the times. It started as a joke, recalled Molly Martin, '72. She roomed at the Rosa Luxemburg Collective, a house near Greek Row in which about a dozen men and women students lived and shared politics and cooking chores. "We were well organized," Martin said, "considering our eclectic conglomeration of counter-culturists, and dinner was served nightly at six o'clock sharp by a rotating kitchen crew."

The evening meal would be followed by free-flowing political discussions. One night, someone proposed the League for the Promotion of Militant Atheism, mostly in jest, and somehow word got out. The next thing collective members knew, they were receiving invitations from Christian groups to debate. "We had to read the Bible!" said Martin.

The level of personal commitment on the part of student activists expanded their influence way beyond the proportion of their numbers. At no time did a core group of militants orchestrate marches, plan sit-ins, write and distribute literature, or make public statements on a regular basis. Each group of activists had special causes, but they all embraced and championed the causes of their colleagues out of natural sympathy. Thus, Martin attended Vietnam moratoriums and occasionally helped the Radical Union. "My real radicalization came as I discovered feminism," Martin said.

> I found Betty Friedan's book, [*The Feminine Mystique*] by accident, and searched out other like-minded women on campus. . . . We started a consciousness-raising group and a speaker's group.
>
> We spoke to classes of students, living groups, high school classes, civic groups, even the Pullman Lions Club as I remember. We produced guerrilla theater, staged 'happenings,' protested the student health center's backward position on birth control, supported the struggles of underpaid female faculty members, lobbied for a women's center, worked on the campaign to change the state's abortion law.

Molly Martin said she could laugh about the League for the Promotion of Militant Atheism, but not about feminism. As she searched for attitudes in American culture that led to the oppression of women, she came to feel that, all along, an unseen set of rules worked against her. "You go through a period where you feel very oppressed. You are very, very angry."

IF A YOUNG WOMAN FROM YAKIMA COULD BECOME ALIENATED, DESPITE powerful cultural and traditional forces inviting her to acclimate,* it is not surprising that it could happen to others for whom the campus was a truly alien place. Ernie Thomas, '71, went to high school in Austin, Texas, where his classmates were either black or Chicano. When it came time for him to go to college, he and his high school counselor picked WSU because it had a highly rated program in physical therapy, the field in which Thomas was interested.

Thomas also chose WSU because it was in the North, and young blacks in Texas were always advised to go north. Thomas had the impression that whites in the North were not prejudiced, "and I was really open for some different experiences."

The WSU housing office assigned him to a three-man room in Stimson Hall. When he arrived, his roommates were already there.

---

* When she was a freshman and had to battle the administration's rules about women living off campus, Molly Martin enlisted the aid of her mother. The mother corresponded with President Terrell about the college's rules, and, thereafter, whenever the genial president saw Molly on the campus, he would ask, "How's your mother?"

"They were not ready, when they opened the door, for *me*," Thomas declared. "I had seen that look in people's eyes before, coming from Texas." As he self-consciously threw his suitcase on the bed and began to unpack, the other two men went to a corner and conferred. Then they came back and told Thomas, politely, that they had never lived with a colored person before and they wondered whether it would be okay if he took the single bunk in the alcove. He shrugged and said sure.

Thomas found that the traditional residence hall process of forming a "sense of family" became an experiment in alienation in his case. He was allowed to "overhear" stereotyping jokes about blacks and

Racism workshop, October 1970.

muttered references to "niggers." Once in the laundry room, he found that another guy had taken his clean clothes out of a washing machine and had stacked them on a table, rather than putting them in the dryer as was customary. When Thomas asked, "Why didn't you put them in the dryer!" the guy "went off into a little spiel about 'nigger this and nigger that.' This was not just two college guys arguing, it was him against Africa."

When Thomas turned out for freshman football, he heard someone say across the lockers, "I didn't know we were going to be playing with niggers." When he walked the streets of downtown Pullman, "People would stand there and stare at you, literally stare at you in a mean sort of way."

A survey conducted by the sociology department in 1969 found that about ten percent of students held hard-core racist attitudes. That translated into 1,300 students. That plus the racial slights given in ignorance meant that the 200 black students were "likely to be exposed to unpleasant attitudes with such frequency that it can be said to condition a general climate for them."

Aside from racist insults, the WSU campus was a strange place for blacks, especially those who, like Thomas, came from parts of the country where they were either a large minority or even in the majority. Such innocuous events as Sadie Hawkins dances, where everyone dressed up in overalls and painted freckles on their faces, had no meaning to blacks as a social outlet. "We stuck out already." At such an event Thomas felt like the fifth wheel, like someone who got an invitation to a party by accident. Everyone came to college expecting a social life, and blacks felt left out of things.

Racial problems at Washington State University in the late sixties and early seventies occurred in a larger context, one in which blacks across the country demanded their civil rights. Angered over continued white bigotry despite the work of Martin Luther King and others, young blacks became militant out of frustration. They created organizations like the Black Panthers, a paramilitary group that believed blacks would have to usurp civil rights, by violence if necessary. Books about slavery, the black experience, autobiographies by militants like *The Autobiography of Malcolm X* and Eldridge Cleaver's *Soul on Ice*, were read and discussed by blacks and whites on campus. The general message of the times was that things change only through confrontation. Ernie Thomas came to that conclusion, as well. He said he saw some improvements during his years at WSU, "But always through confrontation."

ONE SUCH RACIAL INCIDENT OCCURRED SHORTLY AFTER THE CHRISTMAS recess of the 1968-1969 school year. The intramural basketball team of the Alpha Gamma Rho fraternity was playing a team from Goldsworthy Hall. A dispute after the game ended with a white player from the fraternity hitting a black player from Goldsworthy. The fraternity members said the black man had confronted and slapped a fraternity member, and only then, according to this version of the story, did a second fraternity brother step in to protect his friend. The black player said he had only accused the white player of guarding too closely during the game, and that another fraternity member made a racial slur and then hit him.

Whatever actually happened, it led to the most serious racial clash in the university's history. A week later, a dozen Black Student Union members, three of them carrying guns, went into the Alpha Gamma Rho fraternity at about 10:30 at night. Once inside, they entered a dining room, where Ernie Thomas climbed on a table and started to make a statement. The fraternity president entered the room and told Thomas to get off the table, one of the blacks hit the fraternity president, and a general melee ensued. One of the blacks fired a rifle at an inside door and several more shots were fired outside the fraternity, but no one was hit by gunfire. Four fraternity members were struck with the rifle or other clubs and were taken to Memorial Hospital with minor injuries.

Thomas and those who entered the building with him were arrested later and charged with assault. In court, Thomas and his friends said they had no intention of using the guns. They brought weapons along only because they were outnumbered—a dozen guys going to a fraternity of forty or more members who may have had guns themselves.

The incident rocked the campus community. What no one could say was what would happen next. Was this a climactic incident from which tensions would subside? Or, was it a sign of deep racial tension that would lead to further violence?

Many students thought that, whatever the provocation, people had no reason to carry guns around the campus. A forum, organized to discuss the incident, erupted in angry racial accusations. A white student wrote to the *Evergreen*:

> I think it is about time the Negroes on this campus
> stop using their color as an excuse for their actions.
> . . Maybe if the blacks started acting like responsible
> citizens instead of a bunch of juvenile delinquents the
> situation would improve. . . . The above views are my
> own and in no way represent those of my living
> group. So, please, don't come over and shoot my
> house up.

The campus was still in confusion six weeks later when the five blacks who had pled guilty were scheduled to spend their first of several weekends in the Whitman County jail. When they went to

Colfax to turn themselves in, about seventy-five members of the Black Student Union and a few whites followed and refused to allow them to be incarcerated. The five convicted blacks and the seventy-five supporters moved to a Colfax church for "sanctuary" and spent the night there. Mike Humphreys, Whitman County sheriff, sent for thirty-five state troopers. Things began to look serious and a confrontation appeared to be shaping up.

The following day, Humphreys ordered the thirty-five troopers to stay in the courthouse and, accompanied by one deputy, he went to the church to face the forty-two people still there. The sheriff told them that if they gave up the five convicted blacks and dispersed peacefully there would be no charges. Those inside refused the offer, so Humphreys placed everyone under arrest and asked that they board a waiting bus for jail. The protesters complied peacefully and were booked; they had made their point. The incident ended without further violence. In fact, the Black Student Union later sent Humphreys a bouquet of roses "because Sheriff Humphreys kept his cool."

Protestors, March 1970.

IN ANY COMPARISON WITH WHAT OCCURRED AT MANY OTHER UNIVER-
sities during that time, Washington State was a model of debate
without disruption. There were no riots, no bombs, no state troopers,
no faculty or administrator hostages, and little disruption of classes.
But the tensions of the sixties were there, and in the last semester of
the last year of the decade, spring 1970, they played themselves out
all at once. In the words of one student, "it went crazy."

At the University of Washington basketball game on March 7, a
group of blacks held their fists in the air, the "black power salute,"
while the band played the national anthem. The crowd in Bohler
Gym erupted in a chorus of booing. At half time, a black student was
chatting with someone when a white man came up to him and asked
whether he was one of those holding fists aloft (he wasn't). The black
student said, "is it your business and if it is, what do you plan to do
about it?" The white man pushed the black student roughly and said,
"I'll kick your black ass!" A deputy sheriff witnessed the whole
sequence of events; consequently the white man was charged and
found guilty of assault. As it turned out he was not a student, but his
actions still contributed to heightened campus tensions.

On March 13, a week after the basketball game, an anti-draft march
of approximately 3,000 students paraded through Pullman, pausing
intermittently to listen to angry speeches against the draft, racism,
and the sale of nonunion grapes, which were being boycotted
nationwide in support of migrant workers trying to unionize in
California. After the speeches, some marchers ran into three Pullman
supermarkets and destroyed grapes as a protest. Ralph Atkins, a
black sophomore, was the only one arrested in the incident, and the
charge was not destruction of property, but "inciting a riot."

That suggested Atkins was the leader, which all of those at the
demonstration knew was not true. He did carry a bullhorn and was
easy to remember and identify because he was wearing the Black
Panther uniform: a leather jacket, a black beret, and sunglasses.
Thousands of people participated in the demonstration. At least a
dozen entered the stores. Why was Atkins the only one charged? The
other demonstrators protested the arrest as an example of selective
injustice based on race. The protest exasperated many on campus
who figured that those who destroyed property had a lot of nerve
complaining simply because someone went to jail for it.

There was no single "student body" opinion in the late sixties.
Those attending WSU were deeply divided over issues and over the
methods used to achieve desired ends. A graduate student wrote to
the *Evergreen* in May 1970: "Everything wrong now in society is
blandly attributed not to individuals but to existing institutions—the
'Establishment.' Such an attitude encourages a kind of scape-goatism
that spells the death of any serious kind of individual self-discipline,
or self-reform."

In early April, the east side of Rogers Stadium burned to the
ground; many people assumed that radicals set the blaze (though no
one was ever charged). That same month, four black students,
including the president of the Black Student Union, were charged

Arsonist's burning of Rogers Stadium, April 4, 1970.

with raping a white woman student. Blacks feared they would be convicted because they were black; some whites said they might get away with it because they were black.

There were campus rumors that "rednecks" from the area around Pullman were organizing to terrorize blacks and protesters on campus. "Things around here are really getting heavy," said one black student. "I've got a feeling people will really start shooting if something gets started. Like man, they won't care who you are, they'll only care what color you are." Many white students also feared "redneck" violence; in fact, some otherwise sympathetic students avoided demonstrations and marches because of this fear.

On April 22, Henry M. Jackson, Washington's junior senator, spoke at WSU. Although Jackson was highly regarded for his stands on many environmental issues, he was also a supporter of American involvement in Vietnam. When he started to speak, he was pelted with marshmallows and shouted down by a group of students in the audience. Although most conservatives avoided discussions about the Vietnam War, they did argue with campus radicals over the use of these coercive methods.

They saw Jackson's treatment at the hands of a hostile crowd to be a violation of the doctrine of free speech.

Despite building tension, the events of April 1970 were merely a prelude to what happened the following month. On May 1, President Richard M. Nixon announced on television that American forces in Southeast Asia had launched an offensive that openly took the Vietnam War into Cambodia for the first time. From the government's perspective, seeing the previous five years' effort threatened by Viet Cong advances, the action was an attempt to cut enemy lines of supply and reinforcement. To antiwar students, it was another escalation of a bloody conflict that had been going on for as long as they could remember.

By Monday, May 4, demonstrations were held on hundreds of campuses, from tiny liberal arts colleges to the largest and best-known institutions in the country. At one of them, Kent State University in Ohio, National Guard troops deliberately aimed their rifles at demonstrating students. For reasons that were never determined, an officer gave the order to shoot. The guardsmen opened fire and killed four people.

This fatal event—a deliberate act of shooting on a college campus by military personnel—shocked students as nothing had before. At

Rally following the Kent State tragedy, May 1970.

Marker commemorating one of the Kent State victims whose name and age, "Allison Krause—19," later was handwritten on the cross, May 1970.

Princeton, ninety-five percent of the students observed a strike of classes. At the University of Washington, 5,000 protestors sat down on Seattle's north-south freeway, blocking rush-hour traffic. Someone threw a fire bomb into the ROTC building at Oregon State University. An arsonist destroyed the Navy ROTC building at the University of Idaho. A fire bombing burned twenty-five military vehicles at the National Guard Armory in Lewiston.

At Washington State, between 500 and 800 students and a few faculty members walked into French Administration Building at midday, May 5, and sat down. Student leaders handed Executive Vice President Wallis Beasley (President Terrell was out of town) demands that the administration send a telegram to President Nixon deploring the invasion of Cambodia and that classes be cancelled for a day to protest the incursion.

When President Terrell returned to campus about 5:30 that afternoon, he was conciliatory. After an hour meeting with his advisors, the president agreed to cancel classes for a day (WSU would be one of 227 American colleges and universities to do so that week). He also promised to send a telegram to President Nixon regretting that there had not been a "deeper explanation" of the Cambodian invasion. Students wanted something stronger, so Terrell changed his message to state that Kent State and the Cambodian invasion had "created outrage and dismay on the part of a substantial segment of the campus at Washington State University." It was not an opinion about

Cambodia but a simple statement of the situation at WSU. Nevertheless, protesters were pleased. The *Evergreen* reported, ". . . they cleaned up their litter and left." They had occupied the building for nine hours without any damage. WSU still had not experienced any of the ugly incidents that became common in that era.

A number of WSU students and faculty members, however, believed the administration had caved in to intimidation. Gary Eliassen, the conservative student who succeeded Nola Cross as editor of the *Evergreen*, had deplored the Kent State incident, saying in an editorial, "the carrying of loaded weapons to put down unarmed students is unnecessary." Still, he considered the administration's statement to be a deep disappointment to "those of us who are against threats and ultimatums as a means of bringing about change." Terrell's response to such critics was to the point; a day of discussion about the war would be a good thing and, in any case, "a far better way of letting off steam than through the destructive actions which have occurred on so many campuses."

The moderate student body president, Brian Benzel, and others in student government issued a statement in support of the cancellation of classes and the organization of a "teach-in" for the day after. They said:

> WSU students have been for some time saying that their structure is too rigid; that education is not 50-minute classes, grades, departmental requirements; that education is not merely vocational but learning how to deal with change in an effective manner. . . . Dr. Terrell has not called off the learning process at Washington State; he has eliminated the structure for a day. . . . We fully support the May 7 teach-in as an opportunity to learn and to confront change.

Occupation of the administration building, "Fort French;" President Glenn Terrell at center conversing with a protestor, May 5, 1970.

The "teach-in" lasted a day. Students gathered in the CUB Ballroom for presentations by history and political science professors and students with various opinions. Gary Eliassen remembered being booed when he tried to defend the Nixon policy in Vietnam. "I was only twenty-one years old," he remembered. "I was shaking and almost crying. I just said, 'This [intolerance] is exactly what I've been talking about,' and stepped back." He went back to his desk at the *Evergreen* and found one of the more outspoken radicals on campus had already been there. She left a note that said: "I don't dig what you were saying, but I dig that you had the courage to say it."

Only ten days after the Kent State killings, the nation witnessed another shooting disaster on a campus. State troopers opened fire on students at Jackson State University in Mississippi, killing two and wounding nine others. This time, however, there was no convulsive reaction on campuses, perhaps because the incident came in an emotional trough created by all the activities of the Cambodia-Kent State protests.

One difference between the events at Kent State and those at Jackson State was that the students killed and wounded at the latter campus were black. Black students at Washington State University called a meeting of minority and radical leaders to propose an action similar to the one that followed Kent State. At the meeting in Koinonia House, an unofficial headquarters for antiwar and racial protest, the whites agreed to support this black cause.

On May 18, the Black Student Union and MEChA, the Chicano organization, presented a document containing eleven demands to President Terrell. These demands included: disarming the campus police, establishing a board that would review all judicial proceedings against "Third World people" (minorities), and sponsorship of a ten-day racism workshop that would be mandatory for all faculty and staff.

To back up their ultimatum, protesters called for a strike of classes and a boycott of all businesses in Pullman not posting signs stating that they opposed racism and that they did not use non-union grapes.

President Terrell answered each of the protesters' concerns at length in a three-page letter that was widely distributed on campus. He was sympathetic to all issues, but responded by pointing out that, in every case, things were already being done. He cited the area of minority recruitment as an example. Beyond that, the demands were impossible to meet. He later declared that opposition to racism was "the social problem about which I have the strongest personal commitment."

As many as 3,000 protesters rejected Terrell's response and the strike was on. Leaders set up a temporary cafeteria at the Koinonia House to serve people who wanted to avoid Campus Commons and the CUB. Many students still went to class, despite noisy parades

Students at the president's mansion during a night march protesting events at Jackson State. President Terrell addressed the group.

down hallways by demonstrators spreading the strike throughout campus. "I can remember feeling a little unnerved and frightened by the demonstration," said Louise Ferguson, '71. Her impression was not of students confronting the world's woes but of a bunch of rowdies "jumping on the band wagon for the novelty of it." About a thousand students paraded across campus and blocked traffic in front of French Administration Building. One demonstrator threw a two-by-four at a passing car, injuring the driver. A few bomb threats and three bricks thrown through the bookstore windows added to the general sense of emergency.

President Terrell, after consulting with strike leaders and learning that their demands were negotiable, made a new offer. To combat racism on campus, he offered to add a special assistant to advise him on minority affairs and commit the university to holding two-day racism workshops in each of the semesters of the coming academic year. He said he would also recommend to the faculty that, since many strikers had missed so many classes, students be given the option of taking grades up to the time the strike began or taking final exams.

The strikers accepted the offer, the incident ended, and one of the most tumultuous semesters in WSU's history ended. Graduation was orderly, seniors stood and cheered President Terrell. Some students, to be sure, believed cancelling tests was a capitulation to a minority of protesters. Most, however, were quietly sympathetic or decided to make the most of the situation by skipping finals and heading for home or for the sunny Snake River beaches.

Student strikers at Todd Hall, May 25, 1970.

GIVEN THE PERSPECTIVE OFFERED BY TIME, A GENERATION OF WASH-ington State University students appears as if it had gone crazy. Mean-while, an alumnus wrote to Harold Romburg, chair of the Board of Regents:

> Three years ago we had the finest university in the United States. How the times have changed! Indignity has been heaped upon indignity, insult upon insult and disgrace upon disgrace . . . the stomping of grapes, burning of stands, breaking of windows and forcible occupation of the Administration Building. . . . My morals will not co-exist with the current lack of discipline and morals at WSU and I have found it necessary, almost tearfully, to withdraw my support. I love our school and it rends my heart to see it being poured down the drain.

The saying "you can't see the forest for the trees" also works in reverse; sometimes what looks like a formidable and impenetrable forest is, on closer examination, seen to be a myriad of individual trees, separated by more space than branches. It was that way with the "movement." For one thing, it was never clear how many students opposed the Vietnam War. Active demonstrators never formed more than one-fourth of the student body. Most protesters were opposed to racism or American participation in the war only; they did not approve of the baggage of a social revolution that many radical leaders made a part of the movement.

While outsiders feared that protesters might "take over" the cam-pus, hard-core radicals were spending most of their time lamenting over the fact that they weren't getting enough support from the student body. Some of the more provocative actions, the ones that most upset the general public, were, as one ex-radical admitted, "expressions of frustration—desperate attempts to capture the atten-tion of WSU students." When mildly destructive tactics, such as blocking passages to classrooms or jamming locks were suggested, strike leaders opposed them for reasons the general public might have found surprising, the student body would not have tolerated these actions.

Even the several dozen Washington State University students who declared themselves to be the the most radical probably did not envision a revolution with guns and street fighting, but rather a large-scale change in American attitudes. Mostly they were revolutionaries in theory, but not in practice. The WSU chapter of Students for a Democratic Society severed ties with its radical parent organization in 1969, commenting: "In their perverted desire to build an ultra-left, oh-so ultra-militant 'vanguard,' Weathermen have plunged into the depths of dead-end political extremism." The Pullman revolutionary contingent spoke radically and acted reasonably. "We're not going to try to go in and bash Marine recruiters," said the president of the Radical Union, the organization that succeeded SDS. "They're not our enemies. It's the institutions they serve."

The bomb threats, and bricks with *strike!* written on them that were thrown through windows at the Students Book Corporation, gave the appearance of being revolutionary acts when described in wire service news reports. In fact, they were isolated actions carried out by a few students. The instruments of violence were telephones (no bombs were ever found) and three bricks. One problem with radical activity, as strike leaders admitted later, was that it occasionally appealed to emotional or unstable people. Former radicals claimed, many years later, that none of the destructive events that occurred at WSU were planned; in virtually every case, they were attributed to people acting in isolation—much as the person who threw a smoke bomb during the big panty raid of 1956 acted alone, and yet he drew blame down on everyone. Many people claim to know, for example, who burned Rogers Stadium; most say it was done by someone under the influence of drugs who wanted to see a big fire.

Ultimately the most important thing that sixties students had in common with one another was a general feeling that they should be doing something about the state of the world. This feeling might have been inspired by John F. Kennedy, Ralph Nader, Martin Luther King, Bobby Seale, Mao Tse-tung, Barry Goldwater, Eldridge Cleaver, Betty Friedan, or any number of other activists of the era. The message of the times was that it was wrong to remain uninvolved. Amid the tumult of that spring of 1970, a graduate student, Carolyn Much, wrote a letter to the *Evergreen* expressing her frustration with contemporary Americans:

> They see war, they say nothing.
> They see racism, they say nothing.
> They see pollution, they say nothing.
> They see injustice, they say nothing.
> They see corruption, they say nothing.
> They see starvation, they say nothing.
> They see ugliness, yet they say nothing.
> They have adjusted perfectly.
> They have become mute.
> They are truly tolerant.
> They are the silent majority.

Political cartoon in the Evergreen,
*May 26, 1970, showing President
Glenn Terrell keeping "the lid on"
during the spring semester of 1970.*

IN THE SUMMER OF 1970, A GROUP OF WORRIED WHITMAN COUNTY citizens called a meeting in Colfax at the Palouse Empire Fairgrounds and invited area legislators to address the problem of what was going on at WSU. About 400 concerned citizens and 100 students crowded into a small auditorium to talk over events of the previous spring.

As it happened, a journalist and former assistant to President Lyndon Johnson, Bill Moyers, was touring the United States that summer gathering material for a book, *Listening to America*. On his way up from Lewiston, Moyers dropped by the meeting to hear the discussion. He described a forceful speech by former *Evergreen* student editor Gary Eliassen in defense of the campus as a neutral, academic setting.

When several citizens rose to complain about WSU student behavior, Eliassen declared: "The student movement at WSU has become an absurdity of generalization, rumor, threats of violence, and over-simplification." He then said that:

> If we are not going to allow our college campuses to become an arena simply for political action, irrational dissent, and violence, the taxpayers, students, and most importantly the university administration are going to have to take a long, hard look at the jobs they are doing. The university must be firm in dealing with both college disrupters whose intent and purpose is not in education but merely to create confusion and bring about confrontation.

As the crowd applauded, Moyers recorded the thought: "I wondered if he would ever write another editorial. For in such moments are politicians born. Gary Eliassen has met the people and they are his."

That night, Moyers also recorded the remarks of Nola Hitchcock Cross, Eliassen's immediate predecessor as editor of the *Evergreen*. She told the audience that she had a 3.5 grade point average, but was active against the war and racism because "there's more to an education than simply going to classes." Moyers noted that other students in the room seemed to listen to her with special intensity. "There is something about her they respect. Her role last spring must have been commanding."

"We've heard a lot of talk about students who want to get a real education," Cross declared,

> who don't want to be disturbed, who want to go to their classes and hear lectures and read their books, get their degrees, and go out and make money. But I think there's more to an education than simply going to classes. I know I have rarely missed a class . . . [but] during the strike I skipped every class that week and I learned more than I had ever learned in any other week of school . . . I learned that I must speak out as a concerned citizen. . . .

Moyers's book became a best-seller and a part of the country's permanent literature on that important time in American history. The picture of Nola Cross and Gary Eliassen frozen in time by Moyers's words flattered these WSU students of the sixties, no matter which of their causes a reader might champion.

THE FIRST YEARS OF THE SEVENTIES WITNESSED A SLOW COOLING FROM the heat generated in the sixties. The controversial racism workshop, set up as part of the deal to end the strike, was attended voluntarily by 5,000 students. This event proved to be a purgative for many hostile feelings that had grown between blacks and whites. Blacks, Chicanos, and Native Americans had their chance to say, before an immense crowd, what was difficult about being a minority at Wash-

University sponsored racism workshop, October 1970.

ington State University. Some of the language was accusatory—blacks told off the whites. But at least whites got a genuine reading of the intensity of feelings involved. The general consensus was that the workshop helped both whites and minorities to explore mutual feelings of suspicion, prejudice, and guilt at a critical time in the history of American race relations.

Another thing that helped cool the atmosphere during that tumultuous spring of 1970 was the election of sophomore Carlton Lewis as student body president for the 1970-1971 academic year. An intelligent, savvy, and involved black leader, Lewis knew how to deal with radicals. He also negotiated well with administrators and was not afraid to represent their interests before students. Remarkably, he had the admiration of many conservative students, as well. Roger Madsen, '71, a self-styled conservative who constantly opposed Lewis's student government programs, described Lewis as "charismatic, articulate, dynamic, very confident and well-organized."

At a time when many were questioning the relevance of student government, Lewis managed to place it at the center of the action. He

Minority students talked and white students listened at the racism workshop, October 1970.

pushed vigorously for involvement in social issues and administrative decision making.

When dissidents threatened to occupy the CUB in the spring of 1972 to protest the Vietnam War, Lewis advised against it on the grounds that the action would only put pressure on the administration. And after talking with university officials, he became convinced they wanted peace as much as anyone. He suggested a campaign to seek out and convert those who still supported the war. "I personally think it would be better to occupy the dorms instead of the CUB. That's where the people are."

Protests continued into the early seventies. By then, however, they become routine enough to lose their ability to unsettle the campus. People watched President Nixon being burned in effigy and went on about their business. When the 1972 CUB occupation occurred, protesters spent a night in the building, but committed no acts of violence. About 700 students paraded around campus and proceeded to Stadium Way where they sat down to block traffic. They stopped cars for a few minutes, to make their point, and then let traffic go through. When the antiwar organization demanded that classes be suspended for two hours to commemorate the second anniversary of the Kent State murders, President Terrell said no, and that was the end of it. The same *Evergreen* front page that carried a story announcing the president's decision gave equal space to reporting on upcoming Mom's Weekend festivities.

Carlton Lewis, student body president for 1970-1971 and 1971-1972.

THE SIXTIES BROUGHT DRASTIC CHANGES TO LIFE ON CAMPUS. THE staples of college life had always been big dances, school spirit, athletic competitions, the ancient struggle against administrative social rules, and the power of fraternity row. Formal dances fell victim to hard rock, casual clothes, and a doubling of the student population. When a male student ran successfully for Homecoming Queen, that venerable competition was hastily suspended. Talk of school spirit simply submerged into discussions of larger social and political issues. The administration practically withdrew from the business of regulating student social life.

Fraternities and sororities, which had always been zealous guardians of campus traditions, went out of fashion in the sixties, and some of these social organizations ceased to exist. A 1972 *Evergreen* review of sorority life said, "time consuming activities of former years—song fests, homecoming preparations etc.—have been abandoned," as had serenades for "pinning"—and, for that matter, the tradition of pinning, because "Greeks don't wear their pins as much." Dress codes were gone, and the sorority girls "practically live[d] in jeans and T-shirts."

Once it was difficult to be a big man on campus without being a "Greek"; in the sixties fraternity membership made it more difficult. An *Evergreen* article in the fall of 1969 stated that social fraternities

Cougar cheer-leaders; beards, long hair, and other counter-culture styles and attitudes permeated much of campus life by the early 1970s.

represented a "wave of the past." Fraternity men, thoroughly versed in their own traditions, didn't like the role.

The revolution came to the little world of the WSU campus. Consider the case of Bill Moos, '73, a tall, handsome, farm kid like those who filled out the line since the beginning of WSU football. His dad was a Lambda Chi at Washington State, his mother a Chi Omega. All his life Moos had gone to Cougar football games with his father. Hugh Campbell and Keith Lincoln were his boyhood inspirations, and his father would remind him that if he worked hard he might someday be good enough to wear the Grey W.

Moos won a scholarship to WSU; the trip with his father to register in the fall of 1969 was a highlight of his life. In the spring of 1970, all the strains of the sixties started bursting around him. "Here I was, still in a crew cut, penny loafers, still trying to hold on to my image of what college ought to be."

He always assumed he would be in a fraternity. He joined Pi Kappa Alpha and enjoyed it, but found out, of all things, it was a social liability. In that anti-rules era you had to be careful how you took your leave of a group or someone might crack, "Got to get home for a frat meeting, guys, so you don't get your bottoms spanked?"

Many people were openly experimenting with drugs; Moos even knew football players who smoked marijuana. One day, he was over at the Kappa house and his courting was interrupted by about 1,500 students making a march to President Terrell's house, "which I found scary as hell."

Nothing in college was like Moos imagined it might be. Everyone, it seemed, was letting their hair grow, and pretty soon he was too. "My

Bill Moos, class of 1973.

mom wanted me to get a hair cut and I wasn't one to defy authority, but I was part of a peer group."

When Moos won the Grey W he had coveted all his life, he practically had to keep it a secret. "You did not advertise the fact that you were an athlete." Not only wasn't being a football player an aid to making friends, but the women he dated risked a certain onus. Football players were assumed to be male chauvinists. Apologizing for being a first string football player was not exactly how he had imagined his college career. "I remember thinking," Moos said, "this can't be happening!"

Later Moos decided that being a student during the sixties had its compensations. Having to deal with all sorts of situations that did not conform to his presumptions forced him to contemplate a big, unruly, troubled world. He could see the results when he left campus. "I was a conservative on campus and a liberal everywhere else."

Other members of this peculiar college generation have similar reactions: memories of turmoil eased by a belief that their personal ordeals fostered personal growth. Scott Hendrickson, an honors student who struggled with ethical questions raised by the Vietnam War, said: "I can't imagine being in school any other time. I loved going to philosophy class then going out into the street and having to argue real issues." Roger Madsen, the conservative who did battle with liberals in the Student Senate, commented: "I never remember anybody being hostile to me. Maybe they secretly admired me—as I did them." Black radical Ralph Atkins, '73, reflected: "I don't know what Pullman is like now, but then it was alive. It was a time when people really cared about each other." Bill Walker, skeptical *Evergreen* reporter with a win-or-get-out attitude toward Vietnam, looked back fifteen years later and said: "I think it would be quite safe to say, regardless of your beliefs or actions at that time, it was one hell of a time to live." ■

The Sixties

Student addressing a protest rally, fall 1969.

President Glenn Terrell and Charles Hurst in open discussion.

Sit-in on Pullman's Main Street.

ABOVE: *The peace sign, a symbolic gesture of the sixties generation.*

LEFT: *Folk-rock artist Arlo Guthrie in concert at WSU.*

'SCORN

issue 4
*(formerly,
heretically, 'SBLOOD)*

INSIDE:
Graffiti
Clevenger tells it like it is!
Anti-war propaganda
(War is obscene!)
anD OTher Stuff

15¢

*By the early 1970s, WSU actively
recruited minority and foreign
students to come to Pullman.*

ABOVE: *Behind the clamor, much of campus life continued on as always.*

LEFT: *"Sweeping changes;" two students tending to the recreation room floor, early 1970s.*

University

PAUL CASEY BELIEVES HE MAY HAVE WITNESSED THE LAST ANTI-VIETNAM demonstration on campus. One spring day in 1974 he looked down from the rear catwalk behind the CUB and saw, across the practice football field, a line of about fifty people carrying signs and chanting as they passed Bohler Gymnasium. Casey reacted with a shrug. The draft had ended; the Vietnam War was clearly on its way to some sort of conclusion. The demonstrators seemed like refugees from another era of college life. Things change that quickly on campus.

What did not disappear suddenly, however, was the new view student leaders had of their own status. Not all demands and reforms that students called for in the sixties brought lasting change to the university. The process, however, made student opinion an important topic to college administrators. Students found they could be heard.

Before the 1960s, rules and policies were made by presidents, vice presidents, and deans and issued as proclamations. When students had complaints about those rules—which they often did—they could petition the administration for relief. The student body president would go to the Administration Building and be received by someone designated as the official student contact, usually affable fatherly figures like Earl Foster, assistant to President Holland, or Jack Clevenger, assistant to President French. These individuals were chosen for their ability to get along; they were kind and respectful when they explained to students why they couldn't have what they wanted.

Even moderate student leaders of the sixties had come to reject this essentially parent-child relationship. Everything that had happened in the sixties—the civil rights movement, the feminist movement, and the antiwar movement—urged students to scrutinize their relationship to authority. No longer would they accept the idea that they were indentured to college administrators in exchange for an education.

Sure there were rules. No one had a problem with that; without rules there would be nothing to violate, and another college tradition would die. But agreeing *with* rules was not the same as agreeing to *be* ruled. After the events of the sixties, administrators had to explain their decisions when they affected students. Students could no longer be considered scruffy wards of the college who were called in occasionally and told what was going to happen to them.

That's how students saw it coming out of the sixties. The question   OPPOSITE: *Ferry Hall memorial cupola.*

was, could they maintain this status after the era of sit-ins and marches ended?

Paul Casey, who became student body president that spring of 1974 when he witnessed the last anti-Vietnam demonstration, found that events of the sixties made administrators and state legislators an attentive audience. The fact that eighteen-year-olds could vote in state and national elections after 1972 gave students added leverage. "There was a proposal for a tuition increase, and we were able to defeat that fairly easily," Casey recalled. But legislators soon discovered that students didn't vote in large numbers, and could be ignored. At the same time, college administrators realized that the era of unrest had ended.

From that point, student leaders with agendas found they faced serious problems. For one thing, they were always working against the calendar. Unlike a dance or a pep rally, changing some condition of campus life usually took more than the nine months given student government officers. To make matters worse, elections took place late in the spring, leaving little time to pursue an agenda before summer vacation. In the fall, student government competed with football games and homecoming for attention. Then, suddenly, everyone went home for Thanksgiving and Christmas. After Christmas, student body officers discovered that they had about ninety days to accomplish their programs before a new set of officers took over. University officials, who were around year in and year out, knew this weakness. "They know if they wait you out, you'll be gone," said Casey.

Casey offered as an example the fate of a pet plan of his own. He wanted to continue student involvement in national and world

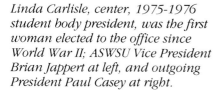

Linda Carlisle, center, 1975-1976 student body president, was the first woman elected to the office since World War II; ASWSU Vice President Brian Jappert at left, and outgoing President Paul Casey at right.

problems through a plan suggested by social reformer Ralph Nader. Nader had set up a program that would allow college students across the country to donate a small sum of money, as part of their regular college fees, to support research into social problems. President Terrell opposed adoption of the plan. Casey decided to fight for it and hastily organized a petition drive to demonstrate student support to the Board of Regents. The signatures were collected and presented. The regents took the petition under advisement. And then? "And then I graduated and that was the end of it."

Another perennial problem for post-sixties student body presidents was that President Terrell was too nice. Even when he disagreed with you "he'd charm you to death," said Casey. Mark Ufkes, student body president 1977-1978, recalled: "You'd go into his office with gripes and thirty minutes later you'd walk out just wanting to hug him. Then, as you walked away, you'd realize, 'Hey! I didn't say what I wanted to say!'" Students who expected to talk their way to influence were pitted against a master.*

The final hitch in maintaining their newly won status, students learned, was that, when it came right down to it, they had no status. If the administration wanted to grant a student request, it would. If it did not want to, the issue would be forwarded to the arbiter of all disputes, the Board of Regents. The regents were accustomed to following the advice of its university president.

---

*Even sixties radicals got along with President Terrell. "I always kind of liked President Terrell," Nola Hitchcock Cross, a leader of the strike of 1970, admitted eighteen years later. "I have to say," reflected Ralph Atkins, the black radical, "the university administration deserves applause. Their handling of various situations kept things from getting totally out of hand."

Mark Ufkes, 1977-1978 student body president, talking with President Glenn Terrell.

Valentine Day, 1983.

Thus, student leaders in the seventies retained much of the ambition of their counterparts in the sixties, but they lacked the clout. "The sixties were over, but I guess we weren't done shouting yet," said Mark Ufkes. Like the club fighter who finds himself matched against the champion, seventies students could only hope to preserve their dignity by putting up a good fight before they went down.

Ufkes is the best example. He opposed the administration's policy of bodily searching students for liquor at concerts and football games. He unsettled the administration by proposing, on behalf of a campus group, divestiture of university investments in South Africa as a protest against that country's apartheid policy. Ufkes and other leaders presented the administration with a real headache when they proposed to rate the teaching competence of WSU faculty members. They undertook a poll of students, asking what they thought of their teachers. The university's attorney said Ufkes and his colleagues would be sued for defamation of character if they published the results. (Indeed, a group of professors, people who make their living by scoring the performance of students, filed a law suit in Colfax to prevent publication of what students thought of them!)

Tim Connor, '79, an *Evergreen* reporter who observed Ufkes's battles with the administration, said that when Ufkes won, it was often by sheer force of personality. Connor recalled going to the student body offices for his first meeting with the new president:

> Ufkes arrives in his office next door with a characteristic thump and roaring mix of blue words and hearty laughs. Ufkes is the most extroverted person I've ever met. Incredible energy. He gives interviews the way Jimmy Connors plays tennis: all out, swinging, diving, running into all the corners, squinting, gesturing, venting, until he wears you down and overwhelms. I am withering under this, unable to keep up with my notes at all, when I look to my left and notice there are tarantulas in cages right next to where we're sitting. Ufkes's pets. I remember thinking that this was a very dangerous fellow. But likeable too.

At regents' meetings, Ufkes, mop-headed and buoyant, entered grinning and hailing friends across the room, then sat down in the front row. Even when Ufkes was quiet, it was the quiet of a suspected bomb. "He obviously had the ability to destroy decorum, which is a lot of what regents want at board meetings," said Connor. Connor suspected regents occasionally conceded to Ufkes a marginal issue here and there simply to duck the energetic rebuttal they would get otherwise.

NEVERTHELESS, "STUDENT POWER" WENT THROUGH A STEADY DECLINE in the seventies, and that was partly by choice of the students themselves. They seemed no longer interested in how administrators ran the university. "I think the theme for the mid- and late-1970s was enjoyment," reflected David Pratt, '76. "We'd all been fighting for so long, we were tired and a little complacent. Streaking was more in our line during that time."

"Streaking" meant running naked through some public place for no reason other than to shock or delight on-lookers. A streaker ran through the gymnasium during halftime of the Husky basketball game at Friel Court in 1974. Whole groups (always or nearly always male) were seen streaking across campus at times, and the custom persisted through the seventies. It was outrageous and utterly without serious motive, a throwback to fifties-era pranks.

In fact, many traditions that had fallen into disfavor during the late sixties now returned. By 1975, sororities and fraternities were again recruiting more members than their houses could accommodate. "Homecoming, a celebration that has oscillated in popularity during the past few years, is back again," said a 1975 *Evergreen* editorial. The editorial noted that thirty-two teams—a record—participated in the

Fifties craze; nostalgia for the 1950s swept through the campus after the tempestuous sixties faded.

Butch.

Greek Row.

ice-block sitting contest, in which contestants in light clothing sat on blocks of ice in fifteen-degree weather to see who would be the last to break and run for a hot shower. The contest had to be called after several hours passed and only one team had "bottomed out."

One tradition, however, came to an end forever. Seventies students made a decision about Butch, the live Cougar mascot. The governor of Washington had presented the first live cougar to WSC at the halftime of a game with the University of Idaho in 1927. Football fans soon named him Butch I, after Butch Meeker, a particularly ferocious Cougar quarterback and All-American of that era. A succession of Butches, each presented by the governor of the state on the demise of its predecessor, spent their days in pampered idleness, alternately sleeping, batting basketballs around their cages, and watching human Cougars pass back and forth on their way to classes.

On game days, the "Butches" would appear on the field in a wheeled chariot, laying their ears back and screaming their warnings with the other Cougars. Occasionally, their excitement began early. Students from Gonzaga and the University of Idaho lured one Butch (alas, all the Butches had a weakness for raw hamburger) into a makeshift cage in the middle of the night and took him away. When the catnapping was discovered the next morning, posses were formed and dispatched to search the likely campus.

Empathy was a highly regarded quality among sixties and seventies students. When they looked at Butch, they saw not only a mascot, but an animal. They saw to it that his cage was greatly enlarged. Still, when they looked into his eyes, they wondered if his motionless aplomb really meant confidence, or was it sadness? The screeching growls that once served as a warning to enemies sounded, to a different generation, more like plaintive cries. When the elderly Butch VI had to be put to sleep August 24, 1978, a debate began whether he should be replaced. A survey of students indicated that sixty-three percent felt that Butch VII, wherever he was, should be left to roam a more natural habitat.

IN THE WAKE OF THE RADICAL SIXTIES CAME THE "MELLOW" SEVENTIES. The sixties expression *"right on!"* was replaced by the more contented "all-*right!*" Long hair for both men and women remained in fashion until the last years of the decade, but then rapidly began to shorten. The flashy, floppy raiment of the hippie era modified into utilitarian sloppiness. The well-dressed seventies male wore faded jeans, running shoes, and a jersey or T-shirt. The shirt would be certain to be decorated with a WSU logo, a picture of Beethoven, Snoopy, or a large number. A blank shirt became as rare as a tie. A coat or ski jacket was added in winter. Women wore much the same outfit.

Washington State University's student body grew from about 10,000 in 1965 to about 17,000 in 1980. Most juniors and seniors lived off campus. There had always been an apartment population among students, but in this era apartment life became the most common

Homecoming tug-of-war, 1984.

college memory. Three, four, or five women would move into a single apartment and find ways to make it liveable with pots and dishes borrowed from mom, beaded curtains for privacy, and posters of rock stars to cover up cracks in the walls. Perhaps the common substitution of bean-bag chairs and big pillows for furniture suggested this generation's favorite description of itself, which was "laid-back."

Some groups of men rented entire houses and gave them names like "Moose Lodge" and "The Mars Hotel." These were like miniature fraternities, except that rules were created only as needed and social events were invariably planned around a keg of beer. In the era of "do your own thing," apartments gave everyone a chance to put together a living group. "Partyers" could room together, but so could diligent engineering students and born-again Christians. Several members of a mid-seventies gymnastics team lived together in a house on Howard Street, and most other members of the team made it a hangout. One of them, David Pratt lived in a separate apartment that was probably more typical of seventies apartment dwellers:

> It was a one bedroom apartment with a closet turned
> into a kitchen. You couldn't turn around in the
> kitchen with a pot in your hand, without running into
> the walls. I shared the apartment with another gym-
> nast, who rotated with me on who slept in the living
> room, and who got the bedroom.

Relaxing at "the Coug"
(a.k.a. Cougar Cottage).

IN THE SEVENTIES, BARS AND TAVERNS BECAME ALTERNATE STUDENT UN-
ions. Of course, this was always true to some extent. In the 1930s it
was the legendary Oriental, whose immigrant Chinese owner avidly
followed WSC sports. In the fifties the four pool tables of the City Club
on Main Street were kept busy by an interesting crowd of college
students and local farmers. In the late sixties some people bragged
that the old City Club, remodeled and renamed Charley Brown's,
served more Olympia beer than any other single tavern in the world.

But the general loosening of rules about drinking, especially
regarding women students, and the tendency toward fragmentation
of on-campus social life, made taverns an especially important part
of college memories in the seventies. The Cougar Cottage, which
served beer in the fifties but stopped in the sixties at the insistence of
the administration, became a tavern again in 1976. It became the
special hangout of Greek Row.

Many fraternity men and athletes had an unofficial headquarters at
Rusty's. That garage-sized space on Grand Avenue will always be
remembered fondly for its grime, smoke, pervading sixty-watt dingi-
ness, and good times. The walls were covered with autographed
pictures of Cougar sports heros, some of whom could be seen
standing at the bar. Each picture was inscribed with the athlete's
honors of "All-Conference" or "All-American," and if Rusty liked them
especially he added, "All-Tavern."

Rico's, located just down from the corner of Main and Grand, was
a favorite graduate student hangout. It was cave-like, full of dark

wood, brick, and dim corners. Undergraduates who could produce an I.D. showing that they were twenty-one also showed up, especially on dollar-pitcher night. "My roommate Leslie Ericson and I would hustle pool for beer," recalled Lori Wheat Beeler, '80. "The guys were usually surprised when we'd win."

Students under twenty-one went to Rathskellers and other bars in Moscow, across the state line. The fact that the legal drinking age was nineteen just six miles from campus was considered, by some, a great advantage over other colleges in the state.

By the early seventies, "discreet" drinking was permitted in dormitory rooms. But the policy had to be refined to outlaw kegs of beer, however, when practical experience suggested to those who ran the university that no drinking that involved a keg was likely to be discreet.

Fraternities and sororities opened each school year with a giant kegger called "The Wheel." All the fraternity houses along Greek Row were divided into four regional groups, each of which sponsored a party with several free-flowing kegs. Meanwhile, sorority members organized themselves into four "platoons," one for each fraternity party. Every hour through the evening, the sororities would rotate to a new party. By the end of the evening, every sorority member had been to four parties and had a chance to meet everyone in every fraternity. By all accounts it was one heck of a party.

A similar custom was continued through the year with "happy hours." On Friday and Saturday nights a couple of fraternities would

AGR Barn Days.

WSU students and a Moscow police-man encourage the drinking of milk, not beer. Eighties students probably were the first to take the hazards of alcohol seriously with "responsible drinking" informational programs.

purchase kegs of beer and hold open house for all Greeks. For three dollars you could have free access to the kegs and mingle endlessly. Since there was usually more than one party going on, party-goers roamed up and down Greek Row. "You would meet more good looking guys during happy hour than you would in a week other-wise," recalled a member of Kappa Alpha Theta sorority.

Beginning in 1979, the school year opened with the annual "Waterbust" sponsored by the Phi Delta Theta fraternity. Thousands of students gathered in Boyer Park on the Snake River for a day of beer swilling and sunbathing. The party grew larger each year until, at the opening of the 1988 school year, 13,000 people, including many non-students, swarmed over the beach. The event was rou-tinely patrolled by local police officers, who found students generally orderly and cooperative. The only incident at the 1988 waterbust was a slight injury to a male student who fell out of a tree while trying to get a better look at Miss Waterbust contestants.

Such events have given WSU the reputation of being something of a "party school." How far afield this reputation extends is impossible to gauge. Many WSU students were convinced that this was a national, or at least, a regional fame. Everyone vaguely remembers that in the mid-seventies *Playboy* magazine ranked WSU as one of the top party schools in the country. What *Playboy* actually said in a 1976 article was that students at *all* schools claim *Playboy* had ranked their school tops in partying. The article said *Playboy* had in fact never made any such ranking. Another doubter was Bill Gruber, vice president of the WSU student body in 1986-1987 and an ATO member: "I've traveled to other campuses and we don't hold a candle to some of those guys." A sorority member said: "We got this 'party school' image because we're out in the middle of nowhere." Saturday night parties are simply more noticeable than they would be in a big city. "Granted," she felt compelled to add, "we've had some *great* parties."

ONE REASON WHY STUDENTS OF THE SEVENTIES WERE NOT INCLINED TO carry on the protests of the sixties is that there was a lot less to protest about. An *Evergreen* reporter surveyed student opinion on *in loco parentis* in early 1976 and found, "A few are staunch supporters of it; some resent it. But the majority appear to be indifferent to it." He concluded that the rules simply weren't interfering with students' lives anymore. A rule that students should not be in rooms of the opposite sex between 2:00 a.m. and 6:30 a.m. "is essentially dead," a dormitory head resident told the reporter. "Even in the women's halls, there is complete knowledge that men are sleeping with women." University administrators had simply withdrawn from the business of regulating the students' moral behavior. Society did not expect it of them anymore.

BUT THAT DID NOT END THE LONG SAGA OF ADMINISTRATION-STUDENT battles over rules. While the university withdrew from monitoring sexual conduct, it became more involved in controlling drinking.

The response students devised to drinking restrictions had an interesting similarity to that used against the "Dean Annie-ism" in the 1920s and 1930s. Just as their grandparents had argued that because they held hands or stayed out until midnight did not mean they were sleeping together, eighties students argued that because they wanted to have a beer party did not mean that they were embracing alcoholic behavior. They argued, as their grandparents had, that the responsible majority was getting blamed for the trouble caused by the irresponsible minority.

But laws against those under twenty-one drinking were not a matter of university rules, as curfews had been. The university could not countenance parties that allowed minors to drink, even if it wanted to. What made this issue more urgent was a changing legal atmosphere. The university might possibly, and the Greeks would probably, be liable for damages if illegal or irresponsible alcohol use

Maureen M. Anderson became Vice Provost for Student Affairs in May of 1986.

resulted in a serious accident. Besides, Greek Row neighbors phoned in hundreds of complaints to police each month about the noise.

Beginning in about 1984, President Terrell and his successor, President Samuel H. Smith, clamped down. They issued new rules for drinking in dormitories and at football games, but the main targets were Greek houses. The Wheel and the wide-open happy hours were outlawed. Greeks could serve alcohol at parties, but the kegs could not be purchased with house funds. This lifted some of the liability from the house. It also made such parties harder to organize.

In May 1986, the administration created a new position to coordinate student affairs. Maureen M. Anderson, a thirty-seven-year-old Ph.D. in higher education, was named Vice Provost for Student Affairs at Washington State University and given the assignment of calming down student life.

Within months of her arrival she outlawed "camping out" at the football ticket booths because students waiting over night for choice seats had been drinking and littering. Six months later the Board of Regents accepted an administrative recommendation that freshmen be required to live in dormitories for a full year rather than just one semester on the grounds that it would give them a better start in college. Though in practice it affected only a handful of freshmen, it caused consternation among students, who did not like to see the university back in the business of arranging their lives for them. An *Evergreen* editorialist called the rule an outline for "post-pubescent daycare service."

In the spring of 1988, administrators announced that when school opened in the fall, dormitories would be accessible only two days before registration, rather than the customary five days. This angered prior residents, who said the extra time was useful for moving in and getting organized for the year—it was not, they argued, just a party

First in line at Beasley Performing Arts Coliseum.

period, as the administration apparently assumed. The student senate passed a resolution condemning the way the change was handled, allowing students almost no warning or chance to discuss the issue. An angry letter to the *Evergreen* said: "Once again, the students at WSU are letting their rights be trampled on, and once again the offensive, condescending 'keeper-of-our-moral-souls' Maureen Anderson is leading the way . . . Maureen has to go, if students' rights are to be protected . . . it's not going to end here."

Unlike the dormitory system, fraternities and sororities were not fully dependent on the administration. There, the administration said, in effect, *please consider calming down your parties, or we will do it for you.* The threat was that the university might withdraw recognition from houses that did not comply, essentially closing them.

Some on Greek Row were of a mind to be defiant, but if they chose that course of action they faced a problem. Even most fraternity men knew the situation had become impossible to defend. Greek Row regularly vibrated with loud music late into the night and periodically erupted in water fights or egg fights that affected Greeks and everyone else in the area. When a student wrote to the *Evergreen* charging that fraternities were rowdy, a fraternity man had to be pretty quick to come up with a defense. "I think you made this statement while you were still a little heated from the accidental hit with the egg," he said, indignant at the insult to his fraternity.

Greeks had few allies in their battle with the administration and had to admit the argument of legal liability was a sound one. Yet, by 1987 there was a feeling of having been pushed and shoved and jostled by the administration for three years. Greeks believed the administration was making them out to be a whole lot worse than they were. The rumor was that "they want us dry"—meaning that the new president, Samuel Smith, would soon drop all pretense and outlaw drinking on campus altogether (a charge that he denied).

Some Greeks cooperated with administrators and drew up plans for reforms. Others remained defiant. When it came time to enact the new drinking policies, defiance won out. The week before school opened in 1987, Greek Row was wilder than ever. "Washington State University Greeks got an F-minus in public behavior last week and they earned it," wrote Steve Massey, an *Evergreen* editor.

> Eggs, beer and other food items were hurled at just about anything that moved.
>
> Unfortunately some alumni, parents and first-time WSU students saw the events—a case study in immaturity and recklessness—and got a skewed first impression of life on campus.
>
> If the university wants to fuel a quickly-forming negative public image of its Greek system, it will brush off the incident and add it to a long list of 'it-happens-every-fall' activities.

President Samuel H. Smith with his wife Pat. President Smith is only the eighth person to serve as president of Washington State University.

Bicycles were something new on campus in the seventies.

As part of its pact with the administration, fraternities agreed to sponsor a program that would educate freshmen rushees about the other, life-threatening, aspects of alcohol. As the freshmen watched, designated Greeks would be administered doses of alcohol on stage so the effects on behavior and reflexes could be demonstrated. But those who were supposed to get the doses of alcohol showed up already drunk, turning the whole thing into a farce that did not warn against excessive use of alcohol but, in fact, delivered the implicit message that drunkenness was fun. "It was," one fraternity member later admitted with a shake of his head, "pretty horrible."

The administration's response was delivered in what came to be called "The Memo from Hell." Instead of reprimanding the fraternities and threatening punishment, Vice Provost Anderson and Director of Residence Life and Housing George Bettas wrote to the officers of the Interfraternity Council (IFC) informing them that the organization had been effectively disbanded. The tone of the five-page memo was imperious:

> Because of the recent collective actions of the IFC Executive Committee, we have concluded that a major restructuring of the IFC is necessary.
>
> Therefore, an IFC Reorganization Committee will be established. Chapter presidents will submit a list of names to us of individuals whom they recommend for appointment to the Committee. These names are to be submitted by September 21, 1987. The Committee will be named on October 1, 1987. A final report will be expected by January 1, 1988.

If the administration had simply informed the fraternities that their behavior was illegal, not to mention irresponsible, and they could expect disciplinary or legal action, the Greeks would have gotten little sympathy from other students. But instead, they said, in effect, "Since you won't agree with us, you don't exist."

Steve Massey, the *Evergreen* editor who two weeks earlier excoriated the Greeks, now came to their defense:

> For Anderson to hand Greek leaders a memo last Thursday informing them that they haven't done their jobs right and that their living system would be placed under 'new management' is ludicrous. Stuffing a new rule down the throats of any group of students—Greek, Residence Hall or Off-Campus—is unacceptable and should be countered with responsible opposition.

What had been an issue of rowdy students now became an issue of student rights. What if the student newspaper didn't abide by a strong recommendation of the administration. Could it be abolished? What if the student government became uncooperative. Could it be abolished? Student body president Kristi Phillips, who had been elected running against a Greek ticket, pledged that student government would stand behind the IFC on the grounds that no students had any rights if their organizations could be abolished by drafting a memo. Students weren't the only ones to construe the situation in these terms. Bill Hall, the Lewiston *Tribune* columnist and sage observer of regional events, wrote that while there was no defending "no-class vulgarians" on Greek Row, that doesn't mean the university administration should act like a "banana republic" in which "the right of the people to elect their leaders is respected as long as the generals agree with what the elected leaders are doing."

IT LOOKED AS IF ONE OF THOSE PERIODIC MARCHES ON FRENCH ADMINIstration Building was in the offing. But it wasn't. Fraternity members, after boycotting a meeting ordered by the administration and holding some steam-releasing meetings among themselves, showed up to do business. It didn't take long to agree on a plan for future drinking policies. Greeks even felt a little sense of victory because Anderson and Bettas had quickly backed away from the threat to replace IFC leaders.

In fact, the administration became downright conciliatory toward students. Here was an important difference between the Holland and French administrations and that of President Smith. The Smith administration had angered off-campus students by the freshman live-in rule, dormitory students with the late opening of the dorms in the fall, and the fraternities with "The Memo from Hell." Yet there had been no real reaction, probably because on many other matters student leaders were satisfied. "Sam Smith calls *me* and asks how things are going," said student body president Kristi Phillips. Her predecessor, Barbara Gorham, said if you could present a reasonable case for a proposal to Smith's administration, you had an excellent chance of getting what you wanted. When students organized a boycott of dining halls in October 1987 to protest how they were charged for meals, the bureaucracy quickly agreed to find alternatives and put them before students for a vote. It produced a new system that students liked.

Yet, when it was all over something about "The Memo from Hell" still nagged. Bill Stauffacher was one of the moderate fraternity leaders during the negotiations over drinking policies. In the spring of 1988 he was elected student body president, continuing the tradition of student leaders who have borne out judgments made by WSU student voters. Stauffacher, soft-spoken and reflective, held no rancor for Anderson and Bettas. He liked them. The situation on fraternity row had been indefensible and the administration had the right to take action. But "the way they did it was bad," Stauffacher said with a little shake of his head. He was disappointed in their behavior, as well.

Student body president Barbara Gorham, 1986-1987.

BARBARA GORHAM

Cartoon in the November 4, 1987,
Evergreen; *after students boycotted the dining halls, the administration designed three new pricing systems and allowed students to vote on which to adopt.*

Kristi Phillips,
1987-1988 student body president.

Students don't resent being disciplined so much as being put in their place. When the first Board of Regents in 1892 ruled that a student petition supporting a fired president was irrelevant, the editor of the student newspaper replied indignantly: "We think that this is a business in which we ought to have some rights." The students who rebelled in 1936 weren't so upset about the social rules as the fact that Dean Annie didn't even have to listen to their side of the story. Mark Ufkes, the ebullient student body president in 1976-1977, explained that he opposed personal searches at Martin Stadium gates, not on any vaulted civil rights grounds, but that, "It was just one more adult telling you what to do."

Of course administrators had points of view too. When they gave students a chance to choose between doing the right thing and doing the wrong thing, they thought it was demonstrable that students usually chose the wrong thing. The student answer to that has always been that an occasional error is the price of learning. "Why do we have these restrictions when freedom would give us a chance for valuable self-development?" an *Evergreen* editorial writer wrote in 1934. More than fifty years later, Bill Gruber, vice president of the student body, made precisely the same point: "I feel if you want somebody to learn responsibility, you have to give it. Students have to fail in order to learn anything." Commenting on the IFC crisis, Kristi Phillips said, "The whole idea of student leadership is to give them a chance to learn through mistakes. If there were some problems, why not work with these student leaders and help them?"

THINGS HAD CHANGED A GOOD DEAL SINCE THE RADICAL SIXTIES. IN THE 1980s, it was the administration that made "non-negotiable de-mands" and students who called for reasonable consultation. The mellow, partying seventies were waning too. In a 1988 article in *Pacific Northwest* magazine, editor Valerie Rogers, '83, looked back on her first years in a sorority:

> A light load my first semester meant I could be a
> party animal, as we said back in 1978 . . . Hellbent for
> the bars of Moscow, I was soon carousing at the
> Spruce Tavern, Rats, the Corner Club, Mort's and the
> Best Western, to name but a few. . . .

When she returned for her junior year in the fall of 1980, however, she said, "I realized that some radical changes had taken place at Old Wazzu since I first matriculated. I hardly recognized the place anymore." Quite suddenly the "unkempt, untucked post-hippie look" was replaced by a trimmer preppy look. Even more shocking, she found the library was buzzing night and day and "Classrooms that were only half full except on exam days were now standing-room-only." Clearly, "Something serious had happened to my beloved university, the prototypical party school."

What had happened was that the mellow seventies had been replaced by what might be called "The Resumé Eighties." College counselors found students more stressed by the pressure to make good grades. The choice of academic majors showed a sudden turn toward courses leading to careers with great financial reward. Teach-ers complained that students were looking at education as mere job training. The number of students studying business and computer

Hard at work, 1985.

science doubled while students taking history, sociology, and philosophy declined.

Mid-eighties student body presidents Barbara Gorham and Kristi Phillips both said students were unlikely to participate in any time-consuming activity unless it looked good on their resumés. Gorham even considered changing the names of committees, such as "Dance Committee" to something like "Social Events Committee," so that it would look more impressive on a resumé. "People don't do things anymore just for the cause," she said. They have their eyes on graduation and the jobs beyond.

These are reasons why many all-campus activities that distinguished campus life thirty years earlier were missing from WSU in 1988. As late as 1982, the annual "Mayfest" filled the mall and CUB with games, exhibitions, demonstrations, and a great variety of performers. Organizing that kind of activity takes thousands of student hours, and it seemed that in the late eighties no one wanted to spare the time.

The eclipse of all-campus activities had even deeper roots. The formal homecoming dance was abandoned in the early eighties because it was so lightly attended. The all-campus dance during homecoming became informal and was attended by singles as well as couples. Since the sixties, it seemed, students didn't care to get dressed up for the kind of formal function that was once the highlight of the campus year. Only fraternities and sororities retained the custom of "the big dance." Perhaps the typical student didn't feel the need anymore. The full sound of a live band was a real treat for a twenties or thirties student. The eighties student probably had a stereo in his or her room.

Students of the eighties were by no means passive shut-ins, however. A survey in 1987 found that over half participated in organized intramural sports competition, ranging from pocket billiards to flag football. There were 375 softball teams alone. Physical conditioning was the "craze" of the eighties. At almost any hour day or night campus visitors can spot runners, alone or in twos or threes, proceeding down the streets leading out from campus. One of the most popular recreational classes sponsored by the student activities center proved to be aerobics. A common eighties recreation, for men and women, on a Friday night or Saturday morning was to get a group of three or four people together and go to the weight rooms in Bohler Gymnasium for a workout.

Since the sixties, campus social life has been broken into smaller social units. The homecoming dance was switched to the night before the homecoming game because students preferred to spend the homecoming night in smaller groups organized around fraternities, dormitory floors, and groups of family and friends in town for the homecoming weekend. When graduates "came home," they reported directly to these subunits of the campus. Dan Maher, '78, a sixteen-year veteran of the WSU student activities office, said, however, that school ties nevertheless retained a strong grip on alumni. At homecoming time, "those first and second year alums come flying

back here." Homecoming rallies, which seemed so muted to alums of different eras, were that way because the noise, excitement, and parties have become scattered across Pullman.

One-on-one at Orton Hall.

IT IS HARDER TO DISCUSS WHAT THE STUDENTS DID IN 1988 THAN WHAT they did in 1938. The students as a collective abstraction has never applied to everyone in school. But in previous eras, the ideal and typical student was easier to characterize. By 1988, there were various ideal students but few if any were typical.

The difference between 1938 and 1988 was not so much in the quadrupling of the student body, from about 4,000 to about 16,000, as in its diversity. In the thirties, the Washington State College student body was remarkably homogeneous: generally white, middle class, eighteen to twenty-two years old, single, and mostly from the state of Washington. Students of the thirties (and to a slightly lesser extent those in the sixties) might as well have grown up in the same neighborhoods and gone to the same high schools, for all the similarities among them.

By 1988, about one out of three Washington State University students weren't "college aged." They were twenty-three years old or older, often considerably older. Thirteen percent were graduate students, a traditionally more serious lot. One out of thirteen was a

Toni White, student.

racial minority. Eighteen percent of the student body came from other regions of the country.

In 1988, 933 WSU students came from ninety-three different nations: countries like Japan, Norway, Saudi Arabia, China, India, France, and Bolivia had students at Washington State. You might carry a cup of coffee to a table in the CUB and pass within hearing of conversations in Swahili, Thai, and Portuguese along the way. "The WSU student" no longer conjured up the clear image it once did. The WSU student might be any person, of any age, from any place in the world. A perfect symbol of this phenomenon was the sight, one spring day in the mid-1980s, of an African woman walking toward her student apartment with her hands at her sides and a Rosauer's grocery sack deftly balanced on her head.

Study partners—
Malaysian and American.

But even foreign students don't remain foreign. When Muhammed Al-Tell of Jordan moved into Goldsworthy Hall in 1986, his American roommate, in the ancient tradition of college roommates, took the new frosh in tow. The roommate helped Al-Tell with his English, introduced him to campus customs, and brought him into his circle of friends. "Every time I see him on campus now," Al-Tell, by now a well-acclimated junior, said of his first roommate, "I think, 'Man, without you it would have been really something!'"

IF A SINGLE THEME EXISTS THAT CLASSIFIES STUDENT LIFE IN THE LAST period of Washington State University's first century, it is diversification: in types of students, in their choices of activities, in their living arrangements, in their orientation to the world. For all the emotion generated by the 1980s conflict between Greek Row and the administration, the squabble was something at the periphery of most students' lives. It was like a modern-day diplomatic quarrel between Britain and France: no longer the earth-shaking affair it once would have been. By the late 1980s WSU had as many students from foreign nations as there were living on Greek Row. There were probably several times as many students unaware of university policies regarding alcohol, simply because they lived off campus and were unaffected.

Yet, this diversification in the WSU community is apparent only when looking at the school's history. From any other perspective, the campus has remained a close-knit, even isolated community in the late twentieth century. Underlying student body diversity there was unity and universality; there was *university*, to adapt an academic term to the society of students. Even in the era of television, campus isolation has remained a source of cohesion. When WSU engineering students repeatedly out-score University of Washington engineers on standardized professional tests, one explanation has been that, at WSU, students are thrown together out of class as well as in, and consequently spend more time studying together.

At a forum in the fall of 1988, an undergraduate rose to ask President Smith how WSU justified the time and money that went into

the football program. The president answered that it was more than justified as a morale builder. "Let me ask you this," Smith said. "Did you feel better last Monday [after the football team had lost a game] or a week ago Monday [after the team had posted a major win]?" The point was not argued, and it proved to be a point well taken in that particular season. When the football team started winning again, some professors paused before starting to lecture Mondays to describe their emotions while watching the key play of Saturday's game. When the Cougars continued to win, everyone from geneticists to cafeteria help were guessing what bowl the team would be invited to. When the Cougars played UCLA, ranked number one in the nation that year, on national television (Keith Jackson, '54, announcing), much of the campus and town fell silent as people withdrew to televisions to watch the football game. When the heart-stopping game finally ended, Cougars winning 34-30, students and town residents emerged from dormitories and houses all at once and a single roar rolled across Campus Hill. ■

Cougars on parade, downtown Pullman.

University

WSU campus in the seventies.

ABOVE: *Front steps of Pi Beta Phi sorority.*   BELOW: *Sorority flag football.*

ABOVE: *University Honors Program seminar.*

RIGHT: *Geology lab class, mid-seventies.*

LEFT: *Motor scooters invaded the campus in the 1980s.*

BELOW: *Time for a study break on the lawn.*

ABOVE: *In the eighties, the number of students studying computer science doubled.*

RIGHT: *Building an architectural model.*

OPPOSITE: *Meeting friends on the Glenn Terrell Friendship Mall.*

The Past Is Always Present

IN A STUDY OF CHANGE OVER TIME, IT IS NATURAL TO SPEAK OF "THE campus of the twenties," "the campus of the fifties," or "the campus of the seventies" in order to focus on differences. This kind of comparison falsely suggests, however, that "eras" are discreet, self-contained places, like towns along a railroad track, so that when a new era appears on the horizon old ones are left behind.

A better metaphor for campus life would be the train itself. It rolls from one era to another, picking up new customs, ideas, and precedents at each stop; then it delivers them all to each new academic year. During the school year of 1987-1988, when this book was being written, students were singing songs, following customs, and citing precedents laid down by their grandparents, parents, and older brothers and sisters. They wore symbols of the cougar mascot chosen by students in 1919; they loitered under the trees planted on "Campus Day" by students of the twenties; they gathered in Compton Union Building, which was planned in many long evening meetings by students during the early fifties; and they enjoyed privileges insisted upon by students of the sixties.

Certainly students are different today than they were a century ago. But the similarities among student generations go deeper. An essay in the 1988 *Chinook* by Susan Miller and Karla Griffin reminded class-mates that the first few days of a new semester are spent "scamming." "When an individual's roving scam computer focuses on someone," the article said, "they begin thinking of ways to meet this likely candidate." Edward Kimel, '97, a member of the first graduating class, left a description of his arrival on campus in a buckboard wagon in 1894. "Considerably later it was learned," Kimel said, "that certain coeds had been tipped off about the coming of these prospects from the south and that they looked out from behind dormitory curtains as the wagon came into view." Terms change, but not people.

The students of 1987 and 1988 even *looked* familiar. Women wore sixties-era miniskirts and fifties-era "anklets," sox folded down over the ankle. Penny loafers were suddenly popular again. Hair styles were eclectic, but generally simple and natural à la fifties, making use of hair clasps and bows.

Men's fashions in 1987 were utilitarian in the extreme. They wore running shoes or top-siders, jeans, and jerseys, T-shirts, or sweat-shirts. It was *the thing* in the late sixties as well as the late eighties not to wear sox, a display of insouciance to show that students are

OPPOSITE: *Felix McLarney, '28, former president of Stimson Hall, revisits the refurbished dormitory, fall 1987.*

ABOVE: *Autumn leaves.*

BELOW: *Winter slush and ice.*

different from the rest of society. Male students in the early thirties refused to launder their cords all semester for the same reason. In 1987, most college men wore hair styles slightly shaggy, sometimes with a single sprig of hair dangling down on the neck. Many, however, wore it trimmed short, as in the fifties, and a few wore it shoulder length, a reminder of the seventies. It didn't seem to make any difference to anyone; hair style had been depoliticized. What a lot of people thought was pretty wild in 1987 were the earrings some males wore in one ear.

In cold weather, seven out of ten students, men and women alike, wore jeans. The most common garment of all for both sexes was the T-shirt, sweatshirt, or jersey emblazoned with a symbol, logo, or saying. Shirts advertised beer, running competitions, rock groups, radio stations, beach resorts, almost anything. Some carried more evocative messages. A variety of WSU sports logos were common, as always. One shirt had a drawing of the Bryan Tower clock and the words, "High Time at WAZZU." Another said, "Happiness is Seeing Pullman in Your Rearview Mirror."

This billboard-shirt-look had been common since the early seventies. In fact, it went back further than that. Florence Chisholm, '27, recalled: "We used to get these sloppy T-shirts, and somebody who was artistic would draw a picture on the back, maybe a fat woman or something, and you would wear that to class. . . . They were an ugly grey, and not very pretty. But we thought it looked great."

THE 1987-1988 SCHOOL YEAR BEGAN WITH THE AGE-OLD PRE-SEMESTER gathering on the beaches of the Snake River, formalized since 1979 as the "Waterbust." About 13,000 people swarmed over Boyer Beach. Back on campus there was a small-scale panty raid on the Delta Delta Delta sorority.

Stimson Hall reopened after being restored to former splendor, complete with the leather couches, bay windows, and carved oak pillars. Its all-male residents invited Stimson alums from previous eras back for the opening and listened intently to the stories of the years when Stimson Hall battled fraternities for campus leadership. Among the many Stimson alums returning for the opening was Felix McLarney, '28, a former hall president.

OCTOBER 1987 ECHOED THE SIXTIES. THE BLACK AWARENESS COMMITtee held a rally on the Mall. One conservative student wrote to the *Evergreen* that the particular "knee jerk liberalism" expressed by another letter writer "went out with black light posters and love beads." A week later, however, an *Evergreen* editorialist asserted that students must take their complaints about high prices on dorm food and other matters to the administration. "If, after exhausting these avenues of recourse, students still do not feel the administration is listening to their concerns, things like strikes, rallies and protests are logical next steps."

United States Senator Daniel J. Evans spoke on campus October 19. In his speech he remembered another visit to WSU. Evans recalled that, when he arrived at WSU fifteen years earlier, instead of the 300

Membership in ROTC increased as memories of the Vietnam era faded.

students expected, about 1,500 had showed up, most of them to express concern about the Vietnam War. News of a mob waiting to hear him made the governor nervous in those volatile times, and he wondered if it had been a mistake to accept the speaking invitation. "In fact, it turned into one of the most moving experiences in my years as governor," Evans told his 1987 audience. After a two-hour exchange, he said, "I came away with the feeling that they understood the situation better than their parents."

Homecoming in October 1987 included a serpentine—a tradition that went back to the turn of the century—but this time they did it with cars. A tug-of-war at Martin Stadium preceded an evening homecoming rally, where new football coach Dennis Erickson and new basketball coach Kelvin Sampson made speeches. About 800 people showed up for the rally. Unfortunately, exactly one Cougar came away from the next day's homecoming game happy: Stanford Coach Jack Elway, WSC class of 1953 (Stanford won the game 44-7).

In November the Cougars played the University of Washington for the Apple Cup in Seattle. A few days before the game the Seattle *Post-Intelligencer* published a three-quarter page article about Cougar fans called "A Breed Apart." The article, written by Bud Withers, '70, said:

The new "Butch."

> There is a certain pervasive nature to the term Cougar, as if you were saying 'diabetic' or 'millionaire.' You don't need to say a lot else. . . .
> Listen to Gary Libey of Colfax, . . . WSU supporter: 'It's easy to be a Husky fan. It's easy to root for the winning team year in and year out. Drive your big, expensive Mercedes. Diamond-laden women in furs. In Pullman, the fans are in rags. They sit out in the snow game in and game out. But they usually stay until the end of the game.'

The Cougars lost to the Huskies 34-19. After the game, Cougar Coach Erickson, irate over scurrilous taunting of his team by Husky players and fans, swore to newsmen that each day until the next Apple Cup, he would ask himself: "What did I do as a football coach [today] to beat the Huskies?" Doc Bohler and Babe Hollingbery lived by the same code and would have approved of how Erickson answered the question in 1988. That fall, his Cougars won the Apple Cup, beating the Huskies 32-31 in a game played before a sellout crowd in Martin Stadium; they finshed their regular season with an 8-3 won-loss record; they were ranked eighteenth in the nation; and they traveled to Hawaii to play the University of Houston in the Aloha Bowl on Christmas day.

The special Husky rivalry continues in basketball, as well. In 1987, the University of Washington *Daily* called Cougar center Todd Anderson a "pencil-necked loser." In the WSU-UW game a week later, Anderson scored 16 points, knocked down seven Husky shots (a school record), and was a vital part of the Cougar effort to beat the

Huskies 70-63. After the game, Anderson said, "I was ticked off." A month later the Huskies had a rematch at WSU and the Cougars beat them again.

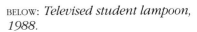

ABOVE: *Student section, Cougar football game.*

BELOW: *Televised student lampoon, 1988.*

IN JANUARY 1988, THE ANCIENT TRADITION OF COLLEGE LAMPOONS reaching back at least to the *Yellow Jacket* of the early twenties, took a new twist when communications students began broadcasting a satirical cable television show called "Live at Eight." In a mock debate over the merits of fraternities versus dormitories, one of the performers said, "Why don't the dormies just come right out and say it? 'Hi, we overstep the boundaries of good taste.'"

That winter Robert McEachern, '37, a member of the Board of Regents from 1981 to 1988, established a fund to help students get through school. McEachern donated $25,000 and friends added another $50,000. The money would be used to make emergency loans to students. McEachern said he established the fund because he heard that students sometimes get caught in temporary, but devastating, financial binds. He was reminded of his own college friends who had to drop out of school for the same reason during the Great Depression.

In the March 1988 student elections Bill Stauffacher, president of Beta Theta Pi, and Mark Luebbers, a resident advisor in Gannon and Stephenson halls, won the offices of president and vice president on a single ticket. It was the third year in a row that a fraternity-dormitory combination won; the living-group rivalry that animated campus politics through the fifties was a thing of the past. Aside from the vote-collecting advantages, these dormitory-fraternity tickets found that they could address the administration and Board of Regents as a united front.

Stauffacher, a communications major, had never intended to go to WSU, but changed his mind after a brief campus visit. One of the reasons was that, on a walk across campus, he noticed the Edward R. Murrow Communication Center and realized, for the first time, that this giant of the journalism profession had attended WSU. The legacy of Nathanial Reeid and Ida Lou Anderson continued to have its effect even in the 1980s.

Ticketed.

IN MARCH 1988, THE CAMPUS CHIEF OF POLICE TOLD AN *EVERGREEN* reporter that heavy metal groups should be barred from performing on campus because their music contained hidden "satanic" themes. "Thirty years ago," wrote *Evergreen* editorialist John Hill, "people were in a tizzy over Elvis Presley for his 'vulgar' hip movements and adults asked 'What's wrong with kids today?' The answer is the same today as it was then. Nothing is wrong with America's kids; it's the so-called grown-ups that continually display narrow-mindedness with their refusal to accept an alternative to their 'higher quality' of music."

In April, a women's dorm, Stephenson East, decided to turn over a wing to men students the following year. The living group thus became coed and almost no one noticed; the big debate about male-female "integration" that began in the fifties had long since been resolved. By 1987, several dorms on campus had side-by-side rooms for men and women; a few living groups had some wings for men and others for women; still other residence halls remained exclusively male or female.

Shortly before the end of the 1987-1988 school year, Associated Press carried a story datelined Pullman about the latest campus craze called "oozeball," a volleyball game played in a mudpit. The result was about the same as the annual tug-of-war across Silver Lake seventy years earlier.

That month, too, Washington governor Booth Gardner signed a bill that allowed sixty-four small wooden crosses to be set along highways 26 and 195 between Vantage and Pullman. The crosses signified the sixty-four people killed in highway accidents along those roadways since 1970. Twenty-one were WSU students. The special legislation arose from efforts made by Mark Ufkes, the effervescent 1977-1978 ASWSU student body president, who returned to campus that year to earn a master's degree. Ufkes, who was studying highway safety, typically decided action ought to follow thought and placed the crosses along the highways to remind students of the hazards. The state's Department of Transportation found this to be illegal and ordered him to remove the crosses. But

1987-1988 students took up the cause and lobbied through the legislature a bill that allowed the safety reminders to be placed along highways at semester breaks.

April 1988 was also the month university administrators announced that dormitories would open a week later in the coming fall. The *Evergreen* was inundated with angry letters from students. "Once again, the university is assuming a parietal role and deciding what is best for the children that attend WSU," wrote Steve Sherrod, president of the Residence Hall Association. Sherrod declared: "We are not children," repeating almost exactly Mimi Frank's statement to the press fifty-two years earlier during the strike of 1936.

In May, John Olerud of the Washington State baseball team was named an All-American, as his father, Dr. John Olerud, Sr., '65, had been in 1965. The younger Olerud, a pitcher with a 15-0 win record, a .464 batting average, and twenty-three home runs, went his father one better a month later by being chosen national College Baseball Player of the Year, the first person from the Pacific Northwest ever to win the title.

Student-sponsored markers alongside cross-state U.S. highway 195.

Library research.

Graduate research.

ONE PURPOSE OF AN INSTITUTION LIKE WASHINGTON STATE UNIVERsity is to carry the past into the future. The existence of an immense physical plant, where buildings were planned, financed, and constructed ten, twenty, or fifty years ago, underscores this point to students of today. But the interaction between the past and present operates on many other levels as well. Practically every building named—Van Doren Hall, Johnson Tower, Thompson Hall, Kimbrough Hall, Bryan Hall—possesses a story, a legacy, a tradition that will benefit each new generation of WSU students. To hundreds of physicians across the country, "Eastlick" was nothing so insubstantial as a brick building; it was Doctor. Herbert Eastlick, a driving disciplinarian who hounded them to work harder, with the warning that if they did not, they might not make it into medical school—and with the promise that they could be, if they would only live up to their abilities, great physicians. They and Eastlick's other students set up a scholarship fund to help current medical students.

In the Bookie that spring of 1988 there was a special table of used books, put up for sale by the English Department to raise funds. All of the books were from the library of Murray Bundy, the flamboyant English department chair and professor from 1928 to 1956. The books were remnants of a huge personal library donated by Bundy to the department's reading room and the university archives. Many of them were annotated in Bundy's own hand (Bundy was, at the time, ninety-seven years old and living in a Moscow nursing home). The sonorous voice that managed to move thousands of preoccupied students to an appreciation of Shakespeare and Milton was almost audible in the underlinings, exclamation points, and mini-lectures scribbled in the margins of these special sale items.

A couple of steps away from the remnants of the Bundy library were displays of national best-sellers. One of them was for a book titled *Rubber Legs and White Tail-Feathers* by Patrick F. McManus, '56. "I took every class Bundy taught," McManus recalled. "He was just a fabulous teacher. He had this shock of white hair and when he lectured he just sent sparks flying off in every direction. He had an almost frightening kind of intensity." Bundy and Milton Peterson, a freshman composition teacher who took the time to cover McManus's first compositions with corrections, made those years "one of the most significant periods in my life."

TWO WEEKS BEFORE GRADUATION, THREE MEMBERS OF THE CLASS OF 1988 sat in the CUB and reflected on their college careers. They sounded about like graduates of previous classes. Stephanie Sasaki, who grew up in western Washington, selected WSU because it had a good communications school, but also because when she visited, "People were so friendly." She was already getting nostalgic about leaving. "I'll be walking to class and suddenly I think, 'I'll never be able to walk across this campus as a student again!'"

Linda Wilson's father graduated from WSC in 1957, a Sig Ep, and her three brothers all belonged to WSU fraternities in the early eighties. "I knew I was going to be a Cougar all my life," she said. At one point, when she was a senior in high school, she horrified her father by sending away for a Stanford brochure. But he was a father who prided himself on broadmindedness. "He said, 'Sis, it's your life, and it's got to be your choice.' He did say, 'If you even think about the University of Washington, you're out of the family will.'" The teenage rebellion soon passed and she enrolled at WSU and pledged Alpha Gamma Delta. Sitting in the CUB two weeks before graduation she said:

> I'm a die-hard Cougar. I want to marry a Cougar. It's like belonging to a big family, like being a member of the Mafia. If I had graduated from the University of Washington and went to Boston and ran into someone else from UW, so what? But if I go to Boston and run into another Cougar, we have an instant connection.

As he prepared to end his career as an undergraduate that spring, Matt Prater was proudest of being the first president of the reconstituted Delta Chi fraternity, one of the houses that went under during the anti-fraternity days of the early seventies. It was restarted on the third floor of Goldsworthy Hall, much as the first WSU fraternity started in Ferry Hall at the turn of the century. The revived fraternity was about to begin building its own house. Since he was graduating, Prater would never live in the house, but "When I walk into it in fifty years, there'll maybe be a picture of me on the wall. You want to be remembered for something."

Sorority rush.

IN THE FINAL HECTIC WEEK OF THE 1987-1988 SCHOOL YEAR, MEMBERS of the class of 1988 hurried around taking their final exams and making preparations for graduation. Some of them might have noticed groups of older people strolling about the campus—the class of 1938 gathered for its fiftieth reunion. The sight of the two groups passing each other on the Mall presented an interesting tableau: the class of 1988 rushing to see what the world holds for it, the class of 1938 strolling calmly about, looking back at college from the other end of life. The latter had completed that immense circle, from the Washington State College campus on graduation day in June 1938, through the perils of World War II, through the postwar boom, through the traumas of the sixties, through children and grandchildren, to retirement, and now back to Washington State *University.*

There is something reassuring about this customary return of fifty-year grads; it serves as a quality check. This was a class that played a big role in the all-campus strike of 1936. Their behavior had deeply disappointed many of their elders, including President Holland, who wondered what would become of a group of kids who believed they were free to defy authority. Yet, here they were, having been tested in the real world and having amounted to something after all. Among the strike ringleaders who returned were Herman "Dutch" Haynor, now an attorney and former regent of the university; Weldon B. "Hoot" Gibson, a founder of the Stanford Research Institute; and Jerry Sage, war hero and educator. When the 1938 grads passed the hat at their Golden reunion they came up with a $650,000 donation to the university.

The Golden Grads visited dormitories, fraternities, and sororities. They walked through Fulmer Hall, Bryan Hall, Murrow Hall, and revisited classrooms. They remembered the Pacific Coast championship basketball game with Stanford when the yelling seemed to rattle the mortar that held Bohler Gym together; the fights of national collegiate boxing champion Roy "Pooch" Petragallo, '38; and the 1937 football victory over UCLA, and how the Intercollegiate Knights kept the Victory Bell ringing most of the night.

Jack Winn remembered, after fifty-four years, that President Holland gave the 1934 incoming freshman class two pieces of advice in his welcome to them: "Never, never feel sorry for yourself, and read at least two good books other than required class reading." "I remember," said Lester B. Johnson, "walking down Linden [Street] on a warm spring afternoon to the Beta house, hearing the Tommy Dorsey recording of 'Marie' . . . blaring through the open windows." Betty Cooper Engbretson recalled, "walking down the hill on Sunday afternoons to watch a movie at the Cordova Theater. We would then go to Strupplers for a steak sandwich, Coke, shared hot fudge sundaes—for 50 cents each!" Winnifred Castle Olsen recalled: "reading page proofs three nights a week as *Evergreen* Night Editor; the early morning parades as an ROTC Sponsor; evening seminars in the home of Dr. Fred Yoder; the fragrance of lilacs in Pullman in the spring; . . . the heavy, heavy snows. . . ."

It is an odd thing about college memories. They are virtually always positive. Terrible weather and frozen hot water bottles on the sleeping porch are remembered as triumphs of the will, while pleasant afternoons on campus were never quite matched. Heartbreaks somehow lose their sting with time—but a fortuitous touchdown pass is emblazoned on the memory.

The campus is a world of its own, where the politics are fun, the enemies are Bears, Ducks, and Huskies, where one can see mild professors as stern adversaries, where one can find thrills, where tragedy is total and love forever, where a touchdown is fulfillment, praise abundant, discovery a daily experience, and friends are plentiful.

It is a world populated by exuberant, handsome, entertaining people: the short guy with a great sense of humor, the young woman with pretty brows who always knew what the class assignment was, the athlete with an oiled stride, the serious young woman who was on all the committees, the raw farm kid who surprised everybody by being utterly smart. You lived with them, played with them, plotted with them, competed with them, and learned with them. You got so

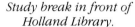

Study break in front of Holland Library.

Graduation, 1988.

used to them, and four years was such a long time when you were twenty, that somehow it never occurred to you that on graduation day the group would scatter, never to be reassembled.

ON MAY 7, THE GRADUATING SENIORS OF THE CLASS OF 1988 GATHERED in Beasley Performing Arts Coliseum to receive their diplomas.* United States Congressman Tom Foley of Spokane, Majority Leader of the House of Representatives, warned them, in the fashion of commencement speakers, that they and their country faced great challenges, but also opportunities. After the ceremony, the graduates gathered outside the Coliseum in large clumps of friends, then gradually sorted into smaller family groups, then by ones and twos, they squeezed into cars pre-packed with belongings and mementos of college careers and took their leave of Campus Hill.

Some already felt a tug. They sensed, even as their cars streamed away from Pullman and student life, that some part of them would always remain *back there.* ■

---

*In various graduation ceremonies that spring, the university bestowed 1,610 bachelor's degrees, ninety-one master's degrees, forty doctoral degrees, and sixty-nine veterinary medicine degrees.

The Past Is Always Present

WSU campus, 1980s.

ABOVE: *Pick-up game at Sigma Phi Epsilon.*

TOP, LEFT: *Rugby player preparing to drop-kick; club sports, such as crew and rugby, are popular at WSU.*

BOTTOM, LEFT: *Skiing the slopes of Rogers-Orton playfield.*

Homecoming rally on the mall.

Students viewing an exhibit in the WSU Museum of Art.

Orchesis dancers in the 1980s are part of a long WSU tradition.

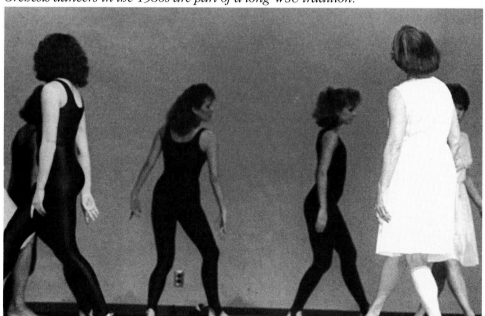

ABOVE: *In many ways, student rooms have changed little since the late 1890s when William Barkhuff photographed his living accommodations.*

RIGHT: *Studying in the 1980s.*

TOP AND BOTTOM:
Students of the eighties.

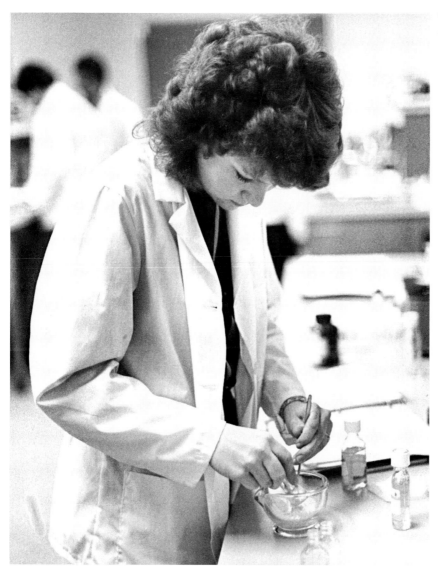

Washington State University's future.

Golden Grads, class of 1938, assembled for a group photograph in the CUB, 1988.

ABOVE: *Students enjoying afternoon sunshine in front of Bryan Hall.*   BELOW: *Happy graduation.*

Further Reading

Balzarini, Stephen E. "The 50th Anniversary of the Time that Will Rogers Didn't Come to the Palouse," *Bunchgrass Historian* 11:2 (Summer 1983): 3-14.

Bjerk, Roger. "Pullman—From Farming Frontier to Urban Center, 1881-1910," *Bunchgrass Historian* 9:2 (Summer 1981): 25-32.

Bowden, Angie Burt. *Early Schools of Washington Territory.* Seattle: Lowman and Hanford Co., 1935.

Brannon, David. "Pullman's Other College," *Landmarks: Magazine of Northwest History and Preservation.* 2/1 (Fall 1982): 17-18.

Bryan, Enoch A. *Historical Sketch of the State College of Washington, 1890-1925.* Pullman: Alumni Association, 1928.

Fiege, Mark T. "Rebellion in the Palouse: The Student Strike at Washington State University, May 1970," *Bunchgrass Historian* 11.1 (Spring 1983): 14-27.

Fry, Richard B. *The Crimson and the Gray: 100 Years with the WSU Cougars.* Pullman: Washington State University Press, forthcoming 1989.

Frykman, George A. *Creating the People's University: Washington State University, 1890-1990.* Pullman: Washington State University Press, forthcoming 1990.

Helton, Harold Elliott. "Wazzu at War: Washington State College During the Great War," *Bunchgrass Historian* 10:3 (Fall 1982): 3-21.

_____. "Wazzu at War, Part II: Washington State College During the Second World War," *Bunchgrass Historian* 12:2 (Summer 1984) 3-23.

_____. "Wilson Hall," *Bunchgrass Historian* 15:1 (Spring 1987): 3-13.

"Historic Resource Survey Analysis. Report of the Task Force for Historic Preservation of the Historic Core of the Washington State University Campus." Task Force for Historic Preservation, Washington State University, February 12, 1985.

An Illustrated History of Whitman County, State of Washington. [n.p.] W. H. Lever, 1901.

Lindsay, Ernest E. "The State College of Washington: A Land-Grant College," *Americana* 34:2 (April 1940): 3-43; reprinted as: *The State College of Washington: Fiftieth Anniversary, 1890-1940.* New York: The American Historical Company, [1940].

Moyers, Bill. *Listening to America: A Traveler Rediscovers His Country.* New York: Harper and Row, 1971.

Neill, Thomas. *Incidents in the Early History of Pullman and the State College of Washington.* Pullman: Pullman Herald, 1922.

Landeen, William M. *E. O. Holland and the State College of Washington, 1916-1944.* Pullman: Washington State University Press, 1958.

Reed, Mary, et al. *Whitman County Historic Resource Survey.* Olympia: Washington State Office of Archaeology and Historic Preservation, 1986.

Slind, Marvin G. "Colfax College and English's Collegiate School: Examples of early higher education in the Palouse," *Bunchgrass Historian* 8:4 (Winter 1980): 20-24.

Stapp, Darby, and Julia Longenecker. *Washington State University Centennial Digs: Report of 1984-86 Investigations.* Pullman: Washington Archaeological Research Center, 1986.

Stark, Lawrence R. "The Founding of Pullman: A Local Folktale," *Bunchgrass Historian* 9:2 (Summer 1981): 4-12; originally published as: "A Local Folktale: the Founding of Pullman," *The Record* 38 (1977): 33-54.

Thornton, Richard S., and Sally Adams. *WSU, the Hill: A collection of pen-and-ink illustrations and an essay highlighting the history of Washington State University.* Second Edition. Pullman: Alumni Association of Washington State University, 1966.

Vogel, O. A. "Wheat Breeding in the Pacific Northwest," *Bunchgrass Historian* 9:1 (Spring 1981): 3-8.

Wilbert, William F. "Political Activities During the Student Strike: Three Recollections," *Bunchgrass Historian* 11:1 (Spring 1983): 28-32.

With the Colors from Whitman County. Pullman: Lou E. Wenham, 1920.

Index

Numbers in italic make reference to photographs.
Numbers followed by an italicized letter *n* make reference to material contained in a footnote.